Paralegal's Handbook
of
Annotated Legal Forms,
Clauses and Procedures

Paralegal's Handbook

of

Annotated Legal Forms, Clauses and Procedures

DEBORAH E. LARBALESTRIER

Legal Assistant

Litigation and Workmen's Compensation Specialist

Executive Director of the American Paralegal Association

Prentice-Hall, Inc.

Englewood Cliffs, New Jersey

Prentice-Hall International, Inc., *London*
Prentice-Hall of Australia, Pty. Ltd., *Sydney*
Prentice-Hall of Canada, Ltd., *Toronto*
Prentice-Hall of India Private Ltd., *New Delhi*
Prentice-Hall of Japan, Inc., *Tokyo*
Prentice-Hall of Southeast Asia Pte. Ltd., *Singapore*
Whitehall Books, *Wellington, New Zealand*

© 1982 by

Prentice-Hall, Inc.
Englewood Cliffs, N.J.

"This publication is designed to provide accurate and authoritative
information in regard to the subject matter covered. It is sold with the
understanding that the publisher is not engaged in rendering legal,
accounting, or other professional service. If legal advice or other expert
assistance is required, the services of a competent professional person
should be sought."
—*From the Declaration of Principles jointly adopted by a
Committee of the American Bar Association and a Committee
of Publishers and Associations.*

Library of Congress Cataloging in Publication Data

Larbalestrier, Deborah E.,
    Paralegal's handbook of annotated legal forms.
    Includes index.
    1. Forms (Law)—United States. I. Title.
KF170.L37   347.73′55   81-15885
ISBN 0-13-648642-8   347.30755   AACR2

Printed in the United States of America

Dedication

To my husband, Yves,
for all of his loyal support,
patience and understanding of
a house cluttered with forms

ABOUT THE AUTHOR

Presently Executive Director of the American Paralegal Association, Los Angeles, C.A., twice past President and recipient of the President's Award for distinguished service to the paralegal profession, Deborah E. Larbalestrier has nearly 20 years of experience as a working and teaching legal secretary and legal assistant to her credit. She has a B.A. in History, Storer College in West Virginia, studied for over 3 years at the Robert Terrell Law School in Washington, D.C., completed the paralegal studies program at the University of West Los Angeles and specialized courses at Woodbury College and the University of California at Los Angeles. She is a Certificated Legal Assistant and Certificated Litigation Specialist, and member of the Advisory Board of the University of West Los Angeles School of Paralegal Studies. Mrs. Larbalestrier is the author of two books *Paralegal Practice and Procedure* and *Paralegal Training Manual*, both published by Prentice-Hall.

Acknowledgments

A special thanks to Linda Bever, Supervising Legal Assistant and teacher of Paralegal Studies at two local colleges, for her help in determining which forms should be utilized in this handbook; and my sincere gratitude to the members of the American Paralegal Association and law firms throughout the country who were kind enough to send me sample forms from which to draw for use in this handbook.

A Word from the Author

This book will aid legal assistants in their job performance and will assist them in understanding the whys and the wherefores of preparing legal documents.

Among other things it covers what elements to incorporate in legal documents; what pitfalls to watch out for; and when to include certain phrases or paragraphs. The book provides the legal assistant with concise general information about each area of law (such as contract, corporate, family law, etc.) and gives guidance in the use and creation of various forms.

There are cautionary measures and hints; and tried and proven guides in creating pleadings and other court documents which have been used successfully by experienced legal assistants in the completion of their duties.

The Format of This Book

The format of this book is designed for easy accessibility by the legal assistant to typical and unusual forms needed for a given task. In addition to setting forth an example of a form, there are comments and annotations to the whys and wherefors of certain paragraphs and phrases; as well as some legal explanation pertinent thereto.

For example: In filing a Worker's Compensation Claim you must include the phrase (or similar language) that the applicant was on the job at the time of injury; or was in the course and scope of said employment, not who was at fault, as is necessary in an ordinary personal injury claim.

Or, *for example:* in preparing a deed, you must include words of conveyance such as "I give," "I transfer," "I convey," etc.

And/or, *for example*: in preparing a deed, be sure you have the intent of the parties set forth thereon as it relates to how the property is being conveyed, tenants in common, joint tenancy, etc.

Benefits to Be Derived From This Book

Most law office forms today have been standardized, tailor-made, and printed to fit a "normal" situation, in an effort to save time and allegedly increase the efficiency and production of the outflow of work in the law office.

It has been my experience, however, that often these types of forms have had to be re-worded, re-worked and in final analysis, re-drafted to fit the current facts; and in so doing, the time and efficiency for which they were initially standardized were negated by the need for re-drafting. A good example of this is the standardized set of adult interrogatories, often mistakenly sent to a minor plaintiff; or to an unknowledgeable passenger or witness; or a corporate set of standardized interrogatories sent to an individual, and vice versa.

Further, by the use of this book you will greatly reduce the need for time-consuming, oral communication and instruction as to how a document should be drawn; or where to find a pleading which is similar in kind; or under what code section to find applicable law governing the pleading.

If used properly, this book can be an effective working tool which will inure to the benefit of a legal assistant, her attorney and the public he serves by simplifying the workload; enhancing a more efficient operation and relaxed working atmosphere.

How to Use This Book

Very simply, and similar to the way you would Shepardize a case in preparing a memorandum of points and authorities:

First, upon receipt of this book you should go through it quickly to get the feel of it, read its contents to see how it is set up.

Second, you should read thoroughly the section dealing with the specialty of your attorney's practice, familiarizing yourself with its forms and comments.

Third, turn to the section dealing with litigation forms, paying particular attention to those forms which are applicable to your attorney's specialty.

Fourth, thereafter when your attorney gives you an assignment, merely turn to the form and comments in the section or chapter you feel applies. Use the contents therein as a guide in preparing your document with the facts of your case in accordance with the laws of your state.

Naturally, *forms vary from state to state*. A form that may be applicable in one state may have no application in another. You are cautioned, in all cases, to check your local codes as a first step before adapting any form for personal use.

Typical examples of what you will find within these covers are annotations and/or comments of pleadings such as:

Affirmative defenses, and when to use them.

How to amend your pleadings and when.

Answers and alternative answers such as general denial, qualified denial, specific denial, and when to use them.

Demurrers, general, specific, and when to use them.

Digesting depositions, various types.

Interrogatories, how to develop and what to include.

Request for admissions, how to develop and the legal ramifications thereof.

In the back of the book you will find a correlation table of code sections to enable you to find the federal code section applicable to your task for those states using the Federal Rules of Civil Practice and Procedure, and much, much more to underscore the immeasurable value of this newest, one of a kind, handbook of annotated forms.

With the *Paralegal's Handbook of Annotated Forms, Clauses and Procedures* you can turn to the Index or Table of Contents to find a guide to the pleading to be prepared, and do it with confidence.

Deborah E. Larbalestrier

CONTENTS

(A detailed outline of its contents precedes each chapter.)

Contents—Chapter 1
Administrative Agencies

1

ADMINISTRATIVE

AGENCIES

1.0   INTRODUCTION

When dealing with documents preparatory to appearances before any administrative agency, you are cautioned to check, not only the state statute applicable, but also the pertinent agency rules and regulations governing the agency before which your attorney is appearing. The foregoing is to be noted because Administrative Law is statutory in most states. Hence, each state may have its own version of the Administrative Act of 1964. For these reasons, a common set of forms is not feasible and those listed below are by way of example only, and are listed to give you an idea of the format and what pleadings can be used before an administrative agency. With this in mind, consider the following:

• In preparing your pleadings before an administrative agency, be sure to first determine the jurisdiction and authority of the agency over the subject matter of the Accusation. The agency must show how and why it has jurisdiction and you should determine if the agency has continuing jurisdiction over the matter being disputed; or if you can appeal to a higher authority or other disciplinary body.

• As to venue, unless otherwise stipulated by state statute directing where a hearing is to be held, if it is a state agency, a hearing on the matter can be held anywhere in the state. If on the other hand, it is a local agency, a hearing will have to be held within the city or local agency offices.

● Finally, it should be noted that the preparation of pleadings to be filed in administrative proceedings are less technical, as can be seen from the forms hereinafter set forth, than those filed in the state and federal court systems. Moreover, there are no filing fees payable when filing pleadings in an administrative agency claim or accusation.

1.1 DOCUMENTS AND PLEADINGS USED IN ADMINISTRATIVE PROCEEDINGS
(As used under the Administrative Act of 1964)

Accusation
Accusation and Petition to Revoke Probation
Alternative Writ of Mandamus
A Motion to Set Aside Default
Answer to Petition to Compel Discovery and Order to Show Cause and Points
    and Authorities
Answer to Petition for Writ of Mandamus
Claim of Privilege
Decision
Declaration to Compel Attendance of Witness
Declaration in Support of a Motion to File a Protest
Declaration in Support of Motion for Pre-Hearing Discovery
Motion to Disqualify Hearing Officer or Agency Member and Supporting
    Declaration
Notice of Defense
Notice of Intent to Introduce Declaration in Evidence
Notice of Motion and Motion to Quash Subpoena, Points and Authorities and
    Supporting Declaration
Notice of Motion and Motion for Continuance, Points and Authorities and
    Declaration in Support of Motion
Notice of Motion and Motion to File a Protest
Notice of Motion for Pre-Hearing Discovery
Notice of Request to Cross-Examine
Notice of Request to Take Official Notice
Notice of Rejection of Proposed Decision
Opposition to a Motion to File a Protest
Opposition to Motion for Continuance
Order to Cease and Desist
Order Granting or Denying a Motion
Order to Show Cause and Stay Order
Order Granting or Denying Petition to Compel Discovery

Order Granting or Denying Motion for Pre-Hearing Discovery
Order Nunc Pro Tunc
Order Granting or Denying Stay
Order of Reconsideration
Order Denying Petition for Reconsideration
Order Granting or Denying Reinstatement
Protest (used when a third party protests issuance of license)
Petition to Compel Discovery
Petition for Writ of Mandamus
Proposed Decision and Order
Petition for Reconsideration
Request for Specification of Issues
Request for Hearing
Request for Discovery
Request for Stay
Request for Stay of Execution
Statement of Issues
Special Notice of Defense
Supporting Declaration for Motion to Set Aside Default

1.2 ACCUSATION

BEFORE THE DEPARTMENT OF CONSUMER AFFAIRS
Bureau of Collection and
Investigative Services

In the Matter of the Accusation against 915 International, Inc., Respondent.	)))))))	No. _____ ACCUSATION

The Department of Consumer Affairs, Bureau of Collection and Investigative Services, for causes of discipline against respondent, alleges:

I

Complainant makes and files this accusation in his official capacity as investigator with the Department of Consumer Affairs, Bureau of Collection and Investigative Services, and not otherwise.

II

At all times since June 1, 19__, respondent has been and now is the holder of a Collection Agency License issued under Section 6908 of the Business and Professions Code.

III

Section __ of the Business and Professions Code provides that a Collection Agency License may be suspended or revoked if the holder of that license:

1. Failed to file financial statements as required by Section __ of the Business and Professions Code;

2. Failed to file supporting photocopies of trust account bank statements as required by Section __ of the Business and Professions Code;

3. Failed to render a written statement of accounts to clients as required by Section __ of the Business and Professions Code;

4. Violated his fiduciary relationship with his clients as set forth in Section __ of the Business and Professions Code;

5. Willfully violated provisions as set forth in Section __ of the Business and Professions Code in the discharge of his duties.

WHEREFORE, complainant prays that a hearing be held on the charges and that 915 International, Inc. (respondent), Collection Agency License, No. 3-2074 be suspended or revoked.

Dated: February 11, 19__.

_____

Investigator
Department of Consumer Affairs
COMPLAINANT

COMMENTS

Form 1.2   Accusation*

In non-administrative Procedure Act hearings, the agency files an Accusation which represents the chief complaint or claim against a company for an alleged violation of its license or operating code.

This Form 1.2 is then investigated by an agent of the agency.

Whether or not a responsive pleading is required will depend on the ordinance or statute governing the agency. When in doubt, file a response to protect the client.

_____

* Text Reference: Administrative Act of 1964 as revised; local Government Code and Business & Professions Code; agency rules and regulations pertinent.

This Accusation sets forth the date and time of hearing in an Administrative Procedure Act hearing. This is not always true in the non-Administrative Procedure Act hearings. You should, therefore, just file a response and obtain a hearing date.

Note: This form must be accompanied by the section of the Government Code or Agency Rules and Regulations giving the agency authority over the business or licensee; and may be accompanied by the section of the Business and Professions Code applicable to the business or licensee which sets forth the violation.

This form must be served by mail, registered or certified, with return receipt requested. The Respondent has 15 days within which to answer, depending on the policy of the agency. You should verify this time limitation.

1.3 NOTICE OF DEFENSE

BEFORE THE DEPARTMENT OF CONSUMER AFFAIRS
Bureau of Collection and
Investigative Services

In the Matter of the Accusation Against SAM SHADY,	))))	NO. _____
	)	NOTICE OF DEFENSE
Respondent.	)))	

I, the undersigned and the respondent named in the above entitled proceeding, hereby acknowledge receipt of a copy of the ACCUSATION, the statement to respondent, a copy of Business and Professions Code sections 6915, 6915.1, 6917, and 6930, and two copies of a blank form notice of defense.

I hereby request a hearing in that proceeding to permit me to present my defense to the charges contained in the ACCUSATION.

DATED: December 2, 19___.

_____

SAM SHADY

_____

GEORGE GOODPERSON,
Attorney for Respondent
5968 Purview Drive
Woodcrest, California

COMMENTS

Form 1.3   Notice of Defense*

This required Notice of Defense (Form 1.3) is filed after the Accusation (Form 1.2) is received.

Whether you can raise new matter by way of defense at the time of the hearing, or whether it should be done at a special hearing, is determined by the provisions of the Administrative Procedure Act. This Act states that you must do it in advance of the hearing. As the law is in a state of flux in this area, you are advised to plead to new matter by way of a special defense before the hearing in both an Administrative Procedure Act hearing and a non-administrative Procedure Act hearing.

Under the Administrative Procedure Act the respondent does not file an "Answer," he merely signs and returns to the agency a "Notice of Defense" (Form 1.3) which is blank in form, stating that respondent will appear without admitting liability.

This Notice of Defense constitutes a request for a hearing and a denial of the allegations or statement of issues.

1.4   SPECIAL NOTICE OF DEFENSE

In the Matter of the   )   BEFORE THE BUREAU OF
Accusation Against   )   COLLECTION AND
915 International, Inc.   )   INVESTIGATIVE SERVICES
)
            Respondent   )
)   NO. _____
)   SPECIAL NOTICE
_____)   OF DEFENSE

I, the undersigned and the Respondent named in the above-entitled proceeding hereby acknowledge receipt of a copy of the Accusation, the statement to Respondent, a copy of Government Code Sections ____, ____, and ____, and two copies of a blank form Notice of Defense.

Under Government Code Section ____, Respondent objects to the Accusation on the grounds that it does not state acts or omissions on which the agency may proceed.

Further, under Government Code Sections ____, Respondent objects to the Accusation in that it is so indefinite and uncertain that Respondent cannot identify the transaction or prepare his defense.

---

* Text Reference: *supra*

I hereby request a hearing in that proceeding to permit me to present my defense to the charges contained in the Accusation.

DATED: February 11, 19___.

915 INTERNATIONAL, INC.

By _____
          Respondent

COMMENTS

Form 1.4   Special Notice of Defense*

At the time of filing the Notice of Defense (Form 1.3) an additional form, Form 1.4, Special Notice of Defense can be filed. This form permits respondent to allege or object to any acts or allegations stated by the agency, or object to the pleading as lacking specificity etc., or to admit to the pleading in whole or in part, rather than just filing a simple Notice of Defense. It further permits new matters to be presented, which is a type of affirmative defense.

This form must be served by mail via the registered or certified mail procedure with return receipt requested. This service constitutes a personal service, if the governing agency requires that the licensee or respondent keeps his address current with the agency.

1.5   NOTICE OF HEARING

Department of Consumer Affairs
Bureau of Collection and
Investigative Services

BEFORE THE DEPARTMENT OF CONSUMER AFFAIRS
BUREAU OF COLLECTION AND INVESTIGATIVE SERVICES

STATE OF FLUX

In the Matter of the Accusation Against 915 International, Inc. Respondent.	CASE NO. 75-71734 NOTICE OF HEARING

---

* Text References: *supra*

TO THE RESPONDENT, 915 INTERNATIONAL, INC. AND TO ITS ATTORNEY:

YOU AND EACH OF YOU, WILL PLEASE TAKE NOTICE that the hearing in the above matter has been set for Monday, March 6, 19___, at 1:30 o'clock P.M. before _____, Hearing Officer, in Room 301 of the Department of Consumer Affairs, located at _____
_____.

DATED: February 11, 19___.

DEPARTMENT OF CONSUMER AFFAIRS
BUREAU OF COLLECTION AND
INVESTIGATIVE SERVICES

BY _____
Deputy
Attorney
State of Flux

COMMENTS

Form 1.5   Notice of Hearing*

This form is self-explanatory and may be filed for an informal hearing; conference type; or a trial hearing; or an argument hearing, the overall purpose of which is to determine whether an Accusation, intervening document or protest can be filed. If the agency agrees with you as to the presence of triable issues of fact, then the agency prepares an order granting or denying the motion to file.

Though the underlying philosophy of administrative agencies is to have a hearing on the merits of a client, they can force the Respondent to come to a hearing or file a Notice of Defense. However, failure to file a Notice of Defense within the time prescribed by law constitutes a waiver of a right to a hearing on the merits.

---

* Text References: *supra*

1.6   STATEMENT OF ISSUES

BEFORE THE _____
(Title of Agency)

In the Matter of the   )   No. _____
Statement of Issues Against   )
)
_____   )   _____
)
)   (Title of pleading, e.g.),
)
                     Respondent.   )   _____
)
_____   )   STATEMENT OF ISSUES

Complainant _____, as
                               (Name of person filing statement of issues)
cause(s) for denial of respondent's application for a _____, alleges:
                                                                            (Type of license)

I

Complainant makes and files this statement of issues in his official capacity
as _____ and
       (E.g.) executive secretary of

                                                         _____
                                                                (Title of agency)
not otherwise.

II

On or about _____, 19__, respondent filed with _____ an
                                                                         (Title of agency)
application for _____ and that
                      (Type of license or permit applied for)
application is now pending before that agency.

III

Respondent's application is subject to denial under _____
                                                                            (Specify statute ordinance
in that on or about _____, 19__, respondent was convicted
of a felony in a proceeding entitled _____in the
                                                    (Title of criminal proceeding)
_____ of _____
    (Court)   (Location)

(Or)

Respondent's application is subject to denial in that respondent has failed to
furnish satisfactory evidence of his good moral character as required by

_____.
    (Statute or ordinance)
(If particular facts are known to agency, add) Respondent lacks good moral
character in that:

a. _____
       (Set forth misconduct showing lack of good moral character)
b. _____

(Or)

The granting of a license to respondent would be contrary to the public welfare and morals within the meaning of _____ in that:
_(Statute)

a. _____
   _(Set forth each particular)
b. _____

WHEREFORE, complainant prays that respondent's application be denied.

DATED: _____

(Signature)
_____
(Typed name)
COMPLAINANT

COMMENTS

Form 1.6 Statement of Issues

This form may be filed by the Respondent (Defendant) by way of mitigating (moderate) circumstances in lieu of filing a Notice of Defense.

For example: A fourteen-year-old girl, heavily made-up with cosmetics to look the age of 18 (or other age of majority), and who stated she was of the age of majority, with false identification to support this statement, is served an alcoholic beverage. This would be considered a mitigating circumstance.

1.7 ACCUSATION AND PETITION TO REVOKE PROBATION

BEFORE THE _____
(Title of Agency)

In the Matter of Accusation
and Petition to Revoke
Probation Against   )
)
) No. _____
_____   )
)
            Respondent.) ACCUSATION AND PETITION
) TO REVOKE PROBATION
_____   )

(Insert allegations in Accusation Form, 1.2, then add). As grounds for revocation of probation complainant alleges:

I

Complainant realleges, and incorporates as though fully set forth here, the allegations contained in paragraphs ___, ___, ___, of the first cause for discipline as set forth above.

II

On _____, 19__, in proceedings entitled "In the Matter of the Accusation Against _____," the _____entered
(Name of respondent)   (Title of agency)
a decision against respondent placing respondent on probation on certain terms and conditions. That decision became final on _____, 19__. A copy of that decision is attached to this petition as Exhibit ___ and is incorporated in this petition by reference.

III

Respondent has subjected his probation to revocation in that he has _____ those conditions of probation in that he has
violated/failed to comply with
_____ more particularly
(Type of conduct, e.g.) failed to obey all laws
as follows: _____
(Set out facts; if same conduct is alleged as

_____
in first cause of action, the paragraph may be incorporated by reference)

WHEREFORE, complainant prays that:

1. Respondent's license be suspended or revoked under the first cause of action.
2. Respondent's probation be revoked and the penalty of _____
suspension/
_____ be placed in full force and effect.
revocation

DATED: _____

_____
(Signature)

_____
(Typed name)
COMPLAINANT

COMMENTS

Form 1.7   Accusation and Petition to Revoke Probation

Form 1.7 is used when, as the result of a hearing, the Respondent was placed on probation and since that time the Respondent has violated the terms of the probation and the agency (or other interested party) is seeking to have the probation and license of the Respondent revoked.

1.8 PROTEST

BEFORE THE _____
(Title of Agency)

In the Matter of the
Protest of _____   )   NO. _____
   (name of   )
)   PROTEST
_____   )
protestant)   )
)
Against the Application of   )
_____   )
(Name of applicant)   )
_____   )

_____ , pursuant to _____
  (Name of protestant)   (Statute authorizing protest)
protests the application of _____ for a _____ on each and all the
following grounds:

I

Issuance of the license would be contrary to the public welfare and morals
within the meaning of Article XX, Section 22, of the California Constitution*
in that the premises sought to be licensed are adjacent to a residential neighborhood and would interfere with the quiet enjoyment of the residents.

WHEREFORE, protestant prays that the protest be sustained.

DATED: _____

                                 (Signature)

                                 (Typed name)
                            PROTESTANT

COMMENTS

Form 1.8 Protest

This Form 1.8, Protest, is self-explanatory and can be filed by any concerned citizen to keep the applicable agency from issuing a business license such
as a liquor license, massage parlor and the like in his immediate neighborhood.

---

* Research your state constitution for the applicable article allegedly being infringed upon.

1.9   PETITION FOR RECONSIDERATION

BEFORE THE _____
(Title of Agency)

)	No. _____
)	
In the Matter of the)	PETITION FOR
)	RECONSIDERATION
_____)	
Accusation/Statement of Issues)	
)	
Against _____)	
Respondent.)	
)	
_____)	

To _____ :
(Title of agency)

Respondent petitions for reconsideration of the decision dated _____
19__, in the above-entitled matter.

The grounds for this petition are as follows:

1. _____
   (Summarize each factual and legal ground)
2. _____

ARGUMENT

1. _____
   (Set out factual and legal argument for each of the above grounds)
2. _____

For these reasons, respondent requests that the decision be set aside and the matter be reconsidered.

DATED: _____

_____
(Signature of attorney)

_____
(Typed name of attorney)

COMMENTS

Form 1.9   Petition for Reconsideration

This form is part of the appellate procedure utilized before administrative agencies. It should be noted that not all agencies have an appellate system. You are therefore cautioned to check the appropriate rules and regulations of the agency with which your are dealing to determine if it has such a system.

In any event, you must exhaust all administrative remedies before you can take advantage of the appellate procedure of the administrative agency involved.

This Petition for Reconsideration is served on all parties interested and a hearing date is set by the agency, if granted. If the agency grants the Petition for Reconsideration, your attorney has earned the right for a ''de novo'' hearing (a new hearing) which takes the place of the former hearing and must be tried with all issues raised, as well as new issues.

If the Petition for Reconsideration is denied, then the agency's original order is final. This gives rise to ''judicial review.'' Do your research of the rules and regulations of the agency and local statutes governing this procedure.

Contents—Chapter 2
The Trial Brief

2

THE TRIAL BRIEF

2.0   INTRODUCTION

The three basic types of trial briefs are:

1) Full-blown trial brief which encompasses all your issues and legal authority in great detail;
2) Trial briefs which encompass liability issues only; and
3) Trial briefs which encompass damage issues only.

The Appellate Brief is an entity all its own.

The timing in filing a brief, whichever type is used, is part of the strategy used by your attorney in prosecuting the lawsuit. At any point during the course of the trial, he may ask you to prepare a brief, just on the issue of liability, to be presented to the court the next morning. This sudden move on his part might catch opposing counsel off-guard since he probably would be unprepared for such an event.

To prepare this brief, you would look to the issues raised in the complaint and the affirmative defenses set forth in the answer to the complaint. Thereafter, it is a matter of legal research to find supporting case authority for each issue.

As a legal assistant you must develop a ''lawyer-like'' approach in preparing trial briefs to be used by the attorney. This preparation will require you to think and argue as a lawyer would. If you adopt this approach, much time and effort will be saved by your attorney in revising the trial brief prepared.

The following sample briefs were chosen from hundreds of possibilities just to give you an idea of what you should include in a brief and in your brief file for reference in the future.

2.1   ONE-ISSUE BRIEF—LIABILITY OF DEFENDANT

SUPERIOR COURT OF THE STATE OF _____
COUNTY OF _____

)	NO. _____
)	
)	
) Plaintiff,	TRIAL BRIEF RE LIABILITY
)	OF DEFENDANT
) vs.	
)	
)	
)	
) Defendants.	
)	
)	

Plaintiff's evidence regarding the negligence of defendant _____ shall consist principally of evidence that _____ was driving while intoxicated and was driving in excess of the posted speed limit. Numerous other acts constituting negligence will also be adduced at the time of trial.

I
DRIVING WHILE INTOXICATED CREATES A
PRESUMPTION OF NEGLIGENCE

Vehicle Code Section 23101(a) provides:

   "(a) It is unlawful for any person ***, while under the influence of intoxicating liquor *** to drive a vehicle upon a highway and when so driving *** do any act forbidden by law or *** neglect any duty imposed by law in the driving of such vehicle, which act or neglect proximately causes bodily injury to any person other than himself ***."

Vehicle Code Section 23102(a) provides as follows:

   "(a) It is unlawful for any person who is under the influence of intoxicating liquor, ... to drive a vehicle upon any highway."

The evidence will establish that defendant _____ was in violation of both of those section of the Vehicle Code at the time of the instant collision.

II
VIOLATION BY _____ OF
THE BASIC SPEED LAW

Defendant violated the basic speed law contained in Vehicle Code Section 22350 which provides as follows:

"§22350. Basic speed law.

No person shall drive a vehicle upon a highway at a speed greater than is reasonable or prudent, having due regard for weather, visibility, the traffic on, and the surface and width of, the highway, and in no event at a speed which endangers the safety of persons or property."

The posted speed on the street on which the collision occurred was 35 miles per hour. There is varying testimony that _____ speed exceeded that speed by as much as 10 or 15 miles per hour. Although such violation does not per se constitute negligence, these facts constitute evidence of negligence. Absent evidence of variance of the 25-mile-per-hour prima facie speed limit (Vehicle Code Section 22352(b)(1)) by local authority (Vehicle Code Sections 22357, 21359), the jury must be instructed that 25-miles-per-hour is the prima facie speed at the place of the collison upon a sufficient showing pursuant to Vehicle Code Section 22352(b) (1), *Cf. Payette v. Sterle* (1962), 202 Cal. App.2d 372, 21 Cal. Rptr. 22, 26-27.

III

THE TRAFFIC ACCIDENT
REPORT IS ADMISSIBLE

Within minutes of the collision, _____ Police Officers arrived on the scene and, in the course of their regular official duties, prepared a four-page Traffic Accident Report with regard to that event. The report itself (and certainly its contents) are admissible.

The Traffic Accident Report is not privileged within the meaning of the Vehicle Code. Section 20008 of that Code requires the driver of an involved vehicle to make a written report of the accident within 24 hours to the _____ Highway Patrol or the police department in the city in which the accident occurred. Some cases have interpreted traffic accident reports to be those referred to in Vehicle Code Section 20008 because in the usual situation the *only* report an involved driver makes is to the investigating officer on the scene. Such a report is privileged. Vehicle Code Section 20012. *E.g., Kramer v. Barnes* (1963), 212 Cal, App. 2d 440, 27 Cal. Rptr. 895 (traffic accident report relating alleged admission of driver inadmissible by virtue of Vehicle Code Sections 20012-20015) ....

IV

THE REPORT OF THE BLOOD SAMPLE TAKEN
OF DEFENDANT _____ IS ADMISSIBLE

Testimony shall be offered to establish the blood sample report to be a business record and an official record of the Los Angeles Police Department, and additional testimony will be offered to establish the trustworthiness of such report. The analyzed evidence report setting forth the blood alcohol level of the defendant _____ is neither a report contemplated by Vehicle Code Section 20008 (deemed privileged under Section 20012) nor one within the scope of

Vehicle Code Section 40833, which provides that certain reports required by Vehicle Code Section 16000, *et seq.*, shall not be referred to in any way nor be evidence of the negligence or due care of any party at the trial of any action at law to recover damages. None of the reports referred to in Section 40833 bears any relation to the analyzed evidence report herein.

Respectfully submitted,

_____

Attorney for Plaintiff

COMMENTS

Form 2.1   One-Issue Brief—Liability of Defendant

In this brief you are merely addressing the liability of the defendant to the plaintiff as alleged in plaintiff's complaint based on a statutory violation, in this instance, violation of the Vehicle Code; together with resultant damages to the plaintiff.

Note that you have to establish the violation with specifics, NOT generalities.

How to develop this form of brief is boilerplate since you only have to look to the code section violated and the supporting court pleadings filed in the action for your contentions, such as interrogatories, depositions, statements of witnesses, etc.

2.2   ONE-ISSUE BRIEF: CONTRIBUTORY NEGLIGENCE AND ASSUMPTION OF THE RISK

SUPERIOR COURT OF THE STATE OF _____

FOR THE COUNTY OF _____

No.

_____,)	
Plaintiff,)	TRIAL BRIEF RE CONTRIBU-
vs.)	TORY NEGLIGENCE AND
)	ASSUMPTION OF THE RISK
)	
_____,)	
)	
Defendents.)	
)	
_____)	

All defendants herein have pleaded the affirmative defense of contributory negligence and defendants _____ have additionally pleaded the affirmative defense of assumption of the risk. As a matter of law there is no merit to any of these defenses.

I

Some evidence may be offered that plaintiff may have been driving without a valid operator's license in her possession at the time of the collision. Defendants may contend that this putative violation of a statute constitutes contributory negligence as a matter of law, but a long-standing exception to the negligence per se rule is that driving without a valid driver's license is not evidence of negligence and is immaterial in a case such as this. In the case of *Crosby* v. *Martinez* (1958), 159 Cal. App. 2d 534, 324 P.2d 26, plaintiff sued for personal injuries arising out of an intersection collision. ..... etc.

II

Evidence may also be offered that plaintiff was not wearing a seat belt at the time of the collision. There is no statutory provision requiring the use of a seat belt or other restraints or that it is unlawful to drive a car not equipped with such restraints or with restraints fastened and in working order. Nor has any California case ever held that a driver of a car is contributorily negligent if he fails to wear a seat belt while operating his vehicle. At most, the failure to wear a seat belt is relevant only to the issue of damages and expert testimony is required to establish whether plaintiff's injuries would have been decreased, diminished, or lessened by the use of such restraints. See *Truman* v. *Vargas* (1969), 275 Cal. App. 2d 976, 80 Cal. Rptr. 373, in which plaintiff testified that he had failed to wear a seat belt at the time of the collision:

> "From what injuries would (Plaintiff) have been saved if he had been using a seat belt? Projected forward by the great force caused by the collision what would have been the effects upon his body if he had been wearing the seat belt? The non-expert could only guess. We will not undertake to enumerate the factors that would be considered by physicists and other experts in answering these questions. We are not certain they would all agree in their opinions but expert opinions are essential to an informed and intelligent determination as to these critical facts."

..... etc.

III

The final basis on which any suggestion has been made of plaintiff's contributory negligence is contained in answers of defendants to interrogatories of plaintiff to the effect that plaintiff's turning of her wheels to the left as she awaited the opportunity to make her left turn at the intersection caused her to move into oncoming traffic when she was struck from behind by defendant.

Such a suggestion is so inherently incredible that it merits no discussion. Whether or not plaintiff did turn her wheels to the left in anticipation of making her left turn, such conduct does not constitute negligence contributing as a proximate cause to the bringing about of injury. Certainly the fact of turning her wheels to the left could not have avoided or minimized the injury to plaintiff occasioned by the initial collision. At most such evidence could only tend to diminish the extent of the injuries occasioned by the collision for which defendant was responsible. Thus, as a matter of law, such facts could not constitute contributory negligence.

IV

Defendants have pleaded the defense of assumption of the risk, but have yet to advance any theory on which such defense is based. It should be noted in this regard that one does not and cannot assume the risk of another's violation of a statute. See generally 2 Witkin, Summary of California Law, Torts Section 352 (3).

Respectfully Submitted,

COMMENTS

Form 2.2   Contributory Negligence and Assumption of the Risk

To draft this type of one issue brief, you have to be familiar with the theory of contributory negligence and the assumption of the risk; and know the elements thereof which must be present to make them valid contentions in your brief. And of course, be able to support them with the appropriate case law and authority.

You are cautioned, however, to check your local codes to determine if these two theories of negligence are still applicable in your state.

2.3   APPEAL

Introduction

An appeal is a procedure whereby a trial court's decision is reviewed by a higher court.

In a civil appeal, the decision being appealed is an injustice done or error committed by the court of original jurisdiction, whose judgment or decision the appellate court is being called upon to correct or reverse. It is generally a re-hearing as to both law and fact of judgments or orders handed down by the lower court. Examples of these appealable orders are:

1. A final judgment;
2. Judgment on appeal in a lower court;
3. An order granting motion to quash service of summons;
4. An order granting a new trial;
5. Orders pertaining to application for injunction; or
6. Interlocutory orders specified by the Code of Civil Procedure or other statutory regulation.

In a criminal appeal, the decision being appealed usually is a judgment convicting a person of a crime and the sentence handed down pertinent thereto. The defendant will now be known as the "appellant" and will be trying to convince the reviewing court that the trial court committed errors which appear in the appellate record; and that because of these errors the trial court's decision was wrong and should be reversed.

For example, if the appeal is from a conviction of an offense, the appellant may argue that he should not have been convicted, either because he was not guilty or because he felt he did not receive a fair trial. Thus, the appellant would argue that the sentence which the trial court imposed was excessive and should be reduced.

In the latter appellate procedure the state's attorney (or attorney general) represents the state on appeal. The state is then known as the "appellee." The state attorney attempts to convince the court on review that the trial court's decision was correct and should be affirmed.

By way of example only, consider the following appellate procedure as used in the State of Illinois:*

SAMPLE APPELLATE PROCEDURE (ILLINOIS)

Notice of Appeal

The first step of an appeal is the filing of a Notice of Appeal. The notice must be filed within 30 days of the date of the order being appealed. In some cases, as when the defendant was not informed of his right to appeal or he has a legitimate excuse for not filing a timely notice, a notice may be filed within six months from the expiration date of the original 30 days.

The Notice of Appeal is filed in the Circuit (trial) Court. Once the notice is filed, the trial judge determines if the appellant can afford to hire an attorney. If he cannot, the judge appoints an attorney to represent him. A late Notice of Appeal is filed in the Appellate Court.

---

* See correlation table in the Appendix (page 371) to determine where you may find appellate rules and regulations as provided under the Federal Rules of Civil Procedure.

Record on Appeal

The next step in the appellate process is the preparation of the Record on Appeal. The Record on Appeal consists of the Report of Proceedings (transcript) and the Common Law Record. The Common Law Record contains all the documents which were filed in the case, e.g., indictment, motions, orders, etc.

An appeal is based on the record. Only issues which appear in the report of proceedings or common law record may be raised in the brief, prepared by the appellant's attorney.

The official court reporter is responsible for preparing the report of proceedings. Although the Rules of the Illinois Supreme Court provide that the reporter has only 49 days in which to prepare the transcript, the Rules also allow the time to be extended. This happens in many cases.

When the court reporter finishes typing the shorthand notes, (s)he files the transcript with the Clerk of the Circuit Court. (S)He files an original and a copy, or (s)he may file only the original and send the copy to the defendant or his attorney.

After the transcript is filed, the Clerk has 14 days in which to prepare the Common Law Record. The Common Law Record and the transcript are then filed in the Appellate Court. The Clerk may also request additional time in which to file the record on appeal.

When the Record on Appeal is filed in the Appellate Court, the case is given an appellate number.

Appellant's Brief and Abstract

Once the Record on Appeal has been filed, the appellant's attorney has 35 days in which to prepare and file the brief and abstract. At times, due to the complexity of the case, it may be necessary to ask for an extension of time. The Abstract is a summary of the Record on Appeal. The Brief is a written argument stating the reasons why the trial court's decision should be reversed. The brief is based on the record and may not contain arguments based on evidence or allegations which are *not* included in the Record on Appeal.

State's Brief

The next step is the preparation of the State's brief. The State's Attorney has 35 days from the date the appellant's brief was due in which to prepare and file his brief. In many cases the State will request and be granted extra time in which to file its brief. The State's brief is also based on the Record on Appeal and contains arguments supporting the trial court's actions.

The State's Attorney is not required to file an abstract.

Reply Brief

The appellant's attorney *may* file a reply brief to answer the State's brief. A reply brief is not filed in every case. The appellant has 14 days from the day the State's brief was due in which to file a reply brief.

Oral Argument

Once all the briefs have been filed, the Appellate Court will set a date for oral argument. On the date set, the appellant's attorney and the State's Attorney appear before three (3) judges and argue the case. The appellant is not brought to court in person for the oral argument. There are no witnesses, and the court does not hear new evidence.

Decision

After the judges of the Appellate Court have read the briefs and the abstract and have heard the oral argument, they decide whether the case should be affirmed or reversed, or if the sentence should be reduced. Once a decision is reached, the judges write an opinion stating their decision and the reasons for it. There is no set time within which the decision must be reached and the opinion written. Usually, the decision is announced within six months after oral argument.

Motions

During the course of an appeal, motions may be filed by the appellant's attorney or by the State's Attorney. For example, sometimes the Record on Appeal as filed in the Appellate Court does not contain everything that it is supposed to contain. In that case, the appellant's attorney will file a Motion to Supplement the Record on Appeal which is a request that the Appellate Court order the trial court personnel to prepare and file the material which was omitted.

In some cases the appellant's attorney or the State's Attorney will need additional time in which to file the brief. The attorney will file a Motion for Extension of Time which requests that the Appellate Court grant additional time in which to file the brief.

Appeal Bond

Ordinarily, bond motions are not filed during the course of an appeal. Until the record on appeal is filed in the Appellate Court, the trial judge retains the authority to entertain such motions, but thereafter such motions are to be filed in the Appellate Court. An appeal bond is rarely granted after a conviction. If the appellate record establishes substantial issues for review *and* if the appellant's background shows that he would be eligible for a bond, the attorney may petition the Appellate Court for his release on bond.

Timetable for an Appeal

(Subject to Motions for Extension of Time)

NOTICE OF APPEAL	Must be filed within 30 days of sentence (or within 30 days of any other final order being appealed).
REPORT OF PROCEEDINGS DUE	49 days after notice of appeal filed.
RECORD ON APPEAL DUE	14 days after report of proceedings filed.
APPELLANT'S BRIEF AND ABSTRACT DUE	35 days after record on appeal filed.
STATE'S BRIEF DUE	35 days after appellant's brief and abstract due.
REPLY BRIEF DUE	14 days after State's brief due.
ORAL ARGUMENT	Date determined by court.
DECISION	Date determined by court.
PETITION FOR REHEARING	21 days from decision date.
PETITION FOR LEAVE TO APPEAL TO SUPREME COURT	56 days from decision date or 35 days from denial of Petition for Rehearing.
PETITION FOR WRIT OF CERTIORARI TO THE UNITED STATES SUPREME COURT	90 days from final order or opinion of Illinois Supreme Court

2.4 NOTICE OF APPEAL

Attorney Information

SUPERIOR COURT OF THE STATE OF _____
IN AND FOR THE COUNTY OF _____

JOHN DOE,	)	No. 326442
	)	
Plaintiff,	)	NOTICE OF APPEAL
	)	
vs.	)	
	)	
JAMES SMITH,	)	
	)	
Defendant.	)	
_____	)	

Appeal is made by defendant _____ to the Court of Appeals of the State of _____, First Appellate District, from the orders entered in this action on December 22, 19__, denying defendant's motion for a preliminary injunction, denying defendant's motion to set aside the default judgment entered on or about November 23, 19__, against defendant and denying defendant's motion to quash the writ of execution served upon defendant on or about December 18, 19__.

December 28, 19__

_____
Attorney for defendant

COMMENTS

Form 2.4   Notice of Appeal*

This form is self-explanatory. A Notice of Appeal is commonly used when a party-litigant is appealing from any judgment or order entered by the court of original jurisdiction.

It is a way of telling the court and all parties interested that the appellant is not satisfied with the judgment as it was unfair, or a gross injustice, the award was excessive and so forth, and another opinion is desired.

2.5   NOTICE TO PREPARE CLERK'S TRANSCRIPT

Attorney's name

COURT CAPTION

PARTIES
)
)
)
)
)

Case No.

NOTICE TO PREPARE
CLERK'S TRANSCRIPT

NOTICE IS GIVEN of a request by defendant and appellant, _____, that the clerk incorporate the following papers and records in the record on appeal:

1. All papers and records on file or lodged with the clerk, including the clerk's minutes, to wit:

(a) Complaint on file in the above action;
(b) Request to enter default;
(c) Writ of execution;
(d) Eviction notice;

_____

* Text references: Your local Civil and Criminal Codes, Appeal Section; Federal Rules of Practice.

    (e) Answer to complaint on file in the above action;

    (f) Cross-complaint for temporary restraining order;

(and any other pleadings or notes your boss may want incorporated)

    Dated:

_____

COMMENTS

Form 2.5   Notice to Prepare Clerk's Transcript*

   (*Note*: the Notice to Prepare Reporter's Transcript is similar in content and form.)

    This form is also self-explanatory and should be served on all parties to the suit. You are asking the clerk of the court of original jurisdiction to pull together all of the within contents to aid your attorney in preparing his appeal by reviewing any and all documents heretofore filed in the action. This may include deposition and interrogatory transcripts if they have been used in the trial of the matter.

2.6   SAMPLE BRIEF—"REAL PARTY IN INTEREST'S BRIEF..."

2nd Civil No.

IN THE SUPREME COURT OF THE STATE
OF _____

A CORPORATION,	)
	)
Petitioner,	)
	)
vs.	)
	)
SUPERIOR COURT OF THE	)
STATE OF _____ FOR	)
THE COUNTY OF _____,	)
	)
Respondent,	)
	)
_____	)
	)
Real Party in Interest.	)
_____	)

_____

* Text reference: *supra*

REAL PARTY IN INTEREST'S BRIEF
IN OPPOSITION TO PETITION FOR WRIT
IN THE NATURE OF MANDATE OR PROHIBITION

This action is an action on behalf of insureds, who paid all of the premiums on group credit insurance, for recovery of a portion of One Million Nine Hundred Thousand Dollars ($1,900,000.00) in premium refunds received and retained by the Petitioner, _____.

(For Petitioner's statement on the scope of liability see pp. 28-29 and p. 40 of Transcript of Proceedings, July 13, 19__, Department 36).

The core of the complaint, as stated above, has been previously determined on the merits in a class action brought twenty (20) years ago. In 19__, the _____ Superior Court entered judgment for a class of persons insured under a group policy in _____ v. _____, Case Number _____. (See p. 84, et seq., of Petitioner's Brief). Immediately after the judgment in _____, in 19__, the _____ Legislature enacted legislation requiring excess dividends on group policies be applied for the benefit of the insureds. (See Insurance Code §§10214 and 10270.65).

The alternative writ should not issue because:

1. Petitioner asks this Court to place the Trial Courts in a procedural straitjacket by mandating notice at a specific time in the proceedings.

2. The _____ Superior Court, after extensive study of the problems involved in the trial of class actions, adopted the ''Manual for Conduct of Pretrial Hearings on Class Action Issues.'' The Manual, directly contrary to Petitioner's representation (see page 2, paragraph 6, of Petition), specifically provides for a procedure in which there may be a bifurcation of the issue of liability from the class issues, and an early trial of the issue of liability. (See Manual, Section 427.7(b) and Section 441 attached hereto as Exhibit.)

3. Plaintiff's motion for bifurcation and early trial of the issue of liability was made pursuant to Section 441 of the Manual; the Court's order granting the motion came only after two (2) hearings, June 1, 19__, and July 13, 19__, and two (2) months of deliberation by the Court. (Motion to Bifurcate filed May, 19__; Order granting motion filed August 3, 19__).

4. Under Manual procedures, a judgment as to liability for or against the plaintiff would not foreclose a later decision on the procedural question of whether a proper class action had been stated.

5. If the petitioner were to prevail in this action, and in the subsequent proceedings, the Court found the action to be a proper class action, the judgment on the liability half of the trial would be res judicata against the class.

6. In other class actions litigated, the procedure was exactly the one contemplated by the Trial Court in this case. In those cases, trial was held on the issue of liability only; after a finding of no liability, the Trial Court went on to determine the class issues and found the actions to be good class actions, and the decision binding upon the class.

7. Petitioner's comment that it is in mortal fear that it might prevail without obtaining a res judicata effect is a fear without foundation.

8. Petitioner's contention that the Fourteenth Amendment of the United States Constitution requires notice is an issue shortly to be decided by the United States Supreme Court. On October 15, 19___, the United States Supreme Court agreed to review the decision upon which petitioner relies in seeking this writ. (*Eisen v. Carlisle & Jacquelin, et al.* (C.A. 2d Cir. 1973); Fed. Sec. Law. Rptr., Para. 93963).

9. Petitioner's position that notice must precede any judgment on liability precludes the possibility of binding summary judgments in class actions; many class action defendants who have secured or may secure judgment summarily, will be in a state of shock to learn they have no binding judgment against the class on petitioner's theory.

10. Petitioner goes too far in contending notice is required at a particular point in the litigation; i.e., before a determination of liability. (*Alameda Oil Co. v. Ideal Basic Industries, Inc.*, 326 Fed. Supp. 98 at 105, 1971).

11. A rigid requirement that notice precede a determination of liability could constitute a threat to a corporate defendant, although no liability might in fact exist, as this requirement could be used by unscrupulous plaintiffs to bring meritless strike suits and exact settlements to avoid circulation of a notice which could have disastrous economic implications.

12. Petitioner's position is inconsistent with Civil Code Sections 1781(c) and (d) which do not make notice to the class in advance of trial on the issue of liability mandatory. That portion of Rule 23 of the Federal Rules of Civil Procedure which makes such notice mandatory prior to trial of the issue of liability is one of the most criticized portions of Rule 23, and the _____ Legislature chose not to adopt the philosophy of Rule 23 in this regard.

13. The issue of class is not a real issue in this case. In 1953, in a California case involving similar issues (set forth in full in Petitioner's Petition for Hearing, commencing at page 84 of the Petition for Hearing in this matter), the court held that all persons insured under a group life disability policy constituted a proper class for the purpose of determination as to whether such insureds were entitled to dividends or experience refunds received by the group policy holder under the group policy.

14. The case in favor of the procedure adopted by the Superior Court was well stated in an article entitled "Class Actions—The Defense Viewpoint," volume 47, no. 11, September 1972, The Los Angeles Bar Bulletin:

> "If the legality of the challenge practice is sustained, the other burdensome questions (existence of class, notice, and so forth) are never reached. This is the procedure suggested in *Alameda Oil Co. v. Ideal Basic Industires* where the court observed facts setting in motion all of the class action machinery prior to a determination of the basic liability question would subject all parties to expense which might be dispro-

portionate to the intrinsic merits of the case. It was then decided that the basic liability issue would be tried first. The court considered its approach 'innovative,' properly observing that F.R.C.P. Rule 23' ... itself is new and requires such efforts.' This bifurcated procedure, with trial of the basic liability issue first, was recently utilized in California in consolidated cases involving retail department stores.''

We respectfully submit that the writ should not issue.

Respectfully submitted,

Attorneys for Real Party in
Interest

COMMENTS

Form 2.6   Sample Brief: ''Real Party In Interest's Brief....''

This is a complete narrative example of a brief which is to be used as a guide only as to its contents and format.

2.7(A)   TOPICAL INDEX

TOPICAL INDEX

STATEMENT OF THE CASE   Page
CONCLUSION
APPENDIX—OPINION OF COURT OF APPEALS

TABLE OF AUTHORITIES

Bixby v. Pierno, 4 Cal. 3d 130.

CODES

California Vehicle Code
Section 12800 through 12804
Section 13353
Section 14109
Section 14400

RULES

California Rules of Appeal—10(b)

2.7(B)   TOPICAL INDEX (ALTERNATIVE)

TOPICAL INDEX

TABLE OF AUTHORITIES   Page

PREFATORY STATEMENT

ARGUMENT

I.   THE DISTRICT COURT ERRED IN
     DENYING PLAINTIFFS LEAVE TO FILE
     THEIR PROPOSED SECOND AMENDED
     COMPLAINT

II. THE DISTRICT COURT ERRED IN
     GRANTING DEFENDANT'S ORDER
     VACATING THE NOTICE OF DEPOSITION
     OF DEFENDANT _____.

III. THE DISTRICT COURT ERRED IN ORDERING
     THAT ALL DISCOVERY BE COMPLETED BY
     NOVEMBER 29, 19__.

IV. THE DISTRICT COURT ERRED IN DISMISSING
     THE ACTION ON THE BASIS OF PLAINTIFF'S
     ALLEGED FAILURE TO EXHAUST
     ADMINISTRATIVE REMEDIES.

CONCLUSION

CERTIFICATE OF SERVICE

APPENDIX

COMMENTS

Forms 2.7(A) and (B)

These are option formats for indexes which can be used in appellate briefs, the utilization of which depends on the nature and extent of the case, as well as the option of your attorney as to how much he wants to include in the brief; and/or the policy of court, or both.

2.8 STIPULATION FOR DISMISSAL OF APPEAL

IN THE COURT OF APPEAL
OF THE STATE OF CALIFORNIA
FOURTH APPELLATE DISTRICT
DIVISION TWO

Petitioner and Appellant,	)	NO. 4 CIV.
vs.	)	
	)	
	)	
Defendant and Respondent.	)	
	)	

STIPULATION FOR DISMISSAL

IT IS HEREBY STIPULATED by the parties, through their respective counsel, that the appeal of _____ from the judgment in favor of defendant and respondent _____ entered pursuant to stipulation and sustaining defendant's demurrer on July 15, 19__, may be dismissed without costs to either party and that the remittitur may be issued forthwith.

IT IS FURTHER STIPULATED that said Dismissal is without prejudice to plaintiff and appellant to file a complaint in Riverside County Superior Court Case Number _____ if said case is reversed by the appellate court in the appeal, No. 4 Civ. _____, now before the Fourth Appellate District.

IT IS FURTHER STIPULATED that the defendant and respondent, _____ will not assert the defense of Res Judicata with respect to the judgment which will become final in the Case No. _____ to a complaint which will be filed if plaintiff and appellant prevails in his appeal in Case No. _____ (4th Civ. No. _____).

IT IS FURTHER STIPULATED that this request for dismissal is made because all of the issues which might be raised by plaintiff and appellant in this appeal have merged with those issues raised by appellant in the companion case, No. 4 Civ. _____ and therefore to perfect an appeal in the instant case would be superfluous.

DATED: February 9, 19__.

By _____
Attorneys for Plaintiff
and Appellant

By _____
Attorneys for Respondent and
Defendant

ORDER FOR DISMISSAL OF APPEAL

The written stipulation of the parties for an order dismissing the appeal of _____ from the judgment of the Riverside County Superior Court, Case No. ____, having been filed, and good cause appearing, the same is hereby ordered dismissed without prejudice and without costs to either party.

DATED: _____

_____
Presiding Justice

2.9 APPEAL RE DISMISSAL OF ACTION

NO. _____

NO. _____

IN THE
UNITED STATES COURT OF APPEALS
FOR THE NINTH DISTRICT

_____	)
_____	)
Plaintiffs-Appellants,	)
vs.	)
_____	)
_____	)
Defendant-Appellee.	)
_____	)
_____	)
Plaintiffs-Appellees,	)
vs.	)
_____	)
_____	)
Defendant-Appellant.	)
_____	)

APPEAL FROM THE UNITED STATES
DISTRICT COURT FOR THE
CENTRAL DISTRICT OF CALIFORNIA

(Re: Dismissal of Action)

PLAINTIFF'S-APPELLANTS'
REPLY BRIEF

By _____
(Local Address)

Attorneys for Plaintiffs) Appellants

_____

_____

By _____
(Local Address)

Plaintiff-Appellant,
in Propria Personal and as
Attorney for _____
Plaintiff-Appellant

)
)
)
)
)
)
)
)
)
)
)
)
)
)
)
)
)
)
)
)
)
)
)
)
)
)

No. _____
No. _____

UNITED STATES COURT OF APPEALS
FOR THE NINTH CIRCUIT

_____, a California
corporation, _____, _____,
and _____,

    Plaintiffs-Appellants,

vs.

_____, ADMINISTRATOR
OF THE SMALL BUSINESS
ADMINISTRATION,

    Defendant-Appellee.

)
)
)
)
)
)
)
)
)
)
)
)
)
)
)

```
_____, a California        )
corporation, _____, _____,  )
and _____,                     )
                                  )
          Plaintiffs-Appellants,  )
                                  )
                                  )
vs.                               )
                                  )
_____, ADMINISTRATOR        )
OF THE SMALL BUSINESS             )
ADMINISTRATION,                   )
                                  )
          Defendant-Appellant.    )
                                  )
_____)
```

PLAINTIFFS'-APPELLANTS' REPLY BRIEF

PREFATORY STATEMENT

For the reasons and authorities set forth in plaintiffs' opening brief and hereinafter, the District Court has jurisdiction of the causes of action set forth in plaintiffs' First Amended Complaint, as well as over defendant's counterclaims. Put somewhat differently, we agree with defendant's contention that the District Court has jurisdiction over defendant's counterclaims [DB. 19-20] and so indicated in the Pre-Trial Conference Order [R. 214] as well as at the hearing which occurred on March 11, 19___, when the District Court announced its intent to dismiss the entire action [T. 8]. Accordingly, plaintiffs shall not reply to defendant's brief relative to defendant's cross-appeal.

Plaintiff's opening brief sufficiently sets forth the statement of the case and defendant's brief has not necessitated any further such statement.

TOPICAL INDEX

TABLE OF AUTHORITIES

ARGUMENT

THE DISTRICT COURT ERRED IN DENYING
PLAINTIFFS LEAVE TO FILE THEIR PROPOSED
SECOND AMENDED COMPLAINT.

II

THE DISTRICT COURT ERRED IN GRANTING
DEFENDANT'S ORDER VACATING THE NOTICE
OF DEPOSITION OF DEFENDANT.

III

THE DISTRICT COURT ERRED IN ORDERING THAT
ALL DISCOVERY BE COMPLETED BY NOVEMBER   , 19___.

IV.

THE DISTRICT COURT ERRED IN DISMISSING THE ACTION ON THE BASIS OF PLAINTIFFS' ALLEGED FAILURE TO EXHAUST ADMINISTRATIVE REMEDIES.

CONCLUSION

For the foregoing reasons, the Orders of the District Court denying plaintiffs leave to file a Second Amended Complaint, denying plaintiffs the right to take a percipient witness' deposition, who is also the defendant, terminating discovery and dismissing the entire action, are erroneous.

Plaintiffs urge:

1. That each of the orders appealed from be reversed; and,
2. The action be remanded to the District Court with directions:

   (a) That plaintiffs be granted leave to file a Second Amended Complaint;

   (b) That upon reasonable notice, plaintiffs be allowed to take the deposition of defendant _____ upon oral examination;

   (c) That the parties be allowed a reasonable time of not less than 90 days to complete necessary discovery before trial; and,

   (d) That after prescribed pre-trial procedure, any unresolved issues be heard on the merits.

Respectfully submitted,

_____

Attorney for Plaintiffs-Appellants

_____

_____, Plaintiff-

Appellant, In Propria
Persona and as Attorney for
Plaintiff-Appellant

CERTIFICATE OF SERVICE

I hereby certify that on the ___ day of _____, 19___, I served a copy of the Reply Brief for Plaintiffs-Appellants, by causing copies to be mailed postage prepaid to:

_____ (2) copies
Assistant Attorney General

_____

_____

Attorneys
Department of Justice
Civil Division, Appellate Section
Washington, D.C. 20530

_____ (2) copies
United States Attorney

_____

_____

Assistant U.S. Attorneys
(Local Address)

_____ (2) copies
Assistant Attorneys General
(Local Address)

CLERK OF THE U.S. DISTRICT COURT (2) copies
Central District of California
312 North Spring Street
Los Angeles, California 90012

Plaintiffs-Appellants claim the three (3) day mailing privilege under Rule 26, F.R. App. P.

_____

APPENDIX

1. Summary of contract agreements
2. Notice of Motion; Motion for an Order Compelling Discovery
3. Memorandum of Points and Authorities in Support of Motion;
4. Affidavits in Support thereof;
5. Application for Order Shortening Time for Service of above-mentioned Motion and Order
6. Deposition Subpoena to Testify or Produce Documents or Things
7. Summary of Contract administration and management

2.10 APPEAL FROM JUDGMENT

IN THE COURT OF APPEAL OF THE STATE OF _____
SECOND APPELLATE DISTRICT
DIVISION THREE

John Smith,	)	2D CIV. NO. ___
Petitioner and Respondent,	)	SUP. Ct. NO. ___
	)	
vs.	)	
	)	
William Holden, Director	)	
of Motor Vehicles of the State of	)	
_____	)	
	)	
Defendant and Appellant.	)	

APPEAL from a judgment of the Superior Court of _____ County, _____ Judge. Reversed with directions.

_____ Attorney General, and _____, Deputy Attorney General, for Defendant and Appellant.
_____ for Petitioner and Respondent.

———————

    The State Director of Motor Vehicles appeals from a judgment directing the issuance of a peremptory writ of mandate commanding him to set aside his order, pursuant to Vehicle Code section 13353, to suspend for six months the privilege of petitioner, _____, to operate a motor vehicle upon highways in this state. The appeal lies. (Code Civ. Proc., §§904.1(a), 1094.5(f).)

    On the basis of the departmental record alone the trial court concluded that the evidence was insufficient to support the Department's findings that _____ refused to submit to a chemical test of his blood, breath or urine to determine the alcoholic content of his blood after being requested to do so by a peace officer following his arrest on probable cause for driving a vehicle on a highway under the influence of intoxicating liquor (Veh. Code, § 23102(a)) and after being advised by the officer that failure to do so would result in the suspension of his driving privilege for six months.

    Such insufficiency was found on the basis that the departmental record was confusing (a) as to whether _____ was actually advised by the officer that he did not have a right to have an attorney present before deciding whether to take a chemical test of his choice and (b) as to precisely the advice the officer gave _____ regarding Section 13353. On the foregoing basis alone the trial court found and concluded that _____ did not refuse to take one of the three chemical tests.

The trial court also found that _____ was honestly and sincerely confused by the advice he received from the officer regarding his *Miranda* rights and the admonition concerning the taking of one of the three chemical tests and therefore had the conscientious and honest belief that he had a right to consult with an attorney before agreeing to submit to one of such tests.

The trial court further found that thereafter _____, pursuant to the advice of his attorney, did offer without success to submit to a chemical test within forty-five minutes to one hour after being detained, that the offer was thereafter unsuccessfully repeated by his attorney approximately one-half to three-quarters of an hour later and that thereafter _____'s personal physician at _____'s request withdrew blood from him for the purpose of such a test, but that such blood sample was also refused by the authorities.

The trial court, in reaching the foregoing conclusion in the manner in which it did, committed reversible error. Our reasons follow.

THE ADMINISTRATIVE RECORD

About 2:00 a.m., September 23, 19___, _____ Highway Patrol Officer _____ arrested _____ on probable cause for driving on a highway under the influence of intoxicating liquor (Veh. Code, § 23102(a)), read from a card his constitutional rights as enunciated in *Miranda* v. *Arizona*, 384 U.S. 436 (including his right to consult an attorney), requested that he waive these rights and then read to him the front of DMV form 367 informing him that he must take his choice of one of the three aforementioned chemical tests to determine the alcoholic content of his blood and that refusal to submit to one of these tests would result in the suspension of his driving privilege for six months.[1]

_____ stated that he understood his *Miranda* rights and that he would like to talk to _____. He answered several questions and then agreed to take a breath test.

When such a test, however, had been set up at a nearby sheriff's substation, _____ said "Book me. Forget any test". He then made some reference to an attorney"[2] whereupon _____ read him the front of Form 367 again and then

---

[1] The front of form 367 reads:

"You are requested to submit to a chemical test to determine the alcoholic content of your blood. You have a choice whether the test is to be of your blood, breath or urine. A refusal will result in the suspension of your driving privilege for a period of six months."

[2] _____'s testimony as to whether _____ made some reference to an attorney varied. He first so testified; he later denied that _____ had said anything to him about an attorney.

read him the back of the form to the effect that his *Miranda* rights did not include the right to refuse a chemical test.[3] _____ then refused all three tests and the officer booked him and left the station at approximately 2:30 p.m. As indicated earlier, in summarizing certain of the findings of the trial court, _____, after talking to his attorney somewhat later, unsuccessfully offered twice to submit to one of the required chemical tests and upon the refusal of these offers, apparently as being too late, had his personal physician withdraw blood for such a test, but this sample was also refused by the authorities, presumably for the same reason.

_____ testified that the only advice he received from the officer at the scene of his arrest was regarding his *Miranda* rights, that nothing was said to him about his being required to take a chemical test until he was at the substation, that he then said that he first wanted to call his attorney, that he was never told that his *Miranda* rights had no application to his decision whether to take a chemical test and that he first learned of the consequences of a refusal on his part to take such a test from his attorney in their telephone conversation an hour or so after his arrival at the substation when the call was first permitted.

DISCUSSION

Since driving a motor vehicle on the highways of this state is a privilege and not a "fundamental vested right of the individual," judicial review under Code of Civil Procedure Section 1094.5(c) of an administrative suspension of the privilege is limited to determining whether the administrative findings are supported by substantial evidence in the light of the whole record. (See *Bixby* v. *Pierno*, 4 Cal. 3d 130, 144.) If the findings are so supported they are binding on reviewing courts. Furthermore, the evidence in the administrative record must be viewed in the light most favorable to the administrative decision which means that it must be given the benefit of every reasonable inference from the evidence and all conflicts in the evidence must be resolved in its favor. (*Beverly Hills Fed. S. & L. Assn.* v. *Superior Court*, 259 Cal.App.2d 306, 317-18.)

The trial court's judgment against the Director apparently rests on the rationale developed in *Rust* v. *Department of Motor Vehicles*, 267 Cal. App. 2d

---

[3] The back of Form 367 reads in pertinent part:

"Your right to remain silent or have an attorney present does not include the right to refuse a chemical test . . ."

Since November 23, 19___, Section 13353(a) has contained the following regarding this advice.

"Such person shall also be advised by the officer that he does not have the right to have an attorney present before stating whether he will submit to a test, before deciding which test to take, or during administration of the test chosen."

The quoted advice given by _____ to _____ is found in _____'s sworn statement, the receipt of which by the Department under Vehicle Code Section 13353(b initiated the suspension proceeding before us. _____ objected unsuccessfully to it being received in evidence, but its receipt in evidence was proper. (See *Fankhauser* v. *Orr*, 268 Cal.App.2d 418, 422-23.)

545, 547, and *West v. Department of Motor Vehicles*, 275 Cal.App.2d 908, 910-11, that if a driver's refusal to submit to a chemical test has been caused by the conflicting advice he has received from the arresting officer, such refusal does not warrant the suspension of his driving privilege under Section 13353(c).

The difficulty with this rationale in this case is that the trial court, in reaching it, exceeded its just delineated power of judicial review under Code of Civil Procedure Section 1094.5. The issue before the Department was solely one of the relative credibility of Officer _____ and driver _____ on the factual point as to whether the officer did advise _____ before he refused to take any chemical test that his prior advice to _____ that he had the right to consult with an attorney had no application to this statutory requirement that he submit to such a test on pain of otherwise having his driving privilege suspended by the Director of Motor Vehicles for six months. The trial court resolved this issue of credibility against the officer on the basis that, according to _____'s testimony, as soon as he had been advised by his attorney that he had to take a test of his choice or otherwise lose his driving privilege for six months, he tried repeatedly but unsuccessfully to do so.

This is a reasonable resolution of the conflict in the testimony of these two witnesses. The resolution of this conflict was, however for the trier of fact at the departmental level and not for the trial court. As we have already indicated, the trial court was obligated under Code of Civil Procedure Section 1094.5(c) to accept the findings of the Department if they were supported by substantial evidence. This they were.

A finding of confusion in the administrative record is not equivalent to a finding of insubstantiality in supporting evidence therein. Moreover, contrary to the trial court's finding, there was no confusion in the departmental record as to precisely what advice Officer _____ gave _____ regarding the nonapplicability of his *Miranda* rights to his duty to take a chemical test. Again, on the crucial point as to whether _____ actually gave this advice to _____, the administrative record was not confused. Instead, a conflict existed between the testimony of the two witnesses, and the trial court, as we have already said, was required to accept the Department's resolution of the conflict.

Finally, any confusion in _____'s mind following _____'s explicit advice on the point was legally unwarranted.[4] (See *Reirdon v. Director of Dept. of Motor Vehicles*, 266 Cal. App.2d 808, 811; *Goodman v. Orr*, 19 Cal.App.3d 845, 857-58.)

---

[4] The situation of _____ in this case is unlike that of Decker in *Decker v. Department of Motor Vehicles*, 6 Cal.3d 903. There, our Supreme Court affirmed the Superior Court's issuance of a peremptory writ of mandate ordering the Director of Motor Vehicles to set aside his order of suspension because the arresting officer advised Decker that if he refused to take one of the three chemical tests, his driving privilege *could* be suspended for a period of six months (905).

The judgment is reversed and the trial court is directed to enter instead a judgment denying to petitioner a peremptory writ of mandate.

_____, Acting P.J.

We concur:

_____, J.

_____, J.

Contents—Chapter 3
Arbitration

3

ARBITRATION

3.0   INTRODUCTION

Although it has been on the statute books since on or about 1927 in the various states throughout the country, and repealed and re-enacted, the methodology of seeking to arbitrate a controversy pursuant to agreement before the courts has just now begun to be widely used by attorneys. Some key definitions are appropriate here:

What is meant by arbitration? Black's Law Dictionary defines arbitration as "the submission for determination of disputed matter to private, unofficial persons selected in a manner provided by law or agreement."

What are the types of arbitration? Primarily used are compulsory arbitration and voluntary arbitration.

Compulsory arbitration occurs when consent of one of the parties involved in the dispute is enforced by statutory provisions.

Voluntary arbitration speaks for itself. It is done by way of mutual and free consent of all parties involved.

It should be noted that submission is done by way of agreement wherein the parties agree to submit their differences to the decision of a referee or arbitrator. One key point should be added to this statement; when the parties agree or are forced to submit their dispute to arbitration, a valid award by the arbiters settles all claims and disputes and precludes any future litigation on the facts or the cause of action arising therefrom.

When is it determined that the submission to arbitration is the only way to go?

1. Arbitration may be used by attorneys on behalf of their clients where the defendant has insurance but the parties for whatever reason, cannot agree on a

monetary settlement. In this instance, application may be made to the court to appoint a neutral arbiter to hear the claim and award a binding settlement.

2. Arbitration may be used by the attorney where the plaintiff is involved in an uninsured motorist claim and the plaintiff's insurance company cannot agree on what the case is worth. In this instance, if the plaintiff's insurance company is not listed with the American Arbitration Association and the plaintiff's insurance company does not agree to have this association arbitrate the matter, the claim may be submitted to the court to appoint an arbiter or the plaintiff's insurance company may seek to get an independent arbiter, such as an attorney, to act as the arbitrator or the plaintiff's insurance company may have a clause providing for a different or other procedure.

3. Moreover, it should be noted that arbitration is most often used to expedite the trial or hearing of the triable issues of fact and to hasten the settlement of the claim.

If the arbitration of a controversy is to be conducted by the American Arbitration Association, the *application* form supplied by this association is used and filed with the association with the appropriate filing fee which, as a general rule, is set forth at the bottom of this form.

This association sets forth the date and time and place of the hearing. Further, the American Arbitration Association normally sends out a list of registered attorneys who have heretofore volunteered to act as arbitrators on behalf of the American Arbitration Association. This entire procedure is handled by the American Arbitration Association. Your job, therefore, would merely be to consult with your attorney at to which of the names on the list sent to you by the American Arbitration Association he feels would be appropriate under the circumstances. This is similar to having your attorney pick jurors for jury trial. Accompanying this list of attorneys, is a calendar of dates. Once again, your job would be to pick out the date most convenient to your boss's calendar.

If it is determined between the parties, defendant and plaintiff, that the controversy is to be conducted and arbitrated by a neutral arbitrator, chosen by the parties, the following is the step-by-step procedure to be conducted: You as the legal assistant, and as the moving party, after a consultation with your boss, should prepare a list of attorneys he feels would be competent as arbitrators under the circumstances and willing to serve as such. This list, with a covering letter, should be sent to the defendant for him to approve or send a counter-list of attorneys he feels would be competent under the circumstances.

As a general rule, these independent voluntary attorneys set their own fees, dates and place of the arbitration hearing.

Another method for arbitrating a matter is the request for arbitration of a controversy with the superior court. This method of arbitrating a dispute in controversy is accomplished by filing a formal pleading with the court; however, the complaint, answer and the at-issue memorandum, if applicable, must have been filed prior to the filing of these documents, since the parties are asking the court, in essence, to intervene to help them either:

1. To settle the case;
2. Or reduce the triable issues of fact.
   (You should check your local codes and court rules for this procedure in your state.)

(*Note*: Whichever procedure is used, the award is binding upon all parties, though under certain conditions the award of the neutral arbitrator or the award of the American Arbitration Association may be appealed to the superior court. You should check with your attorney or with your local state codes.)

In any event, once it has been determined that the matter will be arbitrated, regardless of which method is used, the step-by-step procedure for handling the claim and the discovery process is the same; except that the subpoenas for witnesses and documents are prepared by you are mailed to the arbitrator for his signature, and thereafter served on the necessary and appropriate witnesses. For this reason, you should know well in advance the witnesses that your attorney is going to use and the documents that he will be needing to adequately present the client's claim before the arbitrator.

Note: You have the responsibility for supplying the court reporter to take down the testimony at the arbitration hearing. This is often overlooked and at the day of the hearing, it has been our experience that a court reporter has not been ordered. Add this to your checklist when preparing the other documents set forth hereinabove.

As to all of the above, you are once again advised to check your local court rules and regulations as to the step-by-step procedure hereinabove set forth.

See examples of the various types of requests or demands for arbitration hearings at the end of this section.

3.1   AGREEMENT TO ARBITRATE BETWEEN BUILDER AND OWNER

All disputes, claims or questions subject to arbitration under this contract, are to be submitted to arbitration, and the decision of the arbitrators shall be a condition precedent to any right of legal action that either party may have against the other.

Notice of the Demand for Arbitration of a dispute shall be filed, in writing, with the architect and the other party to the contract. If the arbitration is an appeal from the architect's decision, the demand shall be made within _____ days of its receipt; in any other case, the Demand for Arbitration shall be made within a reasonable time after the dispute has arisen.

BUILDER

Dated: _____   BY: _____

Dated: _____   OWNER

BY: _____

COMMENTS

Form 3.1 Agreement to Arbitrate Between Builder and Owner*

This form is a voluntary agreement as between the parties to arbitrate any dispute, and as such, any decision reached by way of arbitration is binding, though the same does not negate the parties' right to have any judgment or award rendered by the arbitrators entered in any federal or state court having jurisdiction thereof. However, the parties may mediate their dispute.

The parties must have had a mediation clause in their contract, or by way of stipulation, to have a dispute so settled to allow them to submit the dispute under the Voluntary Mediation Rules of the American Arbitration Association. This is done by filing a written request (Form 3.2) to arbitrate an existing dispute.

Or,

The initiating party shall, within the time set forth in the contract (agreement), file with the other party a Notice of Intention to arbitrate (Demand for Arbitration).

3.2 AMERICAN ARBITRATION ASSN. CLAUSE (Existing Disputes)

We, the undersigned parties, hereby agree to submit to arbitration under the Commercial Arbitration Rules of the American Arbitration Association the following controversy:

(Here, you should state succinctly and clearly, though briefly, the reasons for the arbitration.)

We further agree that the above controversy be submitted to the arbitrators herein selected from the panels of arbitrators of the American Arbitration Association.

(At this point, your attorney would have selected from a list provided for him by the American Arbitration Association, names of persons willing to act as arbitrators. Under the rules, he can select either one or three.)

---

* Text Reference: Construction Industry Arbitration Rules American Arbitration Association, New York, New York.

We further agree that we will faithfully observe this agreement and the rules, and we will abide by and perform any award rendered by the arbitrator(s) and that a judgment of a court having jurisdiction may be entered upon the award.

Dated: _____   _____

COMMENTS

Form 3.2   American Arbitration Association Clause re: Existing Disputes*

Under the rules of the American Arbitration Association, parties to any existing dispute may commence arbitration hearings under the American Arbitration Rules by filing a written request to so arbitrate their dispute under these rules, which should be signed by both parties.

Here again, no right to judicial proceedings related to the subject matter of the arbitration is forestalled and the same may be entered in any federal or state court having jurisdiction thereof.

3.3   SELECTION OF THIRD ARBITRATOR FROM LIST

To: _____

PLEASE TAKE NOTICE that pursuant to Rule _____ of the Commercial Arbitration Rules, the following list of names of persons selected from the panels of arbitration herein provided, is submitted for the purpose of enabling the arbitrators heretofore designated by the parties to select a third arbitrator, in accordance with the agreement of the parties.

The undersigned, an arbitrator in the above-entitled arbitration, hereby selects from the above list those persons whose names are not crossed off, and authorizes the Tribunal Clerk of the American Arbitration Association to obtain the acceptance of an arbitrator therefrom to serve as the third arbitrator in the above-entitled proceeding.

Dated: _____   _____

COMMENTS

Form 3.3   Selection of Third Arbitrator from List

This form is self-explanatory and should be served on all interested parties, with an accompanying letter.

The original should be sent to the arbitrator so selected and carbon copies sent to all other parties.

---

* Text Reference: Commerical Arbitration Rules, American Arbitration Association, New York, New York.

3.4 ACCIDENT CLAIMS RULES*
DEMAND FOR ARBITRATION

Date:

TO: (Name) _____
(Send original to party upon whom the Demand is made)

(Address) _____

(City and State) _____

The filing party, a party to an Insurance Policy providing for protection against loss sustained in accidents involving Uninsured or Hit-and-Run Motorists which provides for arbitration of disputes arising thereunder in accordance with the Rules of the American Arbitration Association, hereby demands arbitration thereunder.

Issuing Company: _____

Name of Policyholder: _____

Policy Number: _____Effective Dates: _____ to _____

Claim Number: _____

Applicable Policy Limits: _____

NAME(S) OF CLAIMANT(S)	CHECK IF A MINOR	AMOUNT CLAIMED
	☐	
	☐	
	☐	

Date of Accident: _____ Location: _____
(City and State)

CHECK ONE: Uninsured Motorist ☐   Hit-and-Run ☐
NATURE OF INJURY:

HEARING LOCALE REQUESTED: _____
(City and State)

You are hereby notified that copies of our Arbitration Agreement and of this Demand are being filed with the American Arbitration Association at its _____ Regional Office, with the request that it commence the administration of the arbitration.

Signed _____
(May be Signed by Attorney)

_____

* American Arbitration Association.

Name of Attorney _____ Name of Filing Party _____

Address _____ Address _____

Telephone _____ Telephone _____

The original of this Demand should be sent to the other party. Three copies should be filed with a Regional Office of AAA, together with two copies of the Uninsured Motorist Endorsement. The administrative fee of $100 should accompany the initiating papers.

IN ACCORDANCE WITH SECTION 11580.2 (f) OF THE CALIFORNIA INSURANCE CODE, A DECLARATION UNDER PENALTY OF PERJURY MUST BE COMPLETED ... SEE REVERSE

DECLARATION IN ACCORDANCE WITH SECTION 11580.2 (f) OF THE CALIFORNIA INSURANCE CODE, AS AMENDED BY SENATE BILL NO. 66 AND EFFECTIVE SIXTY-ONE (61) DAYS AFTER FINAL ADJOURNMENT OF 1972 REGULAR SESSION.

Insured(s) declare(s) under penalty of perjury:

CHECK APPROPRIATE BOXES
FOR I AND
EITHER II OR III, IF APPROP-
RIATE
CLAIMANT(S)   A   B   C   D   E

I. That the insured(s):

(a) does have a Workmen's Compensation claim ☐ ☐ ☐ ☐ ☐

(b) does not have a Workmen's Compensation claim. ☐ ☐ ☐ ☐ ☐

II. Such claim has proceeded to findings and Award or settlement on all issues reasonably contemplated to be determined in that claim; or, ☐ ☐ ☐ ☐ ☐

III. The claim has not proceeded to findings and Award on all issues reasonably contemplated to be determined in that claim for the following reasons amounting to good cause: ☐ ☐ ☐ ☐ ☐

TYPED NAME AND SIGNATURE OF CLAIMANT(S)

A _____

B _____

C _____

D _____

DATE: _____ E _____

COMMENTS

Form 3.4 Accident Claims Rules—Demand for Arbitration American Arbitration Association

This form is commonly used for personal injury claims sustained in a vehicle collison and filed by the party claiming injuries.

Note that for this claim form to be used, the defendant must be "uninsured," and the plaintiff must have uninsured motorist coverage in their own policy; and/or the defendant must have been adjudged as a "hit-and-run", or sometimes called a "phantom car" driver, and once again the claimant should have coverage for this type of incident. (See Para. #1.)

It is important that the effective dates of the claimant's insurance policy coincide with the date of the accident (Paras. #2 & #3) otherwise the claim will fail.

Para. #4 is where you advise the Arbitration Board under which claim you are filing. To this end it is important that you attach a copy of the section of the claimant's policy covering and permitting your claim under the American Arbitration Rules and either the uninsured motorist or hit-and-run section, whichever is applicable.

3.5 COMMERCIAL ARBITRATION RULES*
DEMAND FOR ARBITRATION

Date: _____

TO: (Name) _____
          (of party upon whom the Demand is made)

    (Address) _____

    (City and State) _____ (Zip Code) _____

    (Telephone) _____

---

* American Arbitration Association Form C2 AAA.

Named claimant, a party to an arbitration agreement contained in a written contract, dated _____, providing for arbitration, hereby demands arbitration thereunder.

(attach arbitration clause or quote hereunder)

(Include page number, article, subsection number pertinent to clause quoted or set forth.)

NATURE OF DISPUTE:

CLAIM OR RELIEF SOUGHT: (amount, if any)

HEARING LOCALE REQUESTED: _____
(City and State)

You are hereby notified that copies of our arbitration agreement and of this demand are being filed with the American Arbitration Association at its _____ Regional Office, with the request that it commence the administration of the arbitration. Under Section 7 of the Commercial Arbitration Rules, you may file an answering statement within seven days after notice from the Administrator.

_____

Signed _____ Title _____
(May be Signed by Attorney)

Name of Claimant _____
Address (to be used in connection with this case) _____
City and State_____ Zip Code _____
Telephone _____
Name of Attorney _____
Address _____
City and State_____ Zip Code _____
Telephone _____

To institute proceedings, please send three copies of this Demand with the administrative fee, as provided in Section 47 of the Rules, to the AAA. Send original Demand to Respondent.

3.6   CONSTRUCTION INDUSTRY ARBITRATION RULES*
DEMAND FOR ARBITRATION

Date:_____

TO: (Name) _____
        (of party upon whom the demand is made)

(Address) _____

(City and State) _____

(Telephone) _____

Named claimant, a party to an arbitration agreement contained in a written contract, dated _____, providing for arbitration under the Construction Industry Arbitration Rules, hereby demands arbitration thereunder. (See comment to Form 3.5)

NATURE OF DISPUTE:

(Non-payment of construction lien for example.)

CLAIM OR RELIEF SOUGHT: (amount, if any)

Please indicate category for each party.

Claimant:

☐ Owner ☐ Architect ☐ Engineer ☐ Contractor ☐ Subcontractor,
Specify _____,
Other _____.

Respondent:

☐ Owner ☐ Architect ☐ Engineer ☐ Contractor ☐ Subcontractor,
Specify _____,
Other _____.

HEARING LOCALE REQUESTED: _____
                                                              (City and State)

You are hereby notified that copies of our Arbitration Agreement and of this Demand are being filed with the American Arbitration Association at its _____ Regional Office, with the request that it commence the administration of the arbitration. Under Section 7 of the Arbitration Rules, you may file an answering statement within seven days after notice from the Administrator.

Signed _____Title _____
                    (May be Signed by Attorney)

_____

* American Arbitration Association Form C2CH.

Name of Claimant _____

Address (to be used in connection with this case) _____

City and State_____ Zip Code _____

Telephone _____

Name of Attorney _____

Address _____

City & State_____ Zip Code _____

Telephone _____

To institute proceedings, please send three copies of this Demand and the arbitration agreement, with the filing fee, as provided in Section 48 of the Rules, to the AAA. Send original Demand to Respondent.

3.7   FAMILY DISPUTE SERVICES*

The individuals whose names appear below hereby submit their family dispute for resolution to the American Arbitration Association pursuant to its Family Dispute Services procedures.

Brief statement of conflict:

Resolution sought:

Nature of service requested: ☐ Mediation ☐ Arbitration

Preferred place of meetings (City, State): _____

The administrative fee for providing a mediator is $100, payable in advance. Required fees of mediators will be established with the parties prior to commencement of services. The administrative fee for arbitration services is set forth in the fee schedule of the Rules.

---

* American Arbitration Association.

Name (Print)	Name (Print)
Street address	Street address
City, State Zip	City, State Zip
Telephone number	Telephone number
Signed by	Signed by

Please file two copies with a local regional office of the American Arbitration Association.
and include the appropriate fee.

COMMENTS

Form 3.7   Family Dispute Services
American Arbitration Association

This form of resolution of a family dispute arises when the parties cannot agree as between themselves or with the help of their respective attorneys.

It attempts to settle their differences as to property, real or personal, and in some instances, custody of children, prior to seeking relief in the court system.

This however, does not waive their right to take the award or judgment to a civil court for final dissolution.

3.8   VOLUNTARY LABOR ARBITRATION RULES*
DEMAND FOR ARBITRATION

Date: _____

To: (Name) _____
          (of party upon whom the Demand is made)

(Street Address) _____

(City and State) _____(Zip Code) _____

(Telephone) _____

The undersigned, a party to an arbitration agreement contained in a written contract, dated _____, providing for arbitration, hereby demands arbitration thereunder.

(attach arbitration clause or quote hereunder)

(See comment to Form 3.5)

---

* American Arbitration Association. Form L2 AAA-15M-2-77.

NATURE OF DISPUTE:

        Cost of living increase in salary; retirement and pension plans; medical benefits etc.

REMEDY SOUGHT:
        Appropriate to examples given.

HEARING LOCALE REQUESTED: _____

You are hereby notified that copies of our arbitration agreement and of this demand are being filed with the American Arbitration Association at its _____ Regional Office, with the request that it commence the administration of the arbitration.

Name of Claimant _____

Signed _____

Title _____

Address _____

City and State_____ Zip Code _____

Telephone _____

To institute proceedings, please send three copies of this Demand with the administrative fee, as provided in Section 43 of the Rules, to the AAA. Send original of Demand to Respondent.

        (See Form 3.2 and Comments)

Contents—Chapter 4
Casualty Claims (Tort Actions)

4

CASUALTY CLAIMS
(TORT ACTIONS)

4.0   INTRODUCTION

The assurance of a well-prepared "tight" Complaint includes a valid, non-demurrable cause of action which compels the inclusion of all necessary elements required and applicable under the law governing the cause of your attorney's client.

The following forms deal with tort actions or wrongs committed against an individual and set forth claims for personal injuries and damages, involving strict or products liability issues; legal malpractice; medical negligence and/or medical malpractice; and actions resulting in wrongful death.

In these Complaint forms, the basic elements required to set up a good cause of action for a tort action have been included. You are cautioned, however, as it relates to negligence, to check your local state statute to determine whether or not the theories of comparative negligence, contributory negligence and strict liability are in force and effect in your state, inasmuch as the trend in the law has changed and contributory negligence is no longer a defense in a casualty claim case. However, in some states, imputed negligence and assumption of a risk are still the prevailing theories.

VIP Caution: In preparing your products liability case, include and spell out with clarity the legal liability of a manufacturer, as follows:

1. That he has placed a product on the market;
2. That he knew the product would be used without inspection for defects by the general public;

81

3. That the product was in fact defective and would cause injury or damage to the plaintiff; and,

4. That the plaintiff used the product in the manner for which it was intended.

Absent the above elements being included in your Complaint, it would most certainly be subject to a demurrer. Where products liability incorporates strict liability, Section 402(a) of Restatement of the Law, Second Edition, Torts 2d, states that where special liability of seller of a product for physical harm to user or consumer is involved, you should be aware of and include in your Complaint allegations as to the following:

1. One who sells any product in a defective condition unreasonably dangerous to the user or consumer or to his property, is subject to liability for physical harm thereby caused to the ultimate user or consumer, or to his property, if

   (a) The seller is engaged in the business of selling such a product, and

   (b) It is expected to, and does, reach the consumer or user without substantial change in the condition in which it is sold.

2. The rule stated in sub-section (1) applies, however, if

   (a) The seller has exercised all possible care in the preparation and sale of his product, and

   (b) The user or consumer has not bought the product from or entered into any contractual relation with, the seller. *

The same type of perusal is true when developing a case in medical and legal malpractice. You must be sure to set up the liability of the defendant and the resulting damage of his negligence to the plaintiff.

The following forms will be your guide to determine whether or not you have included these necessary elements in your Complaint.

---

* Student Edition, Restatement of Law, 2d, Torts 2d, American Law Institute, St. Paul, Minnesota.

4.1 COMPLAINT FOR DAMAGES (NEGLIGENCE)

SUPERIOR COURT OF _____
COUNTY OF _____

[or other as appropriate]

_____,	)	NO. _____
Plaintiff,	)	COMPLAINT FOR DAMAGES
vs.	)	(Negligence)
	)	[Code Section]
_____,	)	
Defendant(s).	)	
_____	)	

Plaintiff alleges:

I

Plaintiff is, and at all times herein mentioned was, a resident of _____ County, _____.

II

Defendant is, and at all times herein mentioned was, a resident of _____ County, _____.

III

Doe Clause

IV

Authority of defendants, such as agents, employers, employees.

V

On or about _____, 19__, plaintiff was _____ [allege facts showing status and activity of plaintiff, placing him in the class of persons to whom each defendant's duty was owed, and, if a defendant's breach included failure to conform to a statutory standard, placing plaintiff in the class of persons the statute was meant to protect].

VI

At said time, defendant _____ [name] was _____ [allege facts showing each defendant's status and activity insofar as they help to establish the duty of each to plaintiff].

VII

[Insofar as the following matters help to establish defendants' duty to plaintiff, allege facts showing:

a. The place, site or locale of the accident, transaction, or event;

b. Defendants' ownership, possession, or control of the instrumentality that caused the damage or the property on which it occurred;

c. The contractual, or other special, relationship between plaintiff and defendants;

d. The statute that imposes a special duty on defendant (where a duty would not otherwise exist).]

VIII

At said time and place, defendants, and each of them, so negligently _____ [show the acts or omissions of defendants wherein they failed to conform to the standard of care required to them] as to cause [or, that _____ was caused to] _____ [show the accident or other result of defendant's conduct; and if a defendant's breach was an omission to act, it is well to add allegations showing how the omission caused the result].

IX

Accident or other occurrence clause with injuries and monied damages specified.

X

Medical expenses incurred, present and future clause.

XI

Employment of plaintiff, present and future and effective injury or other occurrence such as future employment possibilities and loss of earnings, present and future.

XII

As a further proximate result of the negligence of defendants, and each of them, plaintiff's _____ [description of property] was damaged; and for the repair or replacement of the damaged property, plaintiff will be required to pay approximately $_____, which is the reasonable value of the repairs and replacements necessitated by the damage.

XIII

As a further proximate result of said negligence and said accident, plaintiff lost the use of _____ [description of personal property] for a period of _____ days, to his damage in the sum of $_____.

WHEREFORE, plaintiff prays for judgment against defendants, and each of them, as follows:

1. General damages [for injuries to his person] in the sum of $_____.
2. Medical and related expenses _____ [either in the sum of $_____ or according to proof].
3. Lost earnings, past and future, _____ [either in the sum of $_____ or according to proof].
4. Repairs to, and replacement of, plaintiff's property in the sum of $_____.
5. Loss of use of said property in the sum of $_____.
6. For costs of suit herein incurred.
7. Such other and further relief as this Court deems just.

_____ [signature]

Attorney for Plaintiff

VERIFICATION

4.2 COMPLAINT FOR DAMAGES BASED ON STRICT LIABILITY IN TORT

(CAPTION, INTRODUCTION.)

I

Plaintiff is, and at all times herein mentioned was, a resident of _____ (county and state; or allege capacity of plaintiff).

II

Defendant _____ (*manufacturer*) is, and at all times herein mentioned was, a corporation organized and existing under the laws of the State of _____, and qualified to do business in _____, with its principal office for the transaction of business in this State in the (City and) County of _____, [or allege other capacity of manufacturer, as a domestic corporation, a partnership, or a sole proprietorship, etc.]

III

Defendant _____ (*manufacturer*) is, and at all times herein mentioned was, engaged in the business of designing, manufacturing, and assembling (or any combination of the foregoing) _____ (name or description of products, e.g., _____ (*name*) automobiles) for sale to and use by members of the general public, and (plaintiff is informed and believes, and thereon alleges that) as a part of its business defendant designed, manufactured, and assembled the specific _____ (defective product, e.g., _____ (name) automobile) hereinafter referred to.

IV

Defendant _____ (*supplier of component part*) is, and at all times herein mentioned was, an individual doing business under the fictitious name of _____ in the (City and) County of _____, State of _____ (or allege other capacity of supplier as a domestic or foreign corporation, or a partnership, etc.).

V

Defendant _____ (*supplier*) is, and at all times herein mentioned was, engaged in the business of designing and manufacturing certain component parts, to wit, _____ [describe, e.g., tires], and supplying them to defendant manufacturer, and [plaintiff is informed and believes, and on information and belief alleges, that] as a part of its business defendant _____ [*supplier*] designed, manufactured and supplied to defendant _____ [*manufacturer*] the specific _____ [defective product, e.g., tire] hereinafter referred to.

VI

Defendant _____ [*retailer*] is, and at all times herein mentioned was, a partnership, sued herein under the name it has assumed and by which it is known, with its principal place of business in the [City and] County of _____, [or allege other capacity of retailer, as a domestic or foreign corporation, or a sole proprietorship, etc.].

VII

Defendants _____ [*names*] are, and at all times herein mentioned were, members of the partnership named in Paragraph VI, above, and are sued herein individually and are joined as parties defendant in this action against defendant _____ [*retailer*].

VIII

Defendant _____ [*retailer*] is, and at all times herein mentioned was, engaged in the business of _____ [selling *or* assembling, inspecting, and selling *or other*] at retail to members of the general public at its principal place of business in the [City and] County of _____, and hereinabove described _____ [*products, e.g.,* _____ *(name)* automobiles] manufactured, designed, and assembled by defendant _____ [*manufacturer*].

IX

(Doe Clause)

X

[If any of the Doe defendants are sued individually as members of a defendant partnership, add]:

Plaintiff is ignorant of the true names of defendants sued herein as Does _____ through _____, and therefore sues these defendants by such fictitious names and will amend this complaint to show their true names when ascertained. Said defendants and each of them are, and at all times herein mentioned were, members of the defendant partnership hereinabove name and are sued herein individually and are joined as parties defendant in this action against defendant _____ [*partnership*].

XI

[Plaintiff is informed and believes, and on information and belief alleges, that [D]efendant _____ [*manufacturer*] intended that the _____ [*products, e.g.,* _____ *(name) automobiles*] manufactured, designed, and assembled by it were to be used for the purpose[s] of _____ [*state, e.g., in the case of automobiles transporting persons and property from one place to another by operation by an individual of the mechanical devices therein installed*] and defendant _____ [*supplier of component parts*] intended that the _____ [*products, e.g., tires*] designed, manufactured, and supplied by it to defendant _____ [*manufacturer*] were to be installed and incorporated by the latter into the _____ [*products, e.g.,* _____ *(name) automobiles*] manufactured, designed, and assembled by it, and specifically that the _____ [*component part, e.g., tire*] hereinafter referred to was to be installed and incorporated in _____ [*specific product, e.g., a* _____ *(name) automobile of the specific size and model*] as that hereinafter referred to.

XII

Each and every defendant, at all times herein mentioned, knew that the _____ [*products, e.g.,* _____ *(name) automobiles*] manufactured, designed and assembled by defendant _____ [*manufacturer*] would be purchased from defendant _____ [*retailer*] and used by the purchaser or user without inspection for defects therein or in any of its component parts.

XIII

On or about _____, 19__, plaintiff purchased from defendant _____ [*retailer*] at its principal place of business in the [City and] County of _____, a _____ [*product, e.g.,* 19__ _____ *(name) automobile,* _____ *(model),* _____ *(size, e.g., four-door Sedan),* manufactured, designed, and assembled by defendant _____ (manufacturer) and which contained _____ (component part, e.g., _____ (size) tire) designed, manufactured, and supplied to defendant _____ (manufacturer) by defendant _____ (supplier) for installation and incorporation therein.

XIV

At the time of plaintiff's purchase, the _____ (product, e.g., _____ (name) automobile) was defective and unsafe for its intended purpose(s) in that _____ (state, e.g., the _____ (size) tire designed, manufactured and supplied to defendant _____ (manufacturer) by defendant _____ (supplier) for installation and incorporation in the automobile purchased by plaintiff was too small for its intended use resulting in its continually being overloaded by the normal and intended use of the automobile).

XV (OPTIONAL)

Plaintiff neither knew nor had reason to know at the time of his purchase or at any time prior to the _____ (accident or occurrence) hereinafter described of the existence of the foregoing described defect.

> *Note:* The foregoing allegation is probably unnecessary since it is both a negative and anticipatory of the affirmative defense of assumption of risk. (Check your applicable references.)

XVI

On or about _____, 19___, at _____ (location), plaintiff was _____ (using or operating) the hereinabove described _____ (defective product, e.g., automobile) for the purpose of _____ (state, e.g., transporting himself from one place to another,) and during the course of said _____ (use or operation) and as a proximate result of the defect hereinabove described, the _____ (state, e.g., left front tire blew out causing the automobile to go out of control and crash).

XVII-XX
(Incorporate damage allegations)

WHEREFORE, plaintiff prays judgment against defendants, and each of them, as follows:

Verification attached client affidavit, if applicable.

4.3   COMPLAINT FOR PERSONAL INJURIES (PRODUCT LIABILITY)

Attorney for Plaintiff

SUPERIOR COURT OF THE STATE OF _____
FOR THE COUNTY OF _____

_____)	NO. _____
)	
Plaintiff,)	COMPLAINT FOR PERSONAL
)	INJURIES
vs.)	(Products Liability)
)	
_____)	
)	
Defendants.)	
_____)	

Plaintiff alleges:

I

Doe Clause

II

Residency Clause

III

The alleged injury to the persons and property occurred in the City and County of _____, State of _____.

IV

Agency Clause

V

Defendants _____, DOE I and DOE III are and at all times herein mentioned engaged in the business of manufacturing, designing, and assembling tires for sale to and use by members of the general public, and as a part of its business defendant manufactured, designed and assembled the specific tire hereinafter referred to.

VI

DOE I AND DOE II CORPORATION AND DOE IV are and at all times herein mentioned engaged in the business of selling and inspecting the hereinabove described tires manufactured, designed and assembled by the defendants _____, DOE I CORPORATION and DOE II CORPORATION at retail to members of the general public at the City and County of _____, State of _____.

VII

Defendant _____, DOE I CORPORATION and DOE II CORPORATION at all times herein mentioned knew that the defective tire would be purchased and used without inspection for defects by the purchaser, user of the tire or by persons fixing and repairing tires.

VIII

On or about September 25, 19___, plaintiff was employed as an automobile mechanic _____ in _____, _____, and was mounting the defective tire which was manufactured and retailed by defendants when said tire exploded.

IX

At the time of plaintiff's handling, the tire was defective as a result of the defendants', and each of them, failure to give directions and warnings as to the mounting of said tire to prevent it from being unreasonably dangerous and unsafe for its purpose in that the bead of the tire split causing said tire to explode.

X

Defendants, and each of them, knew that as a result of the defects in the tire it could not be safely mounted on the wheel for which it was designed and manufactured.

XI

Plaintiff neither knew nor had reason to know at the time he was mounting said tire at any time prior to the occurrence that said tire was defective nor of the existence of the foregoing defect.

XII

As a proximate result of defendants' defective tire, plaintiff sustained serious and permanent injuries to his health, strength, activities and nervous system and was caused to suffer extreme physical and mental pain all to plaintiff's damage in the sum of $_____.

XIII

Medical Damage Clause.

XIV

Loss of Earnings Clause.
Prayer

_____
Attorney for Plaintiff

Verification attached

Affidavit of client, if applicable

COMMENTS

Form 4.3 Complaint for Personal Injuries (Products Liability)

Basic premises for Products Liability:

"The manufacturer of a chattel which he knows or has reason to know to be, or likely to be, dangerous for use, is subject to the liability of a supplier of chattels with such knowledge."

(See Restatement of the Law, Torts 2d, *supra*).

4.4 COMPLAINT FOR DAMAGES (NUISANCE)
(BASIC FORM)

(CAPTION INTRODUCTION)

I

Doe Clause

II

At all times herein mentioned plaintiff was, and now is, the owner of real property (here you describe the scope of real property, the description of the improvements of the property, its legal description and common designation)

III

At all times herein mentioned defendants have been and now are the (owners, lessees, sub-lessees, occupants, users, and so forth) of the premises located at

(here you should place the address and other locations of property setting forth what the land consists of together with any type of improvements thereon as well as legal description thereof).

IV

Plaintiff's property and defendants' property are _____ (show the relative locations).

V

At all times herein mentioned and since (give the date of the contract) defendants, and each of them, have occupied, used and maintained said location in a manner constituting a continuing (permanent) private (or public) nuisance in that _____ (here you should set forth the pertinent facts which your client believes constitutes the nuisance).

VI

(In this paragraph you should set forth the statutory regulation which defines and constitutes a nuisance within that framework. Also you should set forth the fact that said nuisance is injurious to the health of the plaintiff or that it is indecent and offensive to the senses of the plaintiff; or, an obstruction to the free use of plaintiff's property, so as to interfere with the comfortable enjoyment of said property; or, an unlawful obstruction to plaintiff's free passage or use in the customary manner...).

VII

Note: This is your public nuisance allegation which should set forth specific facts showing the special injury.

VIII

On or about _____ plaintiff gave notice to defendant of the damage caused by said nuisance, and requested the abatement thereof, but defendants had refused and continue to refuse to abate said nuisance.

IX

Defendants have threatened to and will, unless restrained by this court, continue to maintain said nuisance and to continue the acts herein complained of, and each and every said act has been, and will be, without the consent and against the will, and in violation of the rights of plaintiff.

(*Note*, this is an optional paragraph which may be used when seeking a restraining order to enjoin the defendant from continuing said nuisance.)

X

This is your property damage clause and you should set forth with full particulars the property damage involved and the monetary amount.

An alternate allegation re damages is as follows:

(As a result of said nuisance, the value of plaintiff's property has been temporarily diminished in the sum of $_____. Unless said nuisance is abated, plaintiff's property will be progressively further diminished in value.)

Another alternate allegation could be as follows:

"The reasonable costs of repairs and damages to plaintiff's property caused by said nuisance, after the abatement thereof, is the sum of $_____, to plaintiff's damage in that amount."

XI

(Multiplicity of Suits)

(Here again, the following paragraphs are optional unless your complaint is a complaint for damages and injunction.)

(Unless defendants, and each of them, are restrained by an order of court it will be necessary for plaintiff to commence many successive actions against defendants to secure compensation for damages sustained, thus requiring a multiplicity of suits, and plaintiff will be daily threatened with damages caused by said nuisance, such as loss by fire of a part or all the buildings and so forth.)

XII

(Irreparable Injuries)

Unless the defendants, and each of them, are enjoined from continuing their course of conduct, plaintiff will be irreparably injured in an amount which cannot be calculated in terms of money in the following respects:

(a) The usefulness and economic value of said property will be diminished and efforts of plaintiff to sell said property will be an exercise of futility.

(b) Plaintiff will be deprived to a substantial extent of the use and occupancy of said property.

(These are just examples that you can use.)

XIII

Plaintiff has no plain, speedy or adequate remedy at law.

XIV

In maintaining said nuisance, defendants and each of them are acting with full knowledge of the consequences and the damage being caused to plaintiff and their conduct is willful, oppressive and malicious; accordingly, plaintiff is entitled to punitive damages against the defendants, and each of them, in the sum of $_____.

WHEREFORE, plaintiff prays judgment against defendants, and each of them, as follows: ...

_____ (signature)
Attorney for Plaintiff

(Verification to be attached)

(Affidavit of Client may be attached)

4.5 COMPLAINT FOR DAMAGES FOR LEGAL MALPRACTICE

Attorneys for Plaintiff

SUPERIOR COURT OF THE STATE OF _____

FOR THE COUNTY OF _____

_____,	)	NO.
	)	
Plaintiff,	)	COMPLAINT FOR DAMAGES
	)	FOR LEGAL MALPRACTICE
vs.	)	
	)	
_____, and	)	
DOES 1 through 10, inclusive,	)	
	)	
Defendants,	)	
	)	
_____	)	

Plaintiff alleges:

I

Doe Clause.

II

Agency Clause.

III

At all times herein mentioned, defendants, and each of them, were practicing attorneys in the County of _____, State of _____, duly licensed to practice law under the laws of the State of _____. The defendants, and each of them, held themselves out to the public and to this plaintiff as being skilled, careful and diligent in the practice of the profession of the law. At all times herein mentioned said defendants, and each of them, held themselves out to the public and to this plaintiff as being skilled in the practice of general _____ law, and more specifically, that field of the law having to do with personal injuries and other specialities having to do with automobile accidents.

IV

On or about July 15, 19___, plaintiff herein was operating her motor vehicle on Capitol Avenue, near its intersection with Florence Avenue in the County of _____, State of _____; that said Avenues were public highways in the County of _____, State of _____; that at said time and place _____ _____ was driving an automobile and that said

_____ so carelessly and negligently operated, managed, controlled, maintained and drove said vehicle as to cause it to collide with plaintiff's automobile.

V

Damage Clause

VI

Statement of Incident.

VII

Plaintiff contacted the offices of defendants on numerous occasions with regard to the aforesaid accident but experienced difficulty in communicating with defendant _____. Plaintiff was assured by the agents and employees of said defendant _____ that her case was being prosecuted diligently and that they expected to effect a settlement of the matter. Because of her inability to communicate directly with defendant _____ and because of the time lag involved, plaintiff became uneasy about the progress of her case and went to the _____ County Courthouse in June of 19__ to peruse the court file in said matter. At that time plaintiff found that a complaint had been filed and plaintiff obtained a copy of said complaint filed on her behalf by defendants, and each of them.

On October 19, 19__, plaintiff was involved in another automobile accident and because she was dissatisfied with the attorney-client relationship existing between her and the defendants, she sought the services of another attorney with respect to the second accident. On January 2, 19__, she went to the offices of attorney _____ in _____, _____, and set up an appointment with _____ of said office to see attorney _____ on January 5, 19__. In the course of speaking with _____, plaintiff advised her of the accident of July 15, 19__, and showed _____ _____ a copy of the complaint filed by the office of the defendants, and each of them. At that time, to wit, on or about January 2, 19__, said _____ _____ perused the complaint and discovered that said complaint had been filed with the court on July 25, 19__, ten days after the Statute of Limitations had run, and so advised plaintiff. Plaintiff is not at fault for not having made earlier discovery in that she had no prior actual or presumptive knowledge of facts sufficient to put her on inquiry prior to said date. Plaintiff was led to believe by the defendants, and each of them, their agents and employees, that a complaint had been filed for personal injuries sustained by plaintiff and her minor son in the accident of July 15, 19__, and that a settlement of said matter was soon to be effectuated.

VIII

The defendants, and each of them, carelessly, negligently and recklessly failed to prosecute the lawsuit concerning the within automobile accident and permitted the Statute of Limitations to lapse; that in consequence of such negligence and recklessness on the part of the defendants herein, and each of them, plaintiff has been deprived of any legal rights that she might have had against the operators and owners of the automobile in the within accident, all to her damage in the sum of $_____.

WHEREFORE, plaintiff prays judgment against the defendants, and each of them, as follows:

1. For the sum of $_____ as and for general damages;
2. For the costs of suit herein; and
3. For such other and further relief as to this court may seem just and proper.

By _____
Attorneys for Plaintiff

COMMENTS

Form 4.5   Complaint for Damages for Legal Malpractice

In developing this type of complaint you are cautioned to look for the following legal liabilities which may exist and which may have been violated in some way:

1. Breach of contract as between attorney and client;
2. Fiduciary relationship as between attorney and client;
3. Negligence on the part of the attorney; failure to appear at court proceedings; failure to prosecute the claim;
4. Fraud or deceit;
5. Constructive fraud;
6. Violation of Civil Rights Act;
7. Statute of Limitations violation; and, of course,
8. That the plaintiff relied upon the judgment and counsel of the attorney to his detriment and harm.

4.6   COMPLAINT FOR MALPRACTICE
(GENERAL FORM)

CAPTION AND INTRODUCTIONS

I

Doe Clause

II

At all times herein mentioned, defendants _____, and each of them, were physicians and surgeons duly licensed to practice medicine and perform surgery in the State of _____ with offices at _____ [*street address*], _____, _____, and each of them has held himself out to possess that degree of skill, ability and learning common to medical practitioners in said community.

II

[Plaintiff is informed and believes and, on such information and belief, alleges that] defendant _____ [*hospital*] is [a corporation organized and existing under the laws of the State of _____, and now is,] and at all times herein mentioned was, engaged in operating and managing a general hospital in _____.

IV

At all times herein mentioned, defendants _____, and each of them, were the agents and employees of defendant _____ [*hospital*] and defendants _____ [*physicians*], and each of them, and in doing the things hereinafter mentioned were acting in the scope of their authority as such agents and employees and with the consent of their co-defendants.

V

On or about _____, 19___, plaintiff consulted defendants _____ [*physicians*] for the purpose of obtaining diagnosis and treatment of an illness, and employed said defendants to care for and treat plaintiff and do all things necessary in his care and treatment. Said defendants undertook said employment and undertook and agreed to diagnose plaintiff's illness and to care for and treat plaintiff and do all things necessary and proper in connection therewith, and said defendants, and each of them, thereafter entered on such employment, individually, and by and through their employees and agents.

VI

On or about _____, 19___, defendants _____ [*physicians*] arranged to have plaintiff admitted to _____ Hospital. [*For a valuable consideration given by plaintiff,*] defendant _____ [*hospital*] agreed and undertook to care for and treat plaintiff and to assist defendants _____ [*physicians*] in carrying out _____ [*treatment, operation or other procedure*], and to do all things necessary and proper in connection therewith.

VII

From and after said times, defendants, and each of them, so negligently examined plaintiff and diagnosed his condition, and so negligently _____ [show, generally, acts or omissions wherein defendants failed to conform to the standard of care required of them] and treated and cared for plaintiff [in that _____ (show any further acts or omissions constituting the breach of duty)] that plaintiff was caused to and did suffer the injuries and damages hereinafter alleged.

VIII

Injuries Damage Clause

IX

Medical Damage Clause

X

Loss of Employment/Earnings Clause.

[Prayer for damages, costs and general relief]

_____ (Signature)
Attorney for Plaintiff

(Verfication)

(Affidavit of Client)

4.7   COMPLAINT FOR MALPRACTICE, FAILURE TO DIAGNOSE ILLNESS, WRONGFUL DEATH

CAPTIONS AND INTRODUCTION

I

Plaintiffs _____ and _____ are minors, aged _____ years and _____ years, respectively. Plaintiff _____, is the natural father of said minors and heretofore was appointed, and now is, their guardian ad litem for the purpose of this action.

II

Said minors are the surviving children, and plaintiff _____ is the surviving husband of _____, who died in _____ County, _____, on or about _____, 19___, at the age of ____ years, and who was, together with her said minor children and husband, a resident of _____ County at her death. Said minors and plaintiff _____ are the sole surviving heirs-at-law of said _____, deceased.

III

[Fictitious name allegations.]

IV

At all times herein mentioned, defendants _____ were regularly licensed physicians and surgeons in this state, engaged in the practice of medicine and surgery with offices in the City of _____, County of _____, State of _____.

V

On or about _____, 19___, said decedent was in great pain and suffering from a serious illness. At said time, plaintiff _____ [spouse] employed defendants _____, and each of them, to diagnose her sickness and treat and care for her for compensation, which said plaintiff agreed to pay. Defendants _____, and each of them, undertook to diagnose her sickness and treat and care for her. Thereon, said decedent became the patient of defendants _____, and each of them, and remained a patient under their care to and including _____, 19___.

VI

Defendants _____, and each of them, entered on said employment, but did so negligently diagnose her illness and treat and care for said decedent, and did thereafter, with notice and knowledge of her worsening and critical condition, refuse to give her treatment and care, and did in fact abandon her, notwithstanding said employment and said notice and knowledge of her condition, that she was caused to and did suffer the injuries from which she died.

VII

At all times mentioned herein, said _____ was suffering from a condition known as _____ [e.g., a tubal pregnancy], and as a direct and proximate result of said carelessness and negligence of defendants _____, and each of them, and their abandonment of her, said _____ died on or about _____, 19___, thereby depriving plaintiffs, and each of them, of the care, comfort, society, protection, support and services of said decedent, all to their damage in the sum of $_____.

VIII

By reason of said carelessness and negligence of said defendants, and each of them, and as the direct and proximate result thereof, plaintiffs have incurred expenses for medical treatment, hospitalization, and for the funeral and burial of said decedent, the exact value of which is presently unknown, and plaintiffs ask leave to amend their complaint to include the true value thereof when the same is ascertained.

[Prayer for damages, costs and general relief]

_____ [Signature]

[Verification]
[Affidavit of Client]

4.8 COMPLAINT FOR MALPRACTICE, FOR INJURIES OCCURRING AT BIRTH BY GUARDIAN AD LITEM

CAPTIONS AND INTRODUCTION

I

_____ is the _____ [relationship] of _____, a minor, was duly appointed guardian ad litem of said minor on _____, 19___, and has been acting as such guardian ever since.

II

At all times herein mentioned, defendant _____ was a physician and surgeon duly licensed to practice medicine in the State of _____, and did practice in the City of _____, County of _____, State of _____, and held himself out to the public generally and to the parents and natural guardians of minor plaintiff _____ as being qualified and skilled in the practice of medicine, and, more particularly, in the fields of surgery and obstetrics and as possessing and exercising that degree of skill and learning ordinarily possessed and exercised by other skillful physicians, surgeons and obstetricians practicing medicine in the City of _____ County of _____, State of _____.

III

(Fictitious name and agency allegations.)

IV

On or about _____, 19___, plaintiffs _____ [parents] consulted defendant relative to the pregnancy of _____ [mother] and did then and there engage defendant as physician and surgeon for the care and treatment of _____ [mother] during and after pregnancy and, more particularly, for the delivery of the then unborn infant, plaintiff _____, herein.

V

On or about _____, 19___, defendant _____ delivered plaintiff, _____ [minor] at the _____ Hospital in the City of _____, County of _____, State of _____, and in doing so negligently and carelessly failed to use that degree of skill and learning ordinarily possessed and exercised by other skillful physicians, surgeons and obstetricians in the City of _____, County of _____, State of _____, in the delivery of infants at childbirth.

VI

As a direct and proximate result of said negligence of defendant _____, plaintiff _____ [minor] suffered severe and permanent injuries, to wit: _____, _____, _____; and plaintiffs are informed and believe and, on such information and belief, allege that said injuries are permanent in nature; and said negligence and carelessness on the part of defendant did further cause other injuries not presently diagnosed, the allegations of which plaintiffs pray leave to insert by amendment when ascertained.

VII

As a direct and proximate result of the negligence and carelessness of defendant as aforesaid, plaintiff was generally damaged in the sum of $_____.

[Prayer for damages, costs and general relief]

_____ [Signature]

[Verificiation]

[Affidavit of Client]

4.9   DEMAND FOR JURY TRIAL

Attorney Data

Attorneys for defendant

UNITED STATES DISTRICT COURT
CENTRAL DISTRICT OF _____

_____

Plaintiff,	CIVIL ACTION NO.____
vs.	DEMAND FOR JURY TRIAL
Defendant(s).	

Defendant _____, hereby demands a trial by jury in the above-entitled action.

Respectfully submitted,

By _____
Attorneys for Defendant

(Then attach a proof of service
to plaintiffs counsel)

COMMENTS

Form 4.9   Demand for Jury Trial

A little-known fact is that a jury trial is not always automatic. It has to be requested by either counsel. (This statement does not apply to criminal cases.)

If, in a civil action, counsel feels that a trial by "his peers" will be in the best interest of his client, he can petition the court and demand a jury trial.

Or, he may ask for a non-jury trial wherein only the judge hearing the matter is in the courtroom along with the defendant and his counsel. Form 4.9 is one way you can petition the court for a jury trial.

4.10   NOTICE OF ACTION PENDING

Recording requested by and
when recorded return to:

_____

Attorneys for plaintiff

SUPERIOR COURT OF THE STATE OF _____
FOR THE COUNTY OF _____

_____

Plaintiff,	)	Case No.
	)	
	)	
	)	
vs.	)	NOTICE OF ACTION PENDING
	)	(_____ Code of Civil
	)	Procedure, Section _____)
	)	
Defendants.	)	
	)	

PLEASE TAKE NOTICE that the above-captioned action is pending in the Superior Court of the State of _____ for the County of _____, and that this action concerns, and the plaintiff in this action seeks relief affecting, title to that certain real property located in the County of _____, State of _____, and described in Exhibit "A" attached hereto and incorporated herein by this reference.

The object of this action is to declare, impose and enforce a resulting trust upon such property, in favor of plaintiff, a co-tenant in partnership in such property, or in favor of the partnership, *(Name of partnership)* and have such property accounted for as an asset of the partnership with respect to the cause of action for dissolution, accounting and winding up of such partnership.

The parties to this action are the above-named plaintiff and defendants.

DATED: October ____, 19____

_____

Attorneys for plaintiff

EXHIBIT "A"

PROPERTY

_____

Commonly known as:

Legal Description:
Real property in the City of _____, County of _____, State of _____ described as follows:

PARCEL 1:

PARCEL 2:

END OF DOCUMENT

COMMENTS

Form 4.10   Notice of Action Pending

Form 4.10 is normally prepared when the case before the bar involves real property and the title thereto; a petition for partitioning thereof; and/or owner-ship.

It is filed to put the world on notice that there is a dispute as to its ownerhip and that therefore there is a lien (judgment pending) against the interest of the property. This of course, keeps lending institutions from lending money against the property; builders from contracting to build on the property, and/or the parties from trying to sell the property.

This document, together with a complete legal description of the property, (the original of which is filed and recorded in the county where the property is located) is filed with the court of jurisdiction before whom the case is pending, and a copy is served on and opposing counsel.

Contents—Chapter 5
Contracts

5

CONTRACTS

5.0 INTRODUCTION

A breach of contract means that one of the parties has failed and refuses to perform under the contract, and without a valid or a legal reason. As a result, a cause of action may be based upon this failure to perform.

As a general rule, (and please check your local state codes in this area) the party seeking performance of an agreed-upon contract may elect either to rescind the contract, or merely sue to recover money damages expended by him; or, the value of any services rendered by him under the contract. Please note that the injured party may maintain the contract and sue for damages for the breach.

Hence, in preparing a pleading involving a breach of contract, be direct and to the point and use as many theories as you can, as allowed by your local state code.

The theories most often utilized are the common counts. These counts are law relief actions involving contracts for goods sold and delivered, work, labor and services performed; money had and received, and for accounts stated. They are generally known by the following names:

1) *Indebtatus Assumpsit*—Money had and received;
2) *Quantum Meruit*—Work and labor (reasonable value for services);
3) *Quantum Valebant*—Goods, sold and delivered for as much as they were worth (implied contract);
4) Open Book Account (Account Stated).

5.1   COMMON COUNTS

(As Prepared Under the Federal Rules of Civil Procedure)

5.1(A) It is important that the allegation of jurisdiction be included in any complaint filed in the Federal Court system. The following paragraphs are examples of allegation jurisdiction:

(a) Jurisdiction founded on diversity of citizenship and amount.
Plaintiff is a citizen of the State of _____ and defendant is a corporation incorporated under the laws of the State of _____ having its principal place of business in a state other than the State of _____. The matter is controversy, exceeds, exclusive of interests and costs, the sum of $15,0000.00.
(b) Jurisdiction founded on the existence of a federal question and an amount in controversy.
(c) The action arises under (the Constitution of the United States, Article _____, Section ____,); of the United States, Section ____); (the Act of _____, Statute ____, U.S.C., Title ____, Section ____), and so forth, as hereinafter more fully appears. The matter in controversy exceeds, exclusive of interest and costs, the sum of $15,000.00.

Hence, a complaint, with common counts, would be as follows:

5.1(B) Complaint on an Account

1. Allegation of jurisdiction.
2. Defendant owes plaintiff _____ Dollars according to the account hereto annexed as Exhibit "A".
WHEREFORE ...

5.1(C) Complaint for Goods Sold and Delivered

1. Allegation of jurisdiction.
2. Defendant owes plaintiff _____ dollars for goods sold and delivered by plaintiff and defendant between June 1, _____ and December 1, _____.
WHEREFORE ...

5.1(D) Complaint for Money Lent

1. Allegation of jurisdiction.
2. Defendant owes plaintiff _____ dollars for money lent by plaintiff to defendant on April _____, 19___.
WHEREFORE ...

5.1(E) Complaint for Money Had and Received

1. Allegation of jurisdiction.
2. Defendant owes plaintiff _____ dollars for money had and received from D.E.L. on April _____, 19___ to be paid by defendant to plaintiff.
WHEREFORE ...

5.1(F) Complaint for Money Paid by Mistake

1. Allegation of jurisdiction.
2. Defendant owes plaintiff _____ dollars for money paid by plaintiff to defendant by mistake on April 1, 19___ under the following circumstances: (here state the circumstances according to federal Rules of Civil Procedure No. 9(b)).
WHEREFORE ...

COMMENTS

5.1-A Para. (a) is a typical jurisdictional ground in federal common count cases.

Para. (b) sets up the diversity, i.e. State of California ... State of New York The $15,000 is the ''must'' or more monetary value which can be heard and determined in a federal court case.

Para. (c) and (d) are self-explanatory in that you simply determine from your research of the U.S. Codes the authority under which the matter is being filed in the federal court.

5.1-B through F are different common count theories which set forth law relief action involving a contract for goods sold and delivered, work and labor; Practice.

5.2   STATE COURTS—COMMON COUNTS

Introduction

The common counts are very important but are not used as much today as they should be by attorneys. This procedure dates back to old English law during a period when there was no redress to or for an injury. The common count is a law relief action involving a contract for goods sold and delivered, work and labor; services performed, money had and received, etc. It is used for new or additional sources of recovery with any complaint, but will not stand alone if the balance of the complaint is dismissed for cause.

There must be an allegation of breach to show violation of the rights of plaintiff by defendant and the fact that demand has been made for payment and that the same has been refused. The following, therefore, are the types of common counts which are used in the state courts as opposed to the federal counts.

5.2(A) ACCOUNTS STATED

Attorney Information

COURT INFORMATION

	Plaintiff,	)))	NO. _____
vs.		))	ACCOUNTS STATED
	Defendant.	)))	

Within four years last past, on or about _____, 19___ at _____, an account was stated by and between plaintiff and defendant, wherein and whereby it was agreed that defendant was indebted to plaintiff in the sum of _____.

No part of said sum has been paid.

(And the usual closing as with any other complaint unless you are just filing a common count complaint).

5.2(B) OPEN BOOK ACCOUNT

Attorney Information

COURT INFORMATION

	Plaintiff,	)))	NO. _____
vs.		))	OPEN BOOK ACCOUNT
	Defendant.	)))	

Within four years last past, and on or about _____, 19___ at _____, plaintiff furnished to defendant at his special instance and request, upon an open book account, goods, wares, and merchandise of the aggregate agreed reasonable value of _____.

No part of said sum has been paid (except ___ dollars and there is now due, owing and unpaid ___ dollars).

5.2(C)   WORK AND LABOR (COMMON COUNT)

WORK AND LABOR
(The reasonable value thereof)

Attorney Information

                                Court Information

)   Case No. _____
)
)   WORK AND LABOR
)   (COMMON COUNT)
)
Parties   )
)
_____   )

Suggested paragraphs for the above complaint:

Between and during the period _____, 19___ and _____, 19___ at (here you put the city and state) plaintiff rendered the services to defendant as a (name the type of services rendered, maid, housekeeper, companion, etc.). Such services were so rendered and performed at the instance and request of defendant, and the defendant promised to pay plaintiff the reasonable value of such services.

Plaintiff contends that the reasonable value of said services as a (here designate the type of services rendered) at the time they were rendered and at the time defendant promised to pay, was the sum of $___.

Defendant alleges that no part of said sum has been paid (here if there has been a sum paid on the account, then set forth the amount that has been paid) (then thereafter set forth the amount that is due and owing minus the sum that has been paid).

WHEREFORE ...

5.2(A) through (C) are the different common count theories which set forth law relief actions involving contracts under the format of state rules of Civil Practice. You are cautioned to check your local state rules for the applicability of the latter.

5.3 OFFER AND ACCEPTANCE

Dated: _____   City of _____,   State of _____

TO: _____
FROM: _____

I hereby make the following offer:

(This paragraph should include the terms of the offer.)

This offer, when accepted in writing by you,

[If you want a time limit, here is the place where a time limit should be inserted, such as 30 days, 90 days, etc.] shall constitute a contract between us (provided the same be accepted on or before _____).

Accepted at _____, this _____ day of _____, 19___.

_____

_____

WITNESS:

_____

_____

(Address)

_____

COMMENTS

Form 5.3   Offer and Acceptance

This is a basic Offer and Acceptance form. The sentences and phrases in the bracketed areas on Form 5.3 are comments for your guidance as to what should be included in any offer and acceptance agreement and/or contract to make it valid.

5.4   BASIC CONTRACT

This agreement, made at _____, _____, this ____ day of
_____, 19___, by and between

[here, if one of the parties is a corporation, you should insert "a
corporation duly organized under the laws of the State of
_____; or if the party is a partnership, you should insert
"_____ and _____, partners doing business as _____"], of _____,
_____, herein called the Party of the First Part, and _____ and
_____, hereinafter called the Party of the Second Part:

WITNESSETH:

The Party of the First Part, in consideration of the agreements and covenants
of the other party, hereby agrees as follows:

In consideration, the Party of the First Part hereby covenants and agrees

_____

[here set down whatever the agreement was as to the parties].

It is mutually agreed by and between the parties, upon receipt of the
consideration herein set forth, as follows:

[here you should spell out the mutually agreed-upon covenants].

IN WITNESS WHEREOF, the parties have herunto set their hand this _____
day of _____, as above first written.

[In the presence of _____) This Paragraph is optional).]

COMMENTS

Form 5.4   Basic Contract

This is a basic contract form which can be embellished or shortened for
your attorney's purposes, so long as those areas which are bracketed are included.

The bracketed portions of Form 5.4 are the vital points which must be
included in any contract, whatever the length.

Notarization is optional unless required by local statute or is the personal
preference of your attorney.

5.5   SUPPLEMENT TO CONTRACT

This supplement to contract made and entered into this _____ day of
_____, 19___, by and between _____.

(here, if one of the parties is a corporation, you should insert "a
corporation duly organized under the laws of the State of
_____; or if the party is a partnership, you should insert
"_____ and _____, partners doing business as
_____"),

of _____, _____, herein called the Party of the First Part, and
_____ and _____, hereinafter called the Party of the Second
Part:

WHEREAS, the parties hereto entered into an agreement dated _____,
19___, in which it was provided in paragraph _____ thereof, that:

(here set down the specifics of the first contract, if applicable) and

WHEREAS, the parties hereto now desire to amend and change such
provisions;

NOW, THEREFORE, IT IS MUTUALLY AGREED that the following
provisions be added:

(here should be inserted the new additional provisions or provisions
wherein the original contract was changed.)

(If the contract is executed for either party by an agent or attorney, the
signature should be as follows: _____ (Name of the party)

By _____ (Agent or attorney for signing party)

COMMENTS

Form 5.5   Supplement to Contract

See comments for Form 5.4

5.6   CONTRACT RATIFYING DEBT OF INFANT

This agreement, made by and between _____ of the City of
_____, State of _____, hereinafter called Party of the First Part,
and _____, a corporation, duly organized and legally allowed to do
business in the City of _____, State of _____, hereinafter called
the Party of the Second Part, witness as follows:

WHEREAS, on the ___ day of _____, 19___, the Party of the First Part,
being then a minor, purchased of the Party of the Second Part, a stereo for the

sum of $_____, and now having reached his majority, and being desirous of ratifying said purchase for the purpose of giving full effect to his liability for payment of such debt, enters into the following agreement:

NOW THESE PRESENTS WITNESS:

In consideration of the purchase of said stereo, and the agreement on the part of the Party of the Second Part, the Party of the First Part hereby expressly acknowledges the debt to be due to the Party of the Second Part, and agrees to pay the sum in installments within the next _____ months from the date of this agreement, together with interest at the rate of _____ percent (___%).

The Party of the Second Part, in consideration of the promise and agreement herein contained, agrees that they will not sue for or require payment of the debt unless and until default shall be made in the payment thereof at the time and amounts as hereinabove set forth.

IN WITNESS WHEREOF, (etc.)

_____

_____

COMMENTS

Form 5.6   Contract Ratifying Debt of Infant

This form is self-explanatory. The facts would change to suit your purpose(s).

5.7   AVOIDANCE OF INFANT CONTRACT

I, _____, having arrived at the age of majority, do hereby choose to void the contract alleged to have been entered into by and between myself and the Party of the Second Part, by virtue of a _____ executed by me under the date of _____, 19___, and by virtue of which the Party of the Second Part deducted from my account, being Account No. _____, in the amount of _____ Dollars ($_____) on the ___ day of _____, 19___.

I hereby demand that you restore to my account the aforesaid sum or sums as hereinabove set forth.

_____

COMMENTS

Form 5.7   Avoidance of Infant Contract

At #1 should be placed the name of the document attempting to be voided by the "infant," such as a promissory note, sales contract (other than for the necessities of life), car and so forth.

~~Whether the same is witnessed or notarized is optional and should be based~~ on the policy of local state statutes applicable.

5.8 HIGHLIGHTS OF A SONGWRITER'S AND COMPOSER'S AGREEMENT

THIS AGREEMENT, made and entered into this _____ day of _____, 19___, by and between _____, located at _____, hereinafter referred to as "Publisher" and _____, attorneys for composers, located at _____.

WITNESSETH:

For and in consideration of the mutual covenants herein set forth, the parties do hereby agree as follows:

The items to be included in such an agreement should be as follows:

1. Employment;
2. Term;
3. Grants of rights;

   Under the grants of rights in this type of agreement should be additional subdivisions.

   (a) To perform said musical compositions publicly for profit ...

   (b) To substitute a new title or titles for said compositions and to make any arrangements, adaptations, translations, dramatizations ...

   (c) To secure copyright registration and protection of said compositions in publisher's name or otherwise as publisher may desire at publisher's own cost and expense and publisher's election, ...

   (d) To make or cause to be made, master records, transcriptions, sound tracks, pressings, and any other mechanical, electrical or other reproductions of said compositions, in whole or in part: ...

   (e) To print, publish and sell sheet music, orchestrations, arrangements and other additions of the said compositions, in all forms, ...

   (f) Any and all other rights of every and any nature now or hereafter existing under and by virtue of any common law rights and any copyrights and renewals and extensions thereof in any and all of such compositions. ...

4. Exclusivity.
5. Warranties, representations, covenants and agreements.
6. Power of attorney.
7. Compensation. Here in this particular provision of the agreement, should be spelled out with specificity the rights of the parties as they relate to the percentages to be paid to the writer. For example:

(a) Five percent per copy for each piano copy and dance orchestration printed, published and sold in the United States ...

(b) Ten percent of the wholesale selling price for each printed copy ...

(c) Fifty percent of any and all net sums actually received by publisher in the United States from the exploitation in the United States and Canada by licensees of the publisher ...

(d) Writer shall receive his public performance royalties throughout the world ...

The above are examples of the types of information which should be included underneath the compensation paragraph.

8. Advances. (this is a vitally important paragraph as it is intended to insure that the writer gets some types of money for his performance of all the terms and conditions of this agreement; they are commonly called royalties, and as a general rule, are paid in advance.) For example:

(a) Ten Thousand Dollars after the execution of the agreement ...

(b) Twelve Thousand Dollars for the first extension term of the agreement payable in increments of Three Thousand Dollars at the beginning of the first extension and Three Thousand Dollars at the next three months and then six months and then nine months ...

9. Accounting. (it is vitally important that the writer have the right to receive an accounting from his publisher as to the number of copies of his music which have been sold and to whom, and for how much. He or she should have the ability to look at the books or at least have his accountant look at the books.)

10. Collaboration with other writers.

11. The writer's services.

12. Unique services.

13. Actions.

14. Notices.

15. The entire agreement. This agreement supersedes any and all prior negotiations, understandings, and agreements between the parties hereto with respect to the subject matter hereof. Each of the parties acknowledges and agrees that neither party has made any representations or promises in connection with this agreement or the subject matter hereof not contained herein.

16. Modification, waiver, illegality.

17. Suspension and termination.

18. Assignment.

19. Definitions.

20. Attorney's fees.

IN WITNESS WHEREOF, the parties hereto have executed this agreement as of the day and year first above written.

Then, of course, you would have the signature lines, one for each party, or two parties, whichever is applicable. Then depending on the circumstances of the case, it is possible or conceivable that you might have exhibits. These would be attached at the very end and, of course, signed by the parties involved, and to make it tight, it should be notarized.

COMMENTS

Form 5.8   Highlights of a Songwriter's and Composer's Agreement

Form 5.8 sets forth the basic paragraphs which should be included in any songwriter's and composer's agreement for your guidance only.

Please pay particular attention to those paragraphs which have provided examples.

In this type of agreement it is normally mandatory for the protection of all parties concerned that the same be witnessed and notarized. However, this procedure is flexible to the wishes of the parties. We have found it to be the better part of valor to follow this procedure in case of any judicial process.

5.9   PARTNERSHIP AGREEMENT
(Key Phrases)

(*Note:* The following are highlights of a typical partnership agreement and the paragraphs which should be included when preparing such an agreement for your employer).

The initial paragraph reads as follows:

THIS AGREEMENT made as of January 1, 19___ by and between John Doe, hereinafter called ''Doe'' and John Smith hereinafter called ''Smith'' is made with reference to the following facts. Doe and Smith have been associated in the practice of medicine in _____, _____, and now desire to form a partnership as of January 1, 19___.

IT IS MUTUALLY AGREED AS FOLLOWS:

The following are the titles of paragraphs which should be included in the agreement between the parties.

1. Name and business.

2. The term of the business.

3. The capital. It should be spelled out with specificity how much money each party is going to put into the business and the form of that capital, be it cash money, or equipment and how the same shall be paid into the business, since it is conceivable that the same could be done on the installment plan.

4. Profit and loss. (That is, whether or not they shall equally share the profits 50/50 or whether they shall be 65/35 as it relates to profit or loss.)

5. Salaries and drawings.

6. Interest.

This paragraph is important so that each party will know whether or not interest will accrue on his initial contribution to the partnership. For example, ''No interest shall be paid on the initial contributions to the capital of the partnership or any subsequent contributions to capital, or on any undrawn profits of any partner which are credited to his account.''

7. Management, duties and restrictions.

8. Banking.

9. Books.

This of course, would be the books of accounting which shall include the name, address and location of their certified public accountant.

10. Net income.

11. Termination of the partnership.

This should be spelled out with specificity and should include the option of either party to buy out the other in case it is not a mutual termination. It should also include the time limitation for such an option, thirty days, sixty days, ninety days or whatever. In some cases, you might even want to include a clause setting forth that the partner leaving the partnership may or may not practice under his profession within a radius of one hundred miles or two hundred miles, or whatever it is, of the ongoing partnership. This of course, depends on the merits of the case.

12. Disability

13. Death of the partner.

Under the foregoing, disability and death of the partner, it should be spelled out how much money the disabled partner, shall be entitled to receive during his disability since he will not be functioning as a partner, hence bringing in money. The death of the partner should include how much capital he is entitled to, or his wife and dependents are entitled to. Of course, some of the paragraphs should include an accounting of accounts receivable and the deceased partner's interest at such death.

14. Supplemental payment on death.

15. Use of name of disabled or deceased partner.

16. Insurance.

This, of course, could be insurance on the partnership or individual insurance on the partner's life making either one of the partners the beneficiary, or the partners' spouses or dependents.

17. Arbitration.

18. Simultaneous death.

19. Modification.
20. Benefit.

Then of course, the usual closing paragraph:

"IN WITNESS WHEREOF, the parties have signed this partnership agreement this _____ day of _____, 19___" and signatures for both parties and then another paragraph at the bottom which should be for the wives of each of the partners. For example:

"_____, the wife of _____, and _____, the wife of _____, have read the foregoing partnership agreement, approve the same, and on behalf of themselves, their personal representatives, heirs and legatees, agree to be bound there by." Then both wives should sign it.

COMMENTS

Form 5.9   Partnership Agreement

See comments to Form 5.8

Contents—Chapter 6
Corporations

6

CORPORATIONS

6.0   INTRODUCTION

A corporation is a legal entity which has been granted the right to do business by a state or country, which is evidenced by the filing with the appropriate state authority of a corporate charter or articles of incorporation and in some states a certificate of incorporation. This certificate of incorporation may be amended by filing of a Certificate of Amendment, or Articles of Amendment.

The advantages of this legal entity among other things are as follows:

    a. Limited liability of the shareholders;
    b. Lower tax rate on profits;
    c. Perpetual existence;
    d. Transferability of shares;
    e. Ease of raising capital, and so forth

It would be an exercise in futility to set forth herein purported ''common forms'' for this section, as most states have their own Business Corporation Statutes—hence, their own forms and formats—you are cautioned, therefore, to check your local Corporate Codes to determine the applicability of the following examples.

6.1 APPLICATION FOR RESERVATION OF NAME*

HONORABLE _____
SECRETARY OF STATE
STATE OF MISSOURI
JEFFERSON CITY, MO. 65102

The undersigned, pursuant to the provisions of The General and Business Corporation Law of Missouri hereby requests that the following name (or names) be reserved for sixty days:

_____

_____

_____

_____

Check for $5.00 in payment of fee for each name is enclosed.

_____
Signature of Applicant

_____
(If a corporation, by its President or Vice President)

(CORPORATE
SEAL)

ATTEST:

_____
Its Secretary (or Assistant Secretary)

ASSIGNMENT

For value received _____hereby assigns and

transfers unto _____the right to use the name

_____

for corporate purposes in the State of Missouri.

_____
Signature of Applicant

_____
(If a corporation, by its President or Vice President)

(CORPORATE
SEAL)

ATTEST:

_____
Its Secretary (or Assistant Secretary)

_____
* For State of Missouri

I, _____, a Notary Public, in and for the County and State aforesaid, do hereby certify that on the ____ day of ____ A.D., 19__, personally appeared before me _____

_____

to me personally known to be the same persons who executed the foregoing assignment, and severally acknowledged that they executed it for the purposes therein set forth.

IN WITNESS WHEREOF, I have hereunto set my hand and seal the year and day above written.

_____
Notary Public

(NOTARIAL
SEAL)

COMMENTS

Form 6.1   Application for Reservation of Name

This is the first document which must be prepared in forming a corporation. In some states this Reservation of Name is made via the telephone with a follow-up letter to the appropriate agency, i.e., Secretary of State, Corporations Division, etc.

In some jurisdications you have to submit more than one proposed name, one of which must be finalized within a prescribed statutory period. Check your local corporations code for this procedure.

6.2   ARTICLES OF INCORPORATION*
(To be submitted in duplicate by an attorney)

HONORABLE _____
SECRETARY OF STATE
STATE OF MISSOURI
JEFFERSON CITY, MO. 65101

The undersigned natural person(s) of the age of twenty-one years or more for the purpose of forming a corporation under The General and Business Corporation Law of Missouri adopt the following Articles of Incorporation:

ARTICLE ONE

The name of the corporation is: _____

_____

* For State of Missouri

ARTICLE TWO

The address, including street and number, if any, of the corporation's initial registered office in this state is: _____
and the name of its initial agent at such address is: _____

ARTICLE THREE

The aggregate number, class and par value, if any, of shares which the corporation shall have authority to issue shall be:

The preferences, qualification, limitations, restrictions, and the special or relative rights, including convertible rights, if any, in respect of the share of each class are as follows:

ARTICLE FOUR

The number and class of shares to be issued before the corporation shall commence business, the consideration to be paid therefor and the capital with which the corporation will commence business are as follows:

No. of Shares	Class	Consideration to be paid	Par Value (or for shares without par value, show amount of consideration paid which will be capital)

The corporation will not commence business until consideration of the value of at least Five Hundred Dollars has been received for the issuance of shares.

ARTICLE FIVE

The name and place of residence of each incorporator is as follows:

Name	Street	City

ARTICLE SIX

The number of directors to constitute the board of directors is _____

ARTICLE SEVEN

The duration of the corporation is _____

ARTICLE EIGHT

The corporation is formed for the following purposes:

IN WITNESS WHEREOF, these Articles of Incorporation have been signed this _____ day of _____, 19___.

_____

_____

_____

_____

_____

STATE OF _____

COUNTY OF _____

I, _____, a notary public,

do hereby certify that on the _____ day of _____, 19___, personally appeared before me, _____ (and _____,) who being by me first duly sworn, (severally) declared that he is (they are) the person(s) who signed the foregoing document as incorporator(s), and that the statements therein contained are true.

_____
Notary Public

My commission expires _____, 19___.

COMMENTS

Form 6.2   Articles of Incorporation

The purpose of the document is to set forth the purpose of the corporation, as well as to advise the State of the name of its directors and the type of stock to be issued.

It should be prepared in as many copies as are required by local state law. *Note:* The same are not valid unless and until the state seal has been placed thereon and a copy is left with the state; and any others (which you have had certified) are kept in the corporate file for future processing.

See Form 6.3 for alternative Articles of Incorporation.

6.3   ARTICLES OF INCORPORATION (ALTERNATIVE)

I

The name of this corporation is:

II

The purpose of this corporation is to engage in any lawful act or activity for which a corporation may be organized under the General Corporation Law of

_____ other than the banking business, the trust company business or the practice of a profession permitted to be incorporated by the _____ Corporations Code.

III

The name and address in the State of _____ of this corporation's initial agent for service of process is:

IV

This corporation is authorized to issue only one class of stock; and the total number of shares which this corporation is authorized to issue is _____.

Dated: _____, 19___.

_____

I hereby declare that I am the person who executed the foregoing Articles of Incorporation, which execution is my act and deed.

_____

6.4   ARTICLES OF AMENDMENT*
OF THE
ARTICLES OF INCORPORATION
OF

_____

The undersigned officers of _____ (hereinafter referred to as the ''Corporation'') existing pursuant to the provisions of the Indiana General Corporation Act, as amended (hereinafter referred to as the ''Act''), desiring to give notice of corporate action effectuating amendment of certain provisions of its Articles of Incorporation, certify the following facts:

ARTICLE I
Text of the Amendment

The exact text of Article(s) _____of the Articles of Incorporation of the Corporation, as amended (hereinafter referred to as the ''Amendments''), now is as follows:

ARTICLE II
Manner of Adoption and Vote

Section 1. Action by Directors (select appropriate paragraph).

(a) The Board of Directors of the Corporation, at a meeting thereof, duly called, constituted and held on _____, 19___, at which a quorum of

_____
* For State of Indiana

such Board of Directors was present, duly adopted a resolution proposing to the Shareholders of the Corporation entitled to vote in respect the Amendments that the provisions and terms of Article _____ of its Articles of Incorporation be amended so as to read as set forth in the Amendments; and called a meeting of such shareholders, to be held _____, 19___, to adopt or reject the Amendments, unless the same were so approved prior to such date by unanimous written consent.

Section 2. Action by Shareholders (select appropriate paragraph).

(a) The Shareholders of the Corporation entitled to vote in respect to the Amendments, at a meeting thereof, duly called, constituted and held on _____, 19___, at which _____

_____

_____

were present in person or by proxy, adopted the Amendments.

The holders of the following classes of shares were entitled to vote as a class in respect of the Amendments:

(1)

(2)

(3)

The number of shares entitled to vote in respect of the Amendments, the number of shares voted in favor of the adoption of the Amendments, and the number of shares voted against such adoption are as follows:

	Total	Shares Entitled to Vote as a Class (as listed immediately above)		
		(1)	(2)	(3)
Shares entitled to vote:	_____	_____	_____	_____
Shares voted in favor:	_____	_____	_____	_____
Shares voted against:	_____	_____	_____	_____

(b) By written consent executed on _____, 19___, signed by the holders of _____ shares of the Corporation, being all of the shares of the Corporation entitled to vote in respect of the Amendments, the Shareholders adopted the Amendments.

Section 3. Compliance with Legal Requirements.

The manner of the adoption of the Amendments, and the vote by which they were adopted, constitute full legal compliance with the provisions of the Act, the Articles of Incorporation, and the By-Laws of the Corporation.

ARTICLE III
Statement of Changes Made With Request to Any Increase
In The Number of Shares Heretofore Authorized

Aggregate Number of Shares
  Previously Authorized   _____

Increase   _____

Aggregate Number of Shares
  To Be Authorized After Effect of This Amendment _____

IN WITNESS WHEREOF, the undersigned officers execute these Articles of Amendment of the Articles of Incorporation of the Corporation, and certify to the truth of the facts herein stated, this _____ day of ____, 19___.

_____	_____
Written Signature)	Written Signature)
_____	_____
(Printed Signature)	(Printed Signature)

President of   Secretary of

_____	_____
(Name of Corporation)	(Name of Corporation)

STATE OF INDIANA _____
COUNTY OF _____

I, the undersigned, a Notary Public duly commissioned to take acknowledgments and administer oaths in the State of Indiana, certify that _____, the _____ President, and _____, the _____ Secretary of _____, the officers executing the foregoing Articles of Amendment of the Articles of Incorporation, personally appeared before me, acknowledged the execution thereof, and swore to the truth of the facts therein stated.

Witness my hand and Notarial Seal this _____ day of _____, 19___.

_____
(Written Signature)
_____
(Printed Signature)

My Commission Expires:

_____

This instrument was prepared by _____, Attorney at Law,
                              (Name)

_____
(Number and Street or Building)   (City)   (State)   (Zip Code)

COMMENTS

Form 6.4   Amendment to Articles of Incorporation

This document is filed when you have made a change, or there has been a subsequent, material change, in the original articles, such as change of name of the corporation or principal director.

It should be filed and served upon the state and any other pertinent parties to the transaction as indicated in comments to Form 6.2.

6.5   MINUTES OF ANNUAL MEETING OF THE BOARD OF DIRECTORS

The annual meeting of the Board of Directors of _____ was held at _____, ____, on the ___ day of _____, immediately following the annual meeting of Stockholders.

The following persons, constituting all of the Directors, were present and participated throughout the meeting:

_____

_____

_____

_____ acted as Chairman of the meeting and _____ acted as Secretary.

The Chairman stated that since this was the first meeting of the new Board of Directors and was being held immediately following the annual meeting of Stockholders, no notice of the meeting was necessary.

The following persons were nominated for officers of the Corporation to serve for the ensuing year and until their respective successors are chosen and qualify:

_____   _____

_____   _____

_____   _____

_____   _____

All Directors present having voted, the Chairman announced that the aforesaid persons had been unanimously elected to the offices set before their respective names.

_____   _____

_____   _____

_____   _____

_____   _____

There being no futher business to come before the meeting, upon motion duly made, seconded and unanimously adopted, it was adjourned.

_____
_____, Secretary

Approved:

_____
_____, Chairman

COMMENTS

Form 6.5   Minutes of Annual Meeting of the Board of Directors

These minutes are prepared once a year as opposed to the minutes of regular Board of Directors meetings which are prepared once a month (or whenever the regular meeting is scheduled).

The annual meeting minutes are more or less a "state of union" status report of the corporation as to the progress during the past year and its hopes for the future.

Again, as with all other minutes, a copy should be made for the corporate minute book, corporate file and, if applicable, a copy for each shareholder.

6.6   MINUTES OF SPECIAL MEETING BY CONFERENCE TELEPHONE OF THE BOARD OF DIRECTORS

A special meeting of the Board of Directors of _____ was held by conference telephone pursuant to the provisions of Article ____ of the _____ Business Corporation Act, on the ___ day of _____, at _____.M.

The following persons, constituting all of the Directors, participated by telephone throughout the meeting:

_____   _____

_____   _____

[OTHER BUSINESS TO COME BEFORE THE MEETING]

There being no further business to come before the meeting, it was adjourned.

_____,
_____, Secretary

Approved:

_____
, Chairman

COMMENTS

Form 6.6 Minutes of Special Meeting by Conference Telephone of the Board of Directors

The occasion will arise when an emergency matter will necessitate this form of meeting as between the members of the Board of Directors of a corporation. When it does, a record must be kept of those individuals privy to the conference, as well as any resolutions made.

As a general proposition there is only one matter being discussed via this method, but if this is not applicable in your case, perhaps as noted herein, under "other business," you should incorporate the nature and extent of the business discussed via telephone on an emergency basis as well as any other business that was determined by this vehicle. In all cases, minutes of this meeting should also be typed up and placed in the corporate file.

6.7 WAIVER OF NOTICE OF SPECIAL MEETING BY CONFERENCE TELEPHONE OF THE BOARD OF DIRECTORS

We, the undersigned, all being Directors of _____, do hereby waive all the requirements of the Statutes of _____, of the Articles of Incorporation, and of the Bylaws both as to the notice of the time and place, and to notice of the purpose of a special meeting of the Board of Directors of _____, held by telephone conference at _____.M. on _____, and hereby consent to the holding of the holding of the meeting and to the transaction of any business brought before the meeting.

Dated: _____.

_____

_____

_____

COMMENTS

Form 6.7   Waiver of Notice of Special Meeting by Conference Telephone of the Board of Directors.

This is basically a boilerplate waiver form used to negate the prescribed time for notification of special meetings held by a Board of Directors as set forth in the Bylaws, i.e., three days, five days, ten days, etc.

It also protects those members of the Board of Directors who did in fact attend the special meeting and made a determination as to the business for which the meeting was called.

This document should be filed with the minutes of the meeting in the corporate Minute Book.

6.8   BYLAWS

BYLAWS
OF

_____

ARTICLE I

OFFICES

Section 1.1 PRINCIPAL OFFICES. The board of directors shall fix the location of the principal executive office of the corporation at any place within or outside the State of _____. If the principal executive office is located outside this state, and the corporation has one or more business offices in this state, the board of directors shall likewise fix and designate a principal business office in the State of _____.

Section 1.2 OTHER OFFICES. The board of directors may at any time establish branch or subordinate offices at any place or places where the corporation is qualified to do business.

ARTICLE II

MEETING OF SHAREHOLDERS

Section 2.1 PLACE OF MEETINGS. Meetings of shareholders shall be held at any place within or outside the State of _____ designated by the board of directors. In the absence of any such designation, shareholders' meetings shall be held at the principal executive office of the corporation.

Section 2.2 ANNUAL MEETINGS OF SHAREHOLDERS. The annual meeting of shareholders shall be held each year on a date and at a time designated by the board of directors. At each annual meeting directors shall be elected and any other proper business may be transacted.

Section 2.3 SPECIAL MEETINGS. A special meeting of the shareholders may be called at any time by the board of directors, or by the chairman of the board, or by the president, or by one or more shareholders holding shares in the aggregate entitled to cast not less than 10% of the votes at any such meeting.

Section 2.4 NOTICE OF SHAREHOLDERS' MEETINGS. All notices of meetings of shareholders shall be sent or otherwise given in accordance with Section 2.5 of this Article II not less than ten (10) nor more than sixty (60) days before the date of the meeting being notices. The notice shall specify the place, date and hour of the meeting and (i) in the case of a special meeting, the general nature of the business to be transacted, or (ii) in the case of the annual meeting those matters which the board of directors, at the time of giving the notice, intends to present for action by the shareholders. The notice of any meeting at which directors are to be elected shall include the name of any nominee or nominees which, at the time of the notice, management intends to present for election.

• • • •

Section 2.5 MANNER OF GIVING NOTICE; AFFIDAVIT OF NOTICE

Section 2.6 QUORUM

Section 2.7 ADJOURNED MEETING AND NOTICE THEREOF

Section 2.8 VOTING

Section 2.9 WAIVER OF NOTICE OR CONSENT BY ABSENT SHAREHOLDERS

Section 2.10 SHAREHOLDER ACTION BY WRITTEN CONSENT WITHOUT A MEETING

Section 2.11 RECORD DATE FOR SHAREHOLDER NOTICE, VOTING, etc.

Section 2.12 PROXIES

Section 2.13 INSPECTORS OF ELECTION

ARTICLE III

DIRECTORS

Section 3.1 POWERS

Section 3.2 NUMBER AND QUALIFICATION

Section 3.3 ELECTION AND TERM OF OFFICE

Section 3.4 VACANCIES

Section 3.5 PLACE OF MEETINGS AND TELEPHONIC MEETINGS

Section 3.6 ANNUAL MEETING

Section 3.7 OTHER REGULAR MEETINGS

Section 3.8 SPECIAL MEETINGS

Section 3.9 QUORUM

Section 3.10 WAIVER OF NOTICE

ARTICLE IV

COMMITTEES

Section 4.1 COMMITTEES OF DIRECTORS. The board of directors may, by resolution adopted by a majority of the authorized number of directors, designate one or more committees, each consisting of two or more directors, to serve at the pleasure of the board. The board may designate one or more directors as alternate members of any committee, who may replace any absent member at any meeting of the committee. Any such committee, to the extent provided in the resolution of the board, shall have all the authority of the board, except with respect to:

  (a) the approval of any action which, under the General Corporation Law of _____, also requires shareholders' approval or approval of the outstanding shares;

  (b) the filling of vacancies on the board of directors or in any committee;

  (c) the fixing of compensation of the directors for serving on the board or on any committee;

  (d) the amendment or repeal of bylaws or the adoption of new bylaws.

  (e) the amendment or repeal of any resolution of the board of directors which by its express terms is not so amendable or repealable;

  (f) a distribution to the shareholders of the corporation, except at a rate or in a periodic amount or within a price range determined by the board of directors; or ...

ARTICLE V

OFFICERS

ARTICLE VI

INDEMNIFICATION OF DIRECTORS, OFFICERS, EMPLOYEES AND OTHER AGENTS

Section 6.1 INDEMNIFICATION. The corporation shall, to the maximum extent permitted by the General Corporation Law of _____, indemnify each of its directors and officers against expenses, judgments, fines, settlements and other amounts actually and reasonably incurred in connection with any proceeding arising by reason of the fact any such person is or was a director or officer of the corporation and shall advance to such director or officer expenses incurred in defending any such proceeding to the maximum extent permitted by such law. For purposes of this section, a ''director'' or ''officer'' of the corporation includes any person who is or was a director or officer of the corporation, or is or was serving at the request of the corporation as a director or officer of another corporation, or other enterprise, or was a director or officer of a corporation which was a predecessor corporation of the corporation or of another enterprise at the request of such predecessor corporation. The board of directors may in its discretion provide by resolution for such indemnification of, or advance of expenses to, other agents of the corporation, and likewise may refuse to provide for such indemnification or advance of expenses except to the extent such indemnification is mandatory under the _____ General Corporation law.

ARTICLE VII

RECORDS AND REPORTS

Section 7.1 MAINTENANCE AND INSPECTION OF SHARE REGISTER. The corporation shall keep at its principal executive office, or at the office of its transfer agent or registrar, if either be appointed and as determined by resolution of the board of directors, a record of its shareholders, giving the names and addresses of all shareholders and the number and class of shares held by each shareholder.

• • • •

Section 7.2 MAINTENANCE AND INSPECTION OF BYLAWS

Section 7.3 MAINTENANCE AND INSPECTION OF OTHER CORPORATE RECORDS

Section 7.4 INSPECTION BY DIRECTORS

Section 7.5 ANNUAL REPORT TO SHAREHOLDERS

Section 7.6 FINANCIAL STATEMENTS

Section 7.7 ANNUAL STATEMENT OF GENERAL INFORMATION

ARTICLE VIII

AMENDMENTS

Section 8.1 AMENDMENT BY SHAREHOLDERS

Section 8.2 AMENDMENT BY DIRECTORS

CERTIFICATE OF INCORPORATOR

I, the undersigned, do hereby certify:

(1) That I am the duly elected and acting Incorporator of _____, a _____ corporation; and

(2) That the foregoing Bylaws consisting of 26 pages constitute the Bylaws of said corporation as duly adopted by the Incorporator on _____.

IN WITNESS WHEREOF, I have executed this Certificate as of this ___ day of _____.

_____

Incorporator

CERTIFICATE OF SECRETARY

I, the undersigned, do hereby certify:

(1) That I am the duly elected and acting Secretary of _____, a _____ corporation; and

(2) That the foregoing Bylaws consisting of ___ pages constitute the Bylaws of said corporation as duly adopted by the Written Consent of the Board of Directors dated _____, 19___.

IN WITNESS WHEREOF, I have executed this Certificate as of this ___ day of _____.

_____

Secretary

CERTIFICATE OF SECRETARY

I, the undersigned, do hereby certify:

(1) That I am the duly elected and acting Secretary of _____, a _____ corporation; and

(2) That the foregoing Bylaws consisting of ___ pages constitute the Bylaws of said corporation as duly adopted at a meeting of the Board of Directors thereof duly held on _____.

IN WITNESS WHEREOF, I have executed this Certificate as of this ___ day of _____.

_____

Secretary

COMMENTS

Form 6.8   Bylaws (General)

This document is the "constitution" of the business entity which sets forth the rules and regulations by which the Board of Directors are governed and the corporation operated. It outlines the terms of the Board of Directors; penalties for violation of the Bylaws and its directives; times of meetings; when and who can call them, etc.

We have found it to be a better part of valor to supply each member of the board with a copy of these Bylaws, as well as the general membership, if applicable.

6.9   CERTIFICATE OF CORPORATE RESOLUTION

The undersigned, President and Secretary of _____, a corporation, do hereby certify that said Corporation is duly organized and existing under the laws of the State of _____; that there is no provision of the Articles of Incorporation or Bylaws limiting the power of the Board of Directors to pass the resolutions set out below and that the same are in conformity with the provisions of said Articles of Incorporation and Bylaws; that the Secretary is the keeper of the records and minutes of the proceedings of the Board of Directors of said Corporation and that on the ____ day of _____, there was held a meeting of the Board of Directors of said Corporation, which was duly called and held in accordance with the law and the Bylaws of the Corporation, at which meeting the following resolutions were duly and legally passed and adopted and that the same have not been altered, amended, rescinded or repealed and are now in full force and effect:

[RESOLUTIONS]

We further certify that the following persons are the officers of _____ and are the persons authorized to act and sign the foregoing resolutions:

President   _____

Secretary   _____

IN WITNESS WHEREOF, we have hereunto set our hands as President and Secretary, respectively, of said Corporation and have attached hereto the official seal of said Corporation, this the ___ day of _____.

_____

, President

_____

, Secretary

COMMENTS

Form 6.9 Certificate of Corporate Resolution

This form is self-explanatory. You are cautioned however to spell out the resolution exactly as adopted. Thereafter, copies should be mailed to all persons affected by the resolution, as well as shareholders, if applicable.

Copies should be placed in the corporate minute book and corporate file.

6.10 MINUTES OF SPECIAL MEETING OF THE STOCKHOLDERS

A special meeting of the Stockholders of _____ was held at _____, ___, on the ___ day of _____, at _____.M.

The following Stockholders were present at the meeting, with the number of shares held by each being set opposite his name, and the same constituted all the Stockholders of the Corporation:

| | Number of |
Stockholder	Shares
_____	_____
_____	_____
_____	_____

_____, President of the Corporation, acted as Chairman of the meeting, and _____ acted as Secretary.

The Chairman presented to the meeting a Waiver of Notice of the meeting which has been signed by all the Stockholders, and such Waiver was ordered filed with the minutes of the meeting.

(The following paragraphs should incorporate the nature of the business discussed and the resolutions thereof.)

There being no further business to come before the meeting, upon motion made, seconded and unanimously carried, it was adjourned.

_____

_____, Secretary

Approved:

_____

_____, Chairman

COMMENTS

**Form 6.10   Minutes of Special Meeting of the Stockholders
of the Corporation**

The comments to Forms 6 and 7 are applicable here.

6.11   WAIVER OF NOTICE OF SPECIAL MEETING OF THE STOCKHOLDERS

We, the undersigned, being all of the Stockholder of _____, do hereby waive all the requirements of the Statutes of _____, of the Articles of Incorporation, and of the Bylaws both as to the notice of the time and place, and to notice of the purpose of a special meeting of the Stockholders of _____, to be held at _____.M. on _____, at _____, _____, and hereby consent to the holding of the meeting and to the transaction of such business as may be brought up thereat.

Dated: _____.

_____

_____

_____

COMMENTS

Form 6.11   Waiver of Notice of Special Meeting of Stockholders

See comments to Forms 6 and 7.

6.12   STOCKHOLDERS' CONSENT

_____

[Date]

Pursuant to the provisions of Article 9.10 A of the Texas Business Corporation Act, the undersigned, being all of the Stockholders of _____, a Texas corporation, hereby consent to the adoption of the following resolution, and the same shall have the same force and effect as if adopted at a formal meeting duly called and held for the purposes of acting upon a proposal to adopt such resolution:

Dated: _____.

_____

_____

_____

COMMENTS

Form 6.12   Stockholders' Consent

This document is prepared when a formal meeting of the shareholders has not been held and they have been contacted or informed by letter of a resolution adopted at a Board of Directors meeting. Their response is the signing of a consent to the adoption of the resolution.

These consents should be filed in a separate folder in the corporate file and a copy placed in the corporate minute book following the minutes of the meeting of the Board of Directors to which the consent to resolution adopted was discussed.

Note that the consent form should be mailed to the shareholders via a covering letter explaining the resolution, its impact and intent, as well as setting forth the resolution verbatim.

6.13   OATH OF INSPECTORS OF ELECTION

THE STATE OF _____

COUNTY OF _____

We, _____ and _____, having been appointed Inspectors of Election to act at the Annual Meeting of Shareholders of _____, held the ___ day of _____, do solemnly swear that we will fairly and to the best of our ability perform our duties in connection with the election of Directors and in connection with all other matters required of us at such meeting, and we will faithfully and with strict impartiality examine the ballots, canvass the votes cast at such meeting, truthfully and accurately report the results thereof, and discharge all of our responsibilities in accordance with the Bylaws of this Corporation.

COMMENTS

Form 6.13 Oath of Inspectors of Election

At the time of election of a new member to the Board of Directors, or a new Board of Directors, individuals are appointed from the Shareholder membership to be responsible for this election process.

Once appointed, this is the type of oath they are required to take in accordance with, and as set forth, in the bylaws and a copy should be filed in the corporate minute book.

6.14 CERTIFICATE AND REPORT OF THE INSPECTORS OF ELECTION

ANNUAL MEETING OF SHAREHOLDERS

The undersigned, duly appointed Inspectors of Election at the Annual Meeting of the Shareholders of _____ held _____, hereby certify and report:

(1) The Annual Meeting of the Shareholders of _____ was held on _____ at _____.M. located at _____.

(2) The numer of shares of Common Stock issued and outstanding and entitled to vote at such meeting was _____.

(3) There were present at said meeting, in person or by proxy, shareholders of the Corporation who were the holders of _____ shares of Common Stock or _____ percent of the total shares outstanding, which constituted a quorum.

(4) We received the votes of the Shareholders of the Corporation by ballot, in person or by proxy.

(5) We canvassed the votes so cast for the election of Directors at such meeting, in person and by proxy, and the following persons received the number of votes set opposite their respective names:

Names of Candidate	Number of Votes

(6) No other matter was brought before said meeting requiring vote by written ballot.

Dated: _____

COMMENTS

Form 6.14 Certificate and Report of the Inspectors for Election

This form appears to be self-explanatory and should also be filed in the corporate Minute Book; and if it is the policy of the corporation, a copy should be mailed to all Shareholders and the new Board members or new Board of Directors.

6.15 STATEMENT OF _____
REGISTERED OFFICE AND REGISTERED AGENT

TO THE SECRETARY OF _____
OF THE STATE OF _____.

Pursuant to the provisions of Article _____ of the _____ Business Corporation Act, the undersigned corporation, organized under the laws of the State of _____, submits the following statement of registered office and its registered agent in the State of _____:

1. The name of the Corporation is _____.
2. The post office address of its registered office is _____.
3. The name of its registered agent is _____.
4. The name of its alternative registered agent is _____.
5. The post office address of its registered office and the post office address of the business office of its registered agent are identical.
6. The above was authorized by resolution duly adopted by its Board of Directors.

Dated: _____.

_____
[President/Vice-President]

THE STATE OF _____
COUNTY OF _____

I, _____, a notary public, do hereby certify that on this _____ day of _____, personally appeared before me _____, who being by me first duly sworn, declared that he is the [President/Vice-President] of _____, that he signed the foregoing document as [President/Vice-President] of the Corporation and that the statements therein contained are true.

_____
NOTARY PUBLIC IN AND FOR
_____ COUNTY, _____.

COMMENTS

Form 6.15 Statement of Registered Office and Registered Agent

This is a mandatory statement to be filed by a corporation with the Secretary of State in most states. The form and format may be different but all corporations are required to file a document which sets forth the name and address of the agent of the corporation legally able to accept service of process on its behalf. This could be the corporate office headquarters, the office of the attorney of the corporation, or any other person so designated by an adopted resolution of the Board of Directors to accept the responsibility on behalf of the corporation.

6.16 APPLICATION FOR ORDER OF SERVICE OF SUMMONS AGAINST FOREIGN CORPORATION ...

SUPERIOR COURT OF THE STATE OF _____
FOR THE COUNTY OF _____

_____, Plaintiff, vs. _____, Defendant.	No. _____ APPLICATION FOR ORDER FOR SERVICE OF SUMMONS AGAINST FOREIGN CORPORATION BY DELIVERY TO THE SECRETARY OF STATE.

APPLICATION IS HEREBY MADE for an Order directing service of Summons in this action on defendant _____ of Seine, France, by personal delivery to the Secretary of State of California, or to an assistant or deputy Secretary of State of one copy of the Summons, together with one copy of the order applied for herein.

The complaint in this action, which is for injuries, damages, and wrongful death, was filed herein on June 9, 19___; and Summons was duly issued on said date of June 9, 19___.

Said defendant is a foreign corporation owned by the French government, and engaged in the manufacture of automobiles. It sells its products to defendant _____a corporation organized to do business in the County of _____, _____.

Plaintiffs have been unable to find any of the officers or agents of the corporation, as specified in Section ____ of the Corporation Code of the State of _____, on whom service of process may be had, although diligent search has been made therefor in the manner of checking the corporation records in

_____, _____.

The principal place of business of said foreign corporation, and its principal mailing address is:

_____

Seine, France

WHEREFORE, I pray that the court issue its order that service of Summons in this action may be had by personal delivery to the Secretary of State, or to an assistant or deputy Secretary of State of one copy of Summons, together with one copy of the order sought herein.

EXECUTED on this ____ day of October, 19___, in _____, _____.

I DECLARE under penalty of perjury that the foregoing is true and correct.

COMMENTS

Form 6.16   Application for Order for Service of Summons ...
Order for Service of Summons on
Foreign Corporation

Unless your office has the unique status of being an international law firm, the following form is rare.

The 6.16 form is used when the defendant is not a United States citizen; or is a United States citizen residing and domiciled in another country. This description is applicable to corporations and other like business entities with the exception that the business entity may have been licensed to do business in this country. Or it may be the corporation had "an arm" of its corporation in this country.

You normally use this form after you have researched the locality in which the incident occurred; as well as other states throughout the country to locate the culpable corporation or its arm. When all of this has proved to be an exercise in futility, you are then in a position to utilize the procedure and forms hereinabove set forth.

6.17 CHECKLIST FOR THE
CORPORATE LEGAL ASSISTANT

In setting up a corporation, be sure to determine:

1. Who will be the active directors in the corporation?

2. What major changes are expected in the future relative to active participation in the corporation?

3. Are the active parties expected to let loans in the future to the corporation; or will these funds be coming from outside sources be required?

4. Is the corporation to remain within and under the control of the initial promoters in the future?

5. Is each party willing to make full disclosure?

6. How do the parties plan to use the profits of the corporation—put it back into the corporation or take it out?

7. What is anticipated or planned for the profits or shares of a deceased or retiring partner?

8. Did you compute all fees necessary to incorporate?

9. Did you obtain the necessary licenses and permits, dba name statement, attorney's fee, record the certificate of limited partnership, qualifying fee, state recording and county clerk fees and purchase of notebook, seal and so forth?

10. Has an agent been appointed to accept service of process?

Note: Corporations can avoid direct service of process in California. However, there may be instances where it would be preferable for the corporation to designate such agent. You should look to your local code for this or discuss this matter with your attorney.

11. Has the stock been issued and if so, have the shareholders been notified?

12. Determine that the minutes and by-laws have been prepared for signature by the appropriate parties.

13. Prepare adoption of bylaws document showing if there were any restrictions and limitations on the adoption of the bylaws, if applicable.

14. Check to see that the adoption of bylaws document has been executed.

15. Prepare permit to issue stock.

16. Issue the stock and be sure that the red ledger stock has been applied, if applicable.

17. Check to see if you have selected the date on which the corporation is to commence business or if it is an established business, when the income is to be shifted from the owners to the new corporation.

~~18. Check to determine if the date has been set for the new corporation to~~ issue its shares of stock. (There is a question of legal liability involved in the issuance of stock, so be sure to check with your attorney as to the date on which these shares should be issued.)

19. Check and determine if the dates elected and desired for issuance of permit by your state commissioner of corporations is applicable.

20. Check to see if the date selected for filing the application to the commissioner of department of corporations for a permit to issue securities is applicable or required.

21. Check to see if you have set a firm date for the first meeting of the board of directors. (This first meeting of the board of directors should be set as soon as possible after the articles of incorporation have been filed.)

22. Determine if there is a definite date required for the filing of the articles of incorporation.

23. Determine if there is a definite date required for the reservation of the desired name for the new corporation. (There is a time limitation here so try to make your period for reserving a corporate name within the statutory limitation date, which in some states is sixty days, and file your request to coordinate with the selective date for filing the articles of incorporation).

24. Check and determine the date upon which your pre-incorporation subscription agreements should be executed. Be sure that this date falls within the statutory limitation, which is normally ninety days prior to the filing of the articles of incorporation. This statutory time limitation should be governed by the corporation rules and regulations of your state.

25. At the organizational meeting of the incorporating board of directors, be sure that dummy or straw directors file their resignation.

26. Check to be sure that you have filed a report with the secretary of state. This form is the one which should have been automatically mailed to you from the secretary of state when the articles of incorporation were filed. The name given to this document in California is entitled ''Statement by Domestic Corporation.'' You might look to your own local corporation rules and regulations to see if you have an applicable form document set out by your local secretary of state.

Contents—Chapter 7
Criminal Procedure

7

CRIMINAL PROCEDURE

7.0   INTRODUCTION

A legal assistant should not only be familiar with the classification and types of crimes and criminal procedure but should also know how to conduct interviews, know what information is necessary to determine what documents are needed; and then be able to prepare those documents in defense of the defendant's case.

The following are the basic pre-trial and post-trial motions that a legal assistant working for an attorney with a heavy criminal practice, should know.

7.1   CRIMINAL INTERVIEW SHEET

Date in Office _____

CRIMINAL LAW INTERVIEW SHEET

Name _____
          First   Middle   Last

AKA-BOOKED AS: _____

ADDRESS _____
          Street   Apt.   City   Zip

PHONE _____BUS. PHONE _____ NEIGHBOR'S PHONE _____

AGE _____ DATE OF BIRTH _____ SOCIAL SECURITY NO. _____

EMPLOYED: Yes _____ No _____ EMPLOYER _____

ADDRESS: _____
             Street   Apt.   City   Zip

OCCUPATION _____ HOW LONG THERE _____

                                        TIME IN CITY _____

CO-DEFENDANT _____   _____
                       (1)   Attorney

                        _____   _____
                       (2)   Attorney

                        _____   _____
                       (3)   Attorney

FAMILY

MARRIED _____ COMMON-LAW _____ SEPARATED _____

DIVORCED _____ SINGLE _____ WIDOW _____

NUMBER OF DEPENDANTS _____

COURT

DEPARTMENT ____ CASE NO. _____ BAIL _____
                                                                      (Yes or No)

BAIL _____ REDUCTION _____ OWN RECOGNIZANCE _____

BOOKED _____
              Yes or No.   Booking No.   Location

DATE

DATE ARRESTED _____ TIME _____

PRELIMINARY HEARING ARRAIGNMENT _____

PRELIMINARY HEARING _____

COURT ARRAIGNMENT _____

COURT PLEA_____

OTHER CASES PENDING

NATURE _____ WHEN _____ WHERE _____

SENTENCE _____

APPEAL _____ PAROLE _____
     Yes or No   Yes or No

OTHER CASES PENDING

_____
Where   For   Probation Officer

MEDICAL

NEED MEDICINE NOW _____ ON WHAT DOCTOR'S ORDERS ___

NAME OF MEDICINE _____

CONTINUING MEDICAL CONDITION _____
                                          (Epilepsy, Diabetes)

DID POLICE TAKE BLOOD TEST (a) Permission asked _____

                                         (b) Permission given _____

SEARCH AND SEIZURE

WHERE YOU SEARCHED WHEN ARRESTED _____ BY WHOM ___

DID YOU SEE A SEARCH WARRANT _____

DID YOU CONSENT TO THE SEARCH _____

WHAT WAS SCOPE OF THE SEARCH (State Briefly) _____

_____

INTERROGATION—CONFESSION

WERE YOU ADVISED OF RIGHTS (a) To remain silent _____
                                        (b) To have an attorney _____
                                        (c) When _____ Where _____

WAS THERE A LINE-UP _____ AN ATTORNEY PRESENT _____

FACT OF CRIME

FACTS SURROUNDING CHARGE(S)

_____

_____

_____

_____

_____

_____

(Pictures)   NAME _____

ADDRESS _____

PHONE _____

NAME _____

ADDRESS _____

PHONE _____

NAME _____

ADDRESS _____

PHONE _____

NAME _____

ADDRESS _____

PHONE _____

CHARGE

SPONSOR _____

Yes or No

NAME _____

ADDRESS _____

PHONE _____

IT IS UNDERSTOOD AND AGREED THAT MONEY ADVANCED ON THIS CASE IS NOT REFUNDABLE.

UNDER NO CIRCUMSTANCES WILL MONEY BE PAID FOR CONSULATION BE REFUNDED.

DATED: _____ (SIGNATURE) _____

COMMENTS

Form 7.1   Criminal Interview Sheet

This could be considered the most important document to be prepared by you as a legal assistant in an office with a heavy criminal practice.

It is prepared within the privacy of either your office or your attorney's office with the client and contains all of the pertinent information the attorney will need to set the pace for the defense of his client.

Upon completion it should contain all of the statistical background of the family of the defendant and the defendant; his previous "rap sheet," if applicable, of prior offenses and their disposition.

And finally, the defendant's version of the alleged crime for which he has been arrested or accused.

COMMENTS

Form 7.2 Demurrer to Information (See Form 7.10 (page 162) and the section on Demurrers in Chapter 11. Litigation.) (pages 258-262).

A Notice and Motion of Demurrer in a criminal action is similar to the demurrer filed in a civil action which spells out the defects in a complaint, such as lack of a prima facie case, lack of jurisdiction, and so forth.'

Unlike civil actions, the demurrer here is filed at the time of the initial arraignment. A Motion to Quash or Dismiss can be used at this point in the proceeding.

COMMENTS

Form 7.3 Motion to Quash or Set Aside Complaint of Indictment (See Forms 7.6 and 7.7)

This is the motion you would use if there is a lack of probable cause, with the same basic format as any other noticed motion. If you are using it in connection with a grand jury hearing, it should be accompanied by a declaration of your attorney, including the following, among other things:

1. That the grand jury did not have probable cause;
2. That the evidence presented was not properly presented to the grand jury.

If on the other hand, it is for an information charge, then the ground would be "no probable cause to make an arrest".

7.4 MOTION TO REDUCE EXCESSIVE BAIL

Attorney's Name
Address
City, State
Phone

Attorney for Defendant, John Doe

SUPERIOR COURT OF THE STATE OF _____
FOR THE COUNTY OF _____

PEOPLE OF THE STATE OF _____	)))	No. _____
Plaintiff,	))	
vs.	))	MOTION TO REDUCE EXCESSIVE BAIL
JOHN DOE,	))	
Defendant.	)))	
_____	)	

Defendant, John Doe, through his counsel, (Name) _____,
hereby moves the Court for an Order reducing defendant's bail from the
previously set sum of $100,000.00, which is unconstitutionally excessive, to
the sum of $25,000.00, an amount which should guarantee defendant's appear-
ance at all stages of the proceedings.

This motion is based upon the transcript of the preliminary examination,
which the Court has read and considered, the declaration of John Doe, attached
hereto as Exhibit A, the declaration of (Lawyer's Name) attached hereto as
Exhibit B, the points and authorities annexed hereto, and such ...

COMMENTS

Form 7.4 Motion to Reduce Excessive Bail

Bail (money or property to insure the attendance of the defendant on the
date of trial) is normally set at the time of arraignment. It is at this point the
attorney may wish to file Form 7.4, if he feels that the bail being set is excessive
in view of the circumstances, (client's economic condition); or the nature of the
crime.

You may wish to file a declaration of the defendant setting forth his
inability to pay the bail and that of your attorney to collaborate this, together with

a Memorandum of Points and Authorities in Support Thereof if the objection is based on economics. Your attorney, of course, will make this determination.

7.5 and 7.6   NOTICE OF MOTION TO DISMISS

Attorney Information

SUPERIOR COURT OF THE STATE OF _____
FOR THE COUNTY OF _____

PEOPLE OF THE STATE OF _____) Plaintiff,) vs. John Doe, Defendant.)	NO. _____ NOTICE OF MOTION TO DISMISS

TO: DISTRICT ATTORNEY OF THE COUNTY OF _____

PLEASE TAKE NOTICE that on _____, 19___, at _____ A.M. or as soon thereafter as counsel can be heard, in Department _____ of the above-entitled court, located at _____, Defendant JOHN DOE will move the Court for an order dismissing the information filed herein and dismissing the above-entitled action.

Said motion will be made on the grounds that: (specify grounds, e.g., that defendant was deprived of his right to a speedy trial as guaranteed by the Sixth Amendment to the United States Constitution, and by Article ___, Section ___ of the (your state) Constitution in that: (here you should specify the facts pertinent to the violation of the law.)

Said motion will be based on this notice of motion, on the (specify other, e.g., transcript of preliminary examination), and on the declaration of _____, counsel for defendant, on the attached Memorandum of Points and Authorities, served and filed herewith, and on such other oral and documentary evidence as may be presented at the hearing of this motion.

Dated: _____

_____
Attorney for Defendant

Forms 7.5 and 7.6   Notice and Motion to Dismiss

The first paragraph of Form 7.5 is the Notice of Motion to Dismiss and is boilerplate in form.

The second paragraph is Form 7.6 the Motion to Dismiss. You are cautioned to set forth the grounds, not only as legally verbatim as possible from your local code, but to set forth the actual time elapsing from the time of arrest to the date of trial.

7.7   NOTICE OF MOTION FOR SUPPRESSION OF EVIDENCE

(Attorney's Name)
(Address)
(City, State)
(Phone)

Attorney for Defendant John Doe

SUPERIOR COURT OF THE STATE OF _____
FOR THE COUNTY OF _____

THE PEOPLE OF THE STATE OF _____ PLAINTIFF, vs. JOHN DOE, DEFENDANT.	NO. _____ NOTICE OF MOTION FOR SUPPRESSION OF EVIDENCE (Pen. Code ____)

NOTICE IS HEREBY GIVE THAT ON JANUARY 21, 19___, at 11:30 a.m. or as soon thereafter as counsel may be heard, in the Courtroom of Division _____ of the above-entitled court, located at _____ in the City of _____, defendant, JOHN DOE, will move the court for an order suppressing as evidence the following:

All property taken on December 18, 19___, from those certain premises located at 7174 South Broad Boulevard, _____ at the time of the defendant's arrest at said time and place, consisting of the wooden crate, containing ten empty bottles, a pile of rags, two cans of gasoline, two incendiary devices, and four kilos of marihuana; together with all evidence respecting any events that occurred at said time and place and all fruits thereof.

COMMENTS

Form 7.7 Notice of Motion for Suppression of Evidence

This form is, and may be, filed to reduce bail for the charges for which the defendant was arrested.

However, it is generally filed to suppress evidence which may have been obtained as the result of illegal search and seizure of the defendant's house, car or other personal and/or real property.

This is the attorney's bailiwick and he should make this determination based on a conversation with the defendant as to what happened at the time of arrest.

7.8   POINTS AND AUTHORITIES IN SUPPORT OF MOTION TO SUPPRESS EVIDENCE

SUPERIOR COURT OF THE STATE OF _____

FOR THE COUNTY OF _____

THE PEOPLE OF THE STATE
OF _____

                    Plaintiff,

vs.

                    Defendant,

No. _____

POINTS AND AUTHORITIES
IN SUPPORT OF MOTION
TO SUPPRESS EVIDENCE
[Pen. Code _____].

Defendant submits the following points and authorities in support of his motion to suppress evidence on file herein:

I

A CRIMINAL DEFENDANT MAY MOVE TO SUPPRESS EVIDENCE OBTAINED AS THE RESULT OF AN UNREASONABLE SEARCH AND SEIZURE.

Penal Code §_____ provides that the Superior Court may, at a special hearing prior to trial, hear a motion to suppress evidence obtained from an unreasonable search where the warrant is unreasonable because (1) "there was not probable cause for the issuance of the warrant," and (2) where "the method of execution of the warrant violated federal or state constitutional standards." *Pen Code §*_____.

II

A MOTION TO SUPPRESS EVIDENCE WILL LIE WHERE THERE WAS NO PROBABLE CAUSE TO ISSUE A WARRANT.

The courts have defined reasonable or probable cause to mean "such a state of facts as would lead a man of ordinary caution or prudence to believe, and
• • •

COMMENTS

Form 7.8   Points and Authorities in Support of Motion to Suppress Evidence

This is the support document (together with a declaration of the attorney which may be optional in your state) which must be filed with Form 7.7. This document sets forth the authorities upon which you base your motion to suppress evidence obtained illegally and may be found in your Evidence Code or other local state statutes.

7.9   MOTION FOR DISCOVERY AND INSPECTION

Attorney for Defendant

SUPERIOR COURT OF THE _____
FOR THE COUNTY OF _____

THE PEOPLE OF THE STATE
OF _____   )   NO. _____
)
                          Plaintiffs,   )   MOTION FOR DISCOVERY
)   AND INSPECTION
)
vs.   )
)
JOHN DOE,   )
)
                          Defendant.   )
_____   )

Defendant, John Doe, through his counsel, hereby moves the Court for an order requiring the prosecution to do the following:

1. Supply defendant's attorneys, at their expense, one copy (by Xerox reproduction, or other method of comparable quality) of each of the following:

   a) All oral and written statements and/or admissions allegedly made by defendant, whether signed or unsigned.

   b) All written statements, signed or unsigned, of persons known to the People who claim to be witnesses to any transaction or event constituting part of. ...

COMMENTS

Form 7.9   Motion for Discovery and Inspection

Your attorney would need this document prepared should the prosecution, for whatever reason, fail and refuse to share with him any and all pertinent documents, such as confessions, evidence discovered at the scene, etc., they may have turned up during the course of investigation which affect the trial or the defense of the action.

Once again, this determination will be made by your attorney after a review of the arrest record and conversations with the defendant. This procedure would negate any "surprises" at the time of trial.

7.10   NOTICE OF MOTION RE INFORMATION

Attorney for Defendant

SUPERIOR COURT OF THE STATE OF _____
FOR THE COUNTY OF _____

THE PEOPLE OF THE STATE OF _____	)	CASE NO. _____
	)	
Plaintiff,	)	NOTICE OF MOTION RE: INFORMATION
	)	(Section ____, Penal Code)
vs	)	
JANE DOE,	)	
Defendant.	)	
_____	)	

TO ⎯⎯⎯⎯⎯⎯, ~~DISTRICT ATTORNEY OF~~ ⎯⎯⎯⎯⎯⎯⎯⎯

COUNTY, ⎯⎯⎯:

PLEASE TAKE NOTICE that on ⎯⎯⎯⎯, 19⎯⎯, at ⎯⎯⎯⎯A.M., or as soon thereafter as counsel can be heard in Department ⎯⎯⎯⎯⎯⎯ of the above-entitled court, located at ⎯⎯⎯⎯⎯⎯, defendant JANE DOE will move the court for an order *setting aside the information* filed herein.

Said motion will be made on the grounds that ⎯⎯⎯⎯⎯⎯, in that
 (specify grounds)
⎯⎯⎯⎯⎯⎯, as shown on pages ⎯⎯⎯⎯, lines ⎯⎯⎯ of the trans-
 (specify grounds)
cript of the preliminary examination.

Said motion will be based on this notice of motion, on the transcript of the preliminary examination, on the attached declaration of ⎯⎯⎯⎯⎯⎯, and the Memorandum of Points and Authorities served herewith, and on such other oral and documentary evidence as may be presented at the hearing on this motion.

Dated: ⎯⎯⎯⎯⎯⎯⎯⎯

⎯⎯⎯⎯⎯⎯⎯⎯⎯⎯⎯⎯⎯

Attorney for Defendant

(*Note*: A similar form may be used in connection with an indictment, if and where applicable).

COMMENTS

Form 7.10 Notice of Motion Re Information

This motion is normally filed once the defendant has been accused and indicated on a felony count. He is then served with an "Information for Robbery" as an example. This places the defendant on notice that "The People of the State of ⎯⎯⎯" have sufficient evidence to file a felony complaint against him for Robbery, Rape, etc.

These forms are usually served on the defendant at the time of his arrest, though in some jurisdications they are served separately; but in most states the Information and the felony complaint are served simultaneously.

Form 7.10 is presented at the Preliminary hearing to set aside the "Information" all together or at the very least, reduce the charge. See Paragraph Two of Form 7.10 which is the motion.

7.11   MOTION FOR ORDER
APPOINTING PSYCHIATRIST

Attorney Information

SUPERIOR COURT OF THE STATE OF _____
FOR THE COUNTY OF _____

PEOPLE OF THE STAE OF _____	)))	No. _____
Plaintiff,	))))))	MOTION FOR ORDER APPOINTING PSYCHIATRIST _____ Evidence Code, Sections ___, ___, ____.
vs. JOHN DOE,	)))	
Defendant.	))	
_____	)	

TO: _____

_____, counsel for Defendant herein, moves the court for an order appointing _____, M.D., as psychiatrist for Defendant herein, to examine said Defendant and to report the findings to the Defendant's counsel only.

A confidential psychiatric examination is necessary and material, and is authorized by Sections ____, ____ and ____ of the Evidence Code, so that counsel can be fully advised, and can advise defendant, whether to present a defense based on insanity or on Defendant's mental or emotional condition.

DATED: _____

_____
ATTORNEY FOR DEFENDANT

(*Note*: You are cautioned to check your local state Evidence Code for the applicable code sections for use in the above motion.)

7.12   ORDER APPOINTING PSYCHIATRIST

Attorney for Defendant

SUPERIOR COURT OF THE STATE OF _____

FOR THE COUNTY OF _____

THE PEOPLE OF
THE STATE OF _____
 	
                Plaintiff,
 	
vs
 	
JANE DOE,
 	
                Defendant.
	CASE NO.
	
	ORDER

TO DR. _____, _____:
           (name)   (address)

You have been appointed by the Court, under the provisions of Sections ____, ____ and ____ of the Evidence Code, to examine the above-named defendant who is charged with the following offense(s): _____. You are
        (specify)
requested to examine said defendant and report your findings to her attorney only. Counsel for defendant is _____, _____.
                 (name) (address)

You are directed to answer the following questions in your report:

1. Was defendant sane at the time of the commission of the alleged offense?

2. Is defendant presently able to understand the nature and purpose of the proceedings taken against her?

3. Is defendant presently able to cooperate in a rational manner with counsel in presenting a defense?

4. Is she presently of such mental condition that she is dangerous to herself or to the persons or property of others?

5. Did defendant, at the time of the commission of the alleged offense, have the mental capacity to form the specific intent to commit the crime charged (diminished capacity)? To premeditate? To deliberate? To harbor malice? To meaningfully and maturely reflect upon the gravity of her contemplated act?

6. What evidence, if any, is there of a neurological disorder?

7. In your opinion, would defendant benefit from treatment and care in a state hospital?

8. (other) _____?

The defendant is presently detained at _____ and shall be examined there, upon your giving the authorities 24-hour notice of your intention to examine defendant. Copies of the police reports are attached. The trial is scheduled for _____ 19___, and your report should be in the possession of defendant's counsel as soon as possible.

Dated: _____ 19___.

_____

JUDGE OF THE SUPERIOR COURT

COMMENTS

Forms 7.11 and 7.12   Motion for Order Appointing Psychiatrist and Order

These two documents go hand in hand.

Addressed to the court with copies to the prosecution, these forms are prepared and filed when your attorney believes that the defendant may have had some emotional problem causing him to do that for which he has been arrested; or may indeed be legally, mentally ill and therefore not responsible for his action under the law.

This action of course is optional for the attorney but if he intends to use mental illness as a defense, or part of his defense, and has probable cause to believe that the defendant may be suffering from an emotional deficiency, these are the forms you would prepare to obtain a court-appointed psychiatrist who would make this official determination.

7.13   NOTICE OF MOTION TO SEVER ...

Attorney Information

SUPERIOR COURT OF THE STATE OF _____
FOR THE COUNTY OF _____

PEOPLE OF THE STATE OF _____,)	No. _____
)	
Plaintiff,)	NOTICE OF MOTION TO SEVER AND TO
)	DISCLOSE THE IDENTITY
vs.)	OF THE INFORMANT, ...
JOHN DOE,)	
)	
Defendant.)	

TO: DISTRICT ATTORNEY _____.

PLEASE TAKE NOTICE that on the _____ day of _____, 19___, at the hour of _____ A.M. or as soon thereafter as counsel may be heard, in Department _____ of the above-entitled court, the Defendant will move the court for orders to sever defendants, and to disclose the identity of the informant, ...

These motions shall be based on this notice, the pleadings, records, files in this action, the points and authorities attached hereto, and other documentation which may become applicable, and such oral and documentary evidence which shall be presented at the time of hearing on these motions.

DATED: _____

_____
ATTORNEY FOR DEFENDANT

COMMENTS

Form 7.13   Notice of Motion to Sever and to Disclose the Identity of the Informant

This notice and motion is generally prepared and filed when more than one person has been accused and arrested for the same crime.

The attorney for one of said defendants (and/or sometimes more than one attorney for the defendants involved) will file this notice and motion if it is felt that the client's interest would best be served by having separate trials.

Another reason would be to determine which of the defendants would turn state's evidence; or is the informant; or knows an informant who could shed more light on the circumstances of the crime or crimes.

7.14 NOTICE OF MOTION TO DECLARE PRIOR CONVICTION CONSTITUTIONALLY INVALID

Attorney Information

SUPERIOR COURT OF THE STATE OF _____
FOR THE COUNTY OF _____

PEOPLE OF THE STATE OF _____	)))	No. _____
Plaintiff,	)))	NOTICE OF MOTION TO DECLARE PRIOR
vs.	))	CONVICTION
JOHN DOE,	))	CONSTITUTIONALLY INVALID
Defendant.	))))	

TO: CITY ATTORNEY FOR THE CITY OF _____:

PLEASE TAKE NOTICE that on the ___ day of _____, 19___, in _____ of the above-entitled court, at the hour of _____ or as soon thereafter as counsel can be heard, the defendant will seek to have the conviction of _____, 19___, in the _____ Judicial District, (or other appropriate court) being Case No. _____, declared Constitutionally invalid.

Said motion will be based on the following grounds:

a. There was no waiver of right to attorney;

b. There was no advisement of the right to have an attorney appointed to defend;

c. There was no waiver of right to a jury trial;

d. There as no waiver of right against self-incrimination.

(*Note*: These are a few of the grounds which may be used to aid in declaring a prior conviction invalid. Your local code sections may provide for more).

COMMENTS

Form 7.14 Notice of Motion to Declare Prior Conviction Constitutionally Invalid

Paragraph one of this form is the boilerplate Notice of Motion (as with all prior Notices in this section);

Paragraph two herein sets forth the grounds upon which you will be basing your request for hearing.

Particular attention should be made to the authority for these grounds such as defendant's rights under the 4th, 5th, 6th and 14th Amendments of the Federal Constitution as well as state constitutions and local evidence codes.

The point being, if you can get prior convictions declare invalid, then perhaps your attorney can get a reduced charge and/or sentence (or may have it thrown out) for the current alleged offense.

Contents—Chapter 8
Estate Planning

8

ESTATE PLANNING

8.0 INTRODUCTION

Estate planning deals primarily with rights and duties; human needs and emotions: love and hate; fairness and inequity; and the professional lawyer is the mediator. It is his job to help the client plan for the distribution of his property either during his lifetime or after his death; and the giving away of the property he has worked all his life to obtain. Hence, estate planning also involves anxiety, involvement and the need to do the right thing for the deceased's heirs and descendants. The job of the legal assistant, therefore, is to make this procedure more competent; and to make the procedure more competent is to know what facts should be gathered, how they should be gathered, and what documents are needed to be prepared in order to expedite this emotional time for the client. The following forms will aid you in this procedure.

8.1 WILL (WRITTEN/TYPED)

I, _____, a resident of the City of _____, County of _____, State of _____, and residing at _____ Street, being of the age of majority; of sound and disposing mind and memory, and not acting under duress, menace, fraud or undue influence, do make, publish and declare this to be my Last Will and Testament.

FIRST: I direct all my debts, including my funeral expenses and the expense of my last illness together with expenses of the administration of my estate be paid by my executor to be named hereafter out of the first monies coming to his or her hands and available therefor.

SECOND: I hereby declare that I am married; my spouse's name is _____, that I have ____ children, (then set forth the names of each child, together with their birthdates).

THIRD: I give, devise and bequeath all of the rest and residue of my property, after the payment of the debts and expenses hereinabove provided for, be it real, personal or mixed, of whatever kind or character, and wheresoever situated to my _____.

FOURTH: I hereby nominate and appoint _____ the executor of this, my Last Will and Testament.

FIFTH: I hereby revoke all former Wills and Codicils to Wills heretofore by me made.

IN WITNESS WHEREOF, I have hereunto set my hand and seal this _____ day of _____, 19___.

_____

Testator (trix)

(*Note*: In some states, it is required that a seal be attached following the name of testator or testatrix).

The foregoing instrument, consisting of ____ pages beside this, was at the date hereof, by _____, signed, sealed and published as, and declared to be his (or her) Last Will and Testament in the presence of us, who at his (or her) request and in his (her) presence and in the presence of each other, have signed our names as witnesses hereto.

_____

_____

COMMENTS

Form 8.1   Typewritten Will

The underlying purpose in preparing Form 8.1 is to prevent the state from imposing its will upon the estate of the testator.

Paragraph 1, though unnumbered, identifies the testator and the document.

Paragraph 2 normally addresses itself to the payment of any outstanding debts by an Executor (trix) named therein or thereafter to be named.

Paragraph 3 identifies and acknowledges family members, such as husband, wife, children, and so forth.

Paragraph 4 (may be more than one paragraph) sets up the non-residuary legacies, lapsed gifts, bequests, and so forth.

After the closing paragraph and signature of the testator, be sure that the testator initials each and every page of the Will, including the page or pages signed by witnesses.

8.2   INTERVIVOS TRUST

Introduction

In most states the law, as it relates to whether or not the payment of life insurance proceeds should be made to a testamentary trustee, is in a state of flux. As a result, the intervivos trust is considered in those states as ancillary to the testamentary non-estate will. The following is an example of an intervivos trust dealing with insurance proceeds:

8.2(A)   INTERVIVOS TRUST

A. This trust agreement executed by _____, a resident and domicillary of _____ City, _____ County and State of _____, and _____ (which would be the beneficiary), and _____ (which would be the trustee).

The trustor owns and is insured under life insurance policies on which he has caused the trustee hereinabove named to be the contingent beneficiary. The trust property is to be the proceeds of the life insurance policies, which the trustee will be empowered to collect if the contingencies for payment to the trustee occur, and will be distributed by said trustee as provided in this agreement.

****

And/or:

The trustor shall retain during his lifetime all powers under the insurance policy on which the aforementioned trustee is the contingent beneficiary, including the right to assign incidents of ownership in the policy.

This being true, the aforementioned trustee will have no responsibility with respect to these policies of insurance, except to keep copies of the contracts in a safe place when delivered to said trustee.

At the death of the trustor, the trustee shall collect the proceeds of the insurance policy of which it is the beneficiary. Payment of the proceeds to the trustee and the trustee's receipt to the insurance companies shall discharge the insurance companies which have issued policies on which the trustee is the contingent beneficiary.

Then, of course, in all such agreements, they would have to be co-signed by the wife, in which she states her agreement that any community interest she may have in the proceeds of the life insurance shall be part of the trust property.

Alternative Form
(Intervivos Non-Estate Trust):

Residents, domicile and identification are the same as the prior intervivos trust. The second paragraph would be as follows:

B. The trustor owns and is insured under life insurance policies on which he has caused the trustee to be named contingent beneficiary. The proceeds of this policy and other property conveyed to the trustee by the trustor, either during the trustor's life or incorporated within his will, shall be held by the trustee as trust property and be devoted to the purposes described in this agreement.

Then you would have your regular amendment and revocation clauses, trust property spelled out with specificity, the beneficiaries listed, and definitions of what is meant by such terms as legacy, descendants, etc.

Following which, you would have the trust purposes and administration of the trust and the termination therefor; and spelled out in detail, the trustee's powers under the trust and other miscellaneous provisions.

It should be noted that unless the wife is waiving community property interests she need not join in this type of intervivos trust. However, it is sometimes advantageous to use the so-called conflicts clause in your intervivos trust agreements. This would be in your closing formalities.

8.3   INTERVIVOS TRUST (ALTERNATIVE)

INTERVIVOS TRUST
(OF ESTATE-NATURE OF WILL)

I, _____, of the City and County of _____, State of _____, do hereby make, constitute and appoint _____ of the said City and County of _____, State of _____, as trustee for and on behalf of myself to receive, acquire, take and hold title to the following real property situated in the county of, city of, and state of _____, to wit:

(This is where you set out a full and complete description of the real property which will be the subject of the trust estate.),

from and after my death and not before, to execute, transfer and convey title to the above described property and to any and all personal property of which I may die seized or possessed, and I hereby empower said trustee to do any act which I would do if present, upon the following conditions:

1. (Here again, you would set forth all the conditions that the testator would want the trustee to follow such as taking full and immediate possession of the property, both real and personal, and empowering said trustee to pay out all

the debts and general expenses etc. The rest of this intervivos trust would be the same as any other trust or will.)

(Note further that you can have intervivos trusts set up as irrevocable income to grandchildren, income to wife with distribution to the children and you can have irrevocable intervivos trusts with income to wife and income to children; and also you can have irrevocable intervivos trusts for support, maintenance and education of children with power of appointment. The foregoing are just some of the types of intervivos trusts that you can have. And of course, these are all subject to local state statutes relating to wills, trusts and real property; as well as subject to the rules and regulations of the Internal Revenue Service relating to estate taxes.)

COMMENTS

Forms 8.2 and 8.3   Trusts (Intervivos, with Alternative

Form 8.2 is commonly called a "living trust," meaning that it is given during the life of the trustor. It is a present transfer of property or interest now. The interest is now, the possession is in the future.

8.4   TRUSTS (SPENDTHRIFT CLAUSE)

The spendthrift clause, used most often in trust-management cases, is merely a restraint on alienation of assets. You should check with your attorney to see what the client has determined he wants in this regard. The following is the type of clause which should be included in a trust seeking to restrain the client:

"No interest other than the interest of my wife, in my wife's trust, under this Will shall be transferable or assignable by any beneficiary, or be subject to the claims of this creditor.

"I hereby give and authorize my trustee and my executor to defeat by way of prosecution or other means, any attempts to assign or transfer interest by payment or accumulation under this paragraph of this Article."

8.5   (ALTERNATIVE)

SPENDTHRIFT CLAUSE

"Such part of any income payable to any beneficiary as shall at any time, except for the following limitation, become subject to the enforceable claims of his or her creditors shall not be paid to the beneficiary, but shall be held or disposed of as follows:

a. Added to principal if such beneficiary is the only beneficiary then entitled to income from this trust;

b. Go proportionately to augment the income payable to other income beneficiaries if there are any then entitled to income.

Provisions, if any, for payment of periodical benefits, other than income, to any beneficiary shall become inoperative during any period, when, and to the extent that, if paid, they would become subject to the enforceable claims of creditors of the beneficiary.''

COMMENTS

Forms 8.4 and 8.5   Trusts (Spendthrift Clause), with Alternative

This clause is generally placed in a trust to protect the beneficiary against his own ''folly,'' since, under this type of trust, creditors cannot attach property of a beneficiary; and the beneficiary cannot spend and/or encumber the property.

8.6   INTESTATE AND TESTATE PROCEEDINGS

Introduction

The administration of and the step-by-step procedures for probating intestate and testate procedures are generally the same:

A. Search for burial instructions and/or who will dispose of the body;
B. Open safe deposit box for will instructions or will;
C. Determine if a special administrator is needed;
D. Have copies made of the will;
E. Locate witnesses to prove will or if it is a holographic will, someone to prove the handwriting of decedent;
F. Prepare for issuance of letters appropriate, such as Letters of Administration, Letters Testamentary.
G. Determine who is the petitioner and;
H. Ascertain names, addresses and age of heirs, etc.

The following forms will aid you in following through on these procedures; however, you are cautioned to check your local probate code to conform with what your state requires as well as with the Internal Revenue Code, the Tax Reform Act of 1976 and the Economic Recovery Tax Act of 1981.

8.7   PROOF OF DEATH AND OF THE FACTS

No. _____

ESTATE OF)	IN THE PROBATE COURT
)	
_____)	NUMBER _____ OF
)	
DECEASED)	_____ COUNTY, _____

TO THE HONORABLE JUDGE OF SAID COURT:

On this day, _____ (''Affiant'') personally appeared in Open Court, and after being duly sworn, deposes and says that:

1. ''_____ (''Decedent'') died on _____, in _____ County, Texas at the age of _____ years.

2. ''Decedent was domiciled and had a fixed place of residence in this County on the date of death.

3. ''The document dated _____, and now shown to me and which purports to be Decedent's Will was never revoked so far as I know.

4. ''No child or children were born to or adopted by Decedent after the date of this Will.

5. ''Decedent was never divorced.

6. ''I have personal and full knowledge of the financial affairs of Decedent. There is no necessity for any administration of Decedent's estate because there are no debts owed by Decedent which are not secured by liens upon real estate.''

SIGNED this _____ day of _____, 19___.

_____

, Affiant

SWORN TO AND SUBSCRIBED BEFORE ME by _____ on the ___ day of _____, 19___, to certify which witness my hand and seal of office.

_____

CLERK OF PROBATE COURT NUMBER

_____, _____ COUNTY, ___

COMMENTS

Form 8.7 Proof of Death and of the Facts

This form is more or less self-explanatory and merely establishes the death of the decedent and the statistical facts and background of his life.

In some states, this is done by way of a "Certificate of Death," which is furnished by the Coroner's Office; and/or is incorporated in the "Petition for Probate of Will" as used in other states.

8.8   FORM OF ADMINISTRATION (ANCILLARY)

KNOW ALL MEN BY THESE PRESENTS, that _____ of the County and State of _____, died on the ___ day of _____, 19___, at _____, in the City and State of _____, leaving a Will which has been duly proved and probated in the County of _____, State of _____, and I, _____, of the City and State _____, have been duly appointed as executor(trix) of that Will.

And whereas the testator left goods and estate to be administered in the State of _____, all of which he devised and bequeathed to his executor(trix) in trust.

BY THESE PRESENTS:

I appoint _____ of the City and State of _____, as my attorney, to apply for and obtain in his own name from the proper court in the County and State of _____, Letters of Administration with Will Annexed, limited to the property of the testator wherever situated in the City, County and State of _____, and for this purpose to execute and deliver such bond or other obligation as may be required upon the grant of such Letters of Administration.

And further, as administrator of the property (here the legal assistant should set forth all the rights of this appointed administrator in administering this estate which could be some of the following: The right to sue and/or enforce payment of debts; to discharge all monies and goods which belong to the deceased or may hereinafter belong to the deceased and which may be due and owing to the estate from any person or entity; and this administrator may have the right or be given the right to take and retain property, receive rents and/or profits from property in the City and State so designated.)

(The last paragraph should be "In Witness, etc." type of closing.)

_____

Acknowledgment

The legal assistant should check with her attorney to see if there are any other general clauses that the attorney might wish to include.

COMMENTS

Form 8.8   Administration (Ancillary), Form of

This form of Petition for Probate of Will is normally used when the decedent has property (normally real property) in a state other than the state in which he resided and was domiciled.

You should check your local Probate Code to determine when the same is used in your state as it relates to the dollar value of the real property which might affect the feasibility of setting up an ancillary estate.

8.9   NOTICE ON FINAL ACCOUNT, ETC....TO ALL PERSONS INTERESTED IN THE ESTATE

_____, Attorneys.

OF _____

In the Probate Court of Marion County, _____.
_____ Term _____
In the matter of the estate of _____, deceased.

Estate Docket _____ Page _____

Notice is hereby given that _____ as _____ of the above named estate, has filed a report of final accounting together with petition to make distribution of remaining assets to the parties believed entitled thereto. The same will come up for action by the Probate Court on the ___ day of _____, 19___, unless persons interested in said estate appear on or before said date and show cause, if any there by, why such accounting should not be approved or unless such person make proof of heirship and claim any part of such estate now shown by such report.

_____
Clerk of the Probate Court
for _____, _____

COMMENTS

Form 8.9   Notice on Final Account, etc., to All Persons Interested in the Estate

This is a boilerplate and "must" Notice, which should be mailed to all parties interested in the Estate of the decedent. Failure to mail out these Notices could put the Executor and/or your attorney in a position to be sued by one of the heirs or other parties interested. It is their right to be apprised of all matters concerning the Estate, and this proceeding, the final account, is their last chance to see how the money was distributed and to determine if they got their fair share.

8.10   TESTIMONY FOR SELF-PROVEN WILL

On the ___ day of _____, 19___, personally appeared in open court _____, who being by me first duly sworn, deposes and says:

That on _____, the said _____ died in the County of _____, State of _____;

That he/she had his/her domicile in _____ County, _____, at and before his/her death;

That he/she died without having revoked said Will so far as known to affiant;

That no child or children were born to or adopted by the deceased subsequent to the execution of said Will;

That the Testator (trix) _____ was not divorced after signing and publishing said Will;

That four (4) years have not elapsed between the death of the said Testator (trix) _____ and the filing in this docket of Application for probate of said Will.

_____

_____, Witness

_____

_____

SUBSCRIBED AND SWORN TO BEFORE ME by the said _____ on this the ___ day of _____, 19___.

COUNTY CLERK, PROBATE COURT NO.

_____, ___ COUNTY, ___

_____
Deputy

COMMENTS

Form 8.10   Testimony for Self-Proven Will

In some states, this form is called ''Attestation of Witness to Will,'' or ''Subscriber's Affidavit to Signing of Will by Testator.'' By whatever name it is called, it is merely the statement of the witness or witnesses to a Will that the testator in fact did sign the same and that his signature is valid.

When mailing out this form to a witness, it is the common practice to send along a copy of the Will so that he or she can truly identify the testator's signature as being valid or not valid.

8.11   AGREEMENT NOT TO PROBATE WILL

Whereas, on or about the _____ day of _____, 19___, _____ (name of party or petitioner), offered for probate in the aforesaid court a certain will purporting to be the last will and testament of _____ (insert the name of deceased), deceased in which will _____ was named as executor(trix) and to which last will and testament _____ (here name the individual), the heirs at law and distributee of the decedent, did, on the _____ day of _____, 19___, file a caveat or objection to the probating of the last will and testament, and the preceedings relating to the offer of probate of the last will and testament and the objection thereto are now pending in the aforesaid court.

And further, _____ and _____, the executor(trix) named in the last will and testament, have agreed to mutually settle and dispose of the respective objections, relating to the probate or not of the aforesaid last will and testament.

NOW, IT IS AGREED, this _____ day of _____, 19___, that the writing purported to be the last will and testament of _____, deceased, shall not be admitted to probate, and that the aforesaid court shall refuse to admit the purported last will and testament to probate, and that the costs in the aforesaid matter shall be paid out of the estate of the decedent.

(Please note that this is an adaption of a type of form used in the State of Maryland. You should check your local codes to see if the same is applicable.)

COMMENTS

Form 8.11   Agreement Not to Probate Will

This is a type of agreement which can be prepared when there has been a dispute in the Court system between the heirs as to the validity and/or contents of the Will of the decedent.

In this instance, the heirs would have won, the matter would have been settled out of Court; and the Will not admitted to probate.

You should check with your attorney and be advised by him whether or not this type of form is appropriate in such a case.

8.12   ORDER ADMITTING WILL TO PROBATE

NO. _____

IN RE: THE ESTATE	)	IN THE PROBATE COURT
	)	
OF	)	NUMBER _____ OF
	)	
_____, DECEASED)		_____ COUNTY, _____

BE IT REMEMBERED that on this, the ____ day of _____, 19___, came on to be heard the written application of _____, of _____, for the probate of the Last Will and Testament of _____, Deceased, hereinafter called "Decedent," said Will being dated the ____ day of _____, 19___, which Application is also for Letters Testamentary; and due proof being taken in the manner required by law; and

It being proved to the satisfaction of this Court that this Court has jurisdiction and venue over this estate, proceeding and subject matter, and that every citation and notice required by law has been duly issued, served and returned in the manner and for the length of time required by law; and

It also appearing to the Court, after taking sworn testimony in open court, that the application heretofore filed in this cause complies with the _____ Probate Code and that all allegations contained therein are true; that said Will of _____, 19___, was self-proved in accordance with the Probate Code, there being _____ (____) subscribing witnesses to the Will, to-wit: _____, both/all of _____, _____; and to the Will there was attached a self-proving acknowledgment of the Testat _____ and an affidavit of the ___ witnesses; and

That the Decedent died on or about the ____ day of _____, 19___, and that four (4) years have not elapsed since the date of death of the Decedent and filing of said application; that the Decedent was, at the time of his/her death, a resident of and domiciled in _____, _____; that _____, named in said Will as Independent Execut _____, is not disqualified and is entitled to Letters Testamentary; that the Decedent, at the time of execution of said Will, was over the age of eighteen (18) years and was of sound mind, and that Decedent executed said Last Will and Testament with the formalities and solemnities and under the circumstances required by law to make it a valid will, being self-proved in accordance with the provisions of the

_____ Probate Code; that said Will was not revoked by the Decedent prior to his/her death; that the Decedent was never divorced; that the Will is entitled to probate; and that all the necessary proof required for the probate of said Will has been made; and

That _____, of _____, _____, is named in said Will as Independent Executor (trix) to serve without bond, and that such Will provides that no action be had in the County Court with respect to the settlement of such estate other than the probating of said Will and the return of an Inventory Appraisement and List of Claims of said estate; it is, therefore,

ORDERED, ADJUDGED and DECREED by the Court that the said Will on file herein is hereby admitted to probate and is ordered recorded in the minutes of this Court. It is further

ORDERED that the said _____ receive Letters Testamentary upon taking the Oath required by law and that no bond is required, and that when the said _____ shall have so qualified, the Clerk of this Court shall issue Letters Testamentary to him/her in accordance with this judgment; and, that upon the return of an Inventory, Appraisement and List of Claims of said estate, the filing of inheritance tax reports and payment of taxes, if any due, and the payment of costs of Court, this estate be dropped from the docket.

It is further appearing to the Court that _____ and _____ are citizens of _____ County, _____, and disinterested persons in said estate, it is, therefore,

ORDERED that they are hereby appointed to appraise the said estate, either of whom may act.

SIGNED AND ENTERED this the ____ day of _____, 19___.

JUDGE PRESIDING, PROBATE COURT

NO. _____, _____ COUNTY

COMMENTS

Form 8.12   Order Admitting Will to Probate

This Form and Order is self-explanatory, but you are cautioned to incorporate in it the exact wording of the Court's ''Minutes,'' or ''Minute Order,'' or ''Court Notes,'' as rendered by the judge presiding at the hearing of the matter.

If you are not sure of what the Court said, either check with your attorney who may have made notes at the hearing, or pick up the phone and call the Clerk of the Court. He will usually be willing to aid you in this area.

8.13 APPLICATION TO PROBATE WILL AND FOR APPOINTMENT OF INDEPENDENT EXECUTOR (TRIX)

No. _____

IN RE: THE ESTATE OF	)	IN THE PROBATE COURT
	)	
_____	)	NUMBER _____ OF
	)	
DECEASED	)	_____ COUNTY, ___

TO THE HONORABLE JUDGE OF SAID COURT:

COMES NOW, _____ (herein sometimes called "Applicant"), and respectfully shows the court:

I.

That Applicant, _____, resides at _____, _____, _____ County, _____, and is domiciled in the State of _____.

II.

That _____ (herein sometimes called "Decedent") is dead, having died on the _____ day of _____, A.D., 19___, at the age of ___ years, at which time Decedent was domiciled in _____, _____ County, _____. Decedent died in _____, _____ County, _____.

III.

That this Court has venue, since the Decedent's residence was in _____ County, _____, and [he] [she] was domiciled in the State of _____ at the time of [his] [her] death.

IV.

That Decedent owned real estate and personal property generally described as cash, securities, and personal effects of a probable value in excess of _____ ($___) dollars.

V.

That Decedent left a written Will dated _____, 19___. The Will, which is filed herewith, names the Applicant Independent Execut[or] [trix] without bond; and that said Will was witnessed by _____, [both] [all] residents of _____, _____ County, _____; and made self-proving by the acknowledgment thereof by the Testat[or[[trix] and the affidavits of the attesting witnesses, each made before an officer authorized to take acknowledgment to deeds of conveyance and to administer oaths under the laws of this State; such acknowledgment and affidavits being evidenced by the certificate, with official seal affixed, of such officer attached or annexed to said Will, all in compliance with §____ of the _____ Probate Code; that Decedent died without revoking said Will.

VI.

That no child or children were born to or adopted by Decedent after making of said Will by Decedent.

VII.

That the name, age, marital status and residence of the heir and devisee of Decedent, and the relationship to Decedent, if any, is as follows:

Name	Age	Marital Status	Residence	Relationship To Decedent
_____	__	_____	_____	_____
			_____	
			_____	
_____	__	_____		
			_____	
			_____	

VIII.

That Applicant is not disqualified by law from accepting letters.

IX.

That Decedent was not previously divorced.

WHEREFORE, PREMISES CONSIDERED, Applicant prays that citation be issued to all persons interested in the Estate of _____, Deceased, as required by law; and that said Will be admitted to probate; that letters testamentary as Independent Execut[or] [trix], without bond, be issued to _____; and that such other and further orders be made as the Court may deem proper.

RESPECTFULLY SUBMITTED,

_____

COUNSEL FOR APPLICANT

COMMENTS

Form 8.13   Application to Probate Will and for Appointment of Independent Executor(trix)

Here again, you have a typical Application for Probate of Will with the exception that you are also applying for the appointment of an independent Executor.

The key factor in this instance is to be sure of the domicile and residency of the decedent in the state and the jurisdiction of the Court, before whom the Application if filed. Your local Probate Code can help in this regard. And, of course, during the interview with the widow(er); and in reviewing the Will itself, you can obtain all the other pertinent data needed to prepare this form.

8.14   ORDER OF INDEPENDENT EXECUTOR (TRIX)

NO. _____

IN RE: THE ESTATE	)	IN THE PROBATE COURT
OF	)	NUMBER _____ OF
_____, DECEASED	)	_____ COUNTY, _____

I DO SOLEMNLY SWEAR that the writing which has been offered for probate in the above numbered and styled Docket is the Last Will of _____, DECEASED, so far as I know or believe.

FURTHER, I DO SOLEMNLY SWEAR that I will well and truly perform all of the duties of Independent Execut[or] [rix] of said Will of said deceased.

_____
_____, Execut[or] [trix]

SWORN TO AND SUBSCRIBED BEFORE ME on this the _____ day of _____, A.D., 19___.

_____
NOTARY PUBLIC IN AND FOR
_____ COUNTY, _____

COMMENTS

Form 8.14   Oath of Independent Executor(trix)

This form is self-explanatory.

8.15 APPLICATION FOR PROBATE OF WILL AS A MUNIMENT OF TITLE

NO. _____

ESTATE OF	)	IN THE PROBATE COURT
	)	
_____	)	NUMBER _____ OF
	)	
DECEASED	)	_____ COUNTY, _____

TO THE HONORABLE JUDGE OF SAID COURT:

_____ (''Applicant'') hereby furnishes the following information to the Court for the probate of the written Will of _____ (''Decedent'') as a Muniment of Title:

1. Applicant is an individual interested in this Estate, domiciled in and residing at _____ County, _____.

2. Decedent died on _____ in _____ County, _____, at the age of _____ years.

3. This Court has jurisdiction and venue because Decedent was domiciled and had a fixed place of residence in this county on the date of death.

4. Decedent owned real and personal property described generally as home, cash, securities, automobiles, household goods, personal effects, etc. of a probable value in excess of _____.

5. Decedent left a valid written Will (''Will'') dated _____ which was never revoked and is filed herewith.

6. The subscribing witnesses to the Will and their present addresses are _____, _____; _____, _____; and _____, _____.

The Will was made self-proved in the manner prescribed by law.

7. No child or children were born to or adopted by Decedent after the date of this Will.

8. Decedent was never divorced.

9. There are no debts owed by Decedent which are not secured by liens upon real estate and there is no necessity for any administration of this Estate.

WHEREFORE, Applicant prays that citation be issued as required by law to all persons interested in this Estate; that the Will be admitted to probate as a Muniment of Title and without any administration thereon; and that all other orders be entered as the Court may deem proper.

Respectfully submitted,

By _____
ATTORNEYS FOR APPLICANT

COMMENTS

Form 8.15 Application for Probate of Will as a Muniment of Title

In some jurisdictions where a decedent has left a minimal dollar amount estate, $5,000, $10,000, etc., the same does not have to be probated. However, application must be filed to defend or protect the title and interest; and/or legal authority over the assets of the estate for those who have an interest, other than heirs, legatees, etc.

As a general rule, there are none of the foregoing or creditors who may make a claim against the assets of the estate. In most instances, you will find that this Form 8.17 is used when a child, though of majority, and/or who may be living away from home, has died, leaving personal and/or real property and other assets.

It is suggested that you research your local Probate Code as to this procedure before utilizing this form and to determine the dollar figure amount applicable.

8.16 ORDER ADMITTING WILL TO PROBATE AS A MUNIMENT OF TITLE

No. _____

ESTATE OF	)	IN THE PROBATE COURT
	)	
_____	)	NUMBER _____ OF
	)	
DECEASED	)	_____ COUNTY, _____

On this day came on to be heard the Application for Probate of Will as a Muniment of Title filed by _____ ("Applicant") in the Estate of _____, Deceased ("Decedent").

The Court, having heard the evidence and having reviewed the Will and the other documents filed herein, finds that the allegations contained in the Application are true; that notice and citation have been given in the manner and for the length of time required by law; that Decedent is dead; that this Court has jurisdiction and venue of the Decedent's estate; that Decedent left a Will dated _____, executed with the formalities and solemnities and under the circumstances required by law to make it a valid Will; that on such date Decedent had attained the age of at least 18 years and was of sound mind; that such Will was not revoked by Decedent; that no objection to or contest of the probate of such Will has been filed; that all of the necessary proof required for the probate of such Will has been made; that such Will is entitled to probate; that there are no unpaid debts owing by the Estate of Decedent other than those secured by liens on real estate; and that there is no necessity for administration of such Estate.

It is therefore, ORDERED, ADJUDGED and DECREED that such Will is admitted to probate as a Muniment of Title only, and the Clerk of this Court is ORDERED to record the Will, together with the Application in the Minutes of this Court, and this Order shall constitute sufficient legal authority to all persons owing any money, having custody of any property, or acting as registrar or transfer agent, for payment or transfer by them to the persons described in such Will.

SIGNED AND ENTERED this _____ day of _____, 19___.

_____
JUDGE PRESIDING

COMMENTS

Form 8.16 Order Admitting Will to Probate as a Muniment of Title

This form is self-explanatory and should accompany the Application as set forth in Form 8.17

Contents—Chapter 9
Family Law

9

FAMILY LAW

9.0   INTRODUCTION

As the format and statutory procedures utilized in pursuing and amicably settling a family law matter vary from state to state, dyed-in-the-wool, canned forms would be an exercise in futility, if not, immensely impractical.

To assist you in being sure that you have covered all bases, regardless of what state you are in, we have attached hereto a checklist of Functional Duties of a Legal Assistant working with a family law problem for your review and use in preparing the necessary family law pleadings.

9.1   PETITION FOR DISSOLUTION OF MARRIAGE

IN THE CIRCUIT COURT OF THE COUNTY OF _____
STATE OF _____

IN RE:	)	CAUSE NO. _____
	)	
Petitioner,	)	Division No. _____
AND	)	
	)	
Respondent.	)	
_____	)	

PETITION FOR DISSOLUTION OF MARRIAGE

COMES NOW the petitioner and for her cause of action states:

1. That petitioner is and has been a resident of the State of _____ for 23 years immediately preceding the filing of this Petition and is now residing at _____. Respondent, _____, is and has been a resident of the State of _____ for 26 years immediately preceding the filing of this Petition and is now employed at _____, home address unknown.

2. Petitioner and respondent were married September 26, 19___ in _____, _____.

3. The one (1) minor child born of the marriage of petitioner and respondent is living in the custody of petitioner, _____, at _____, and is _____, now 8-1/2 years old, born April 22, 19___. Petitioner is not now pregnant.

4. There is no reasonable likelihood that the marriage of petitioner and respondent can be preserved and, therefore, this marriage is irretrievably broken.

5. Respondent is not a member of the Armed Forces of the United States.

6. Petitioner states that there is marital property of the marriage.

WHEREFORE, petitioner prays that the marriage of _____ _____ and _____ be dissolved, that petitioner be awarded the care, custody and control of the minor child born of the marriage, that petitioner is entitled to marital property, that respondent be ordered to pay petitioner a reasonable sum as and for the support of the said minor child, that the Court make a devision of the marital property, that the respondent be ordered to pay petitioner's attorney's fees and Court costs incurred in this action, and for such other and further orders, judgments and decrees as this Honorable Court deems just and proper.

_____

STATE OF _____

COUNTY OF _____

_____, of lawful age, being duly sworn upon her oath, states that she is the petitioner named above and that the facts stated therein are true according to the best knowledge, information and belief of said petitioner.

_____

Subscribed and sworn to before me this _____ day of _____, 19___.

_____
Notary Public

My Commission Expires:

_____

By _____
Attorney for Petitioner

COMMENTS

Form 9.1   Petition for Dissolution of Marriage

This is a short basic form of complaint for divorce and/or dissolution of marriage. In some states this is a printed form requiring the same (and more) statistical information. In any event, it is normally the first document filed in a divorce action.

You should be aware that in many states the only grounds for divorce is "irreconcilable differences and adultery." You are cautioned therefore to check your local state codes to determine the legitimacy of the grounds the client is seeking to utilize before preparing your dissolution papers.

9.2   PETITION TO DISSOLVE MARRIAGE (ALTERNATIVE)

Attorney(s) for _____

SUPERIOR COURT OF _____, COUNTY OF _____

IN RE THE MARRIAGE OF   )   CASE NUMBER

Petitioner:)

AND)

Respondent:)   PETITION (MARRIAGE)

Note: If Respondent: No Cross Complaint, All Affirmative Relief requested Here

1. This Petition is for:

   Legal separation of the parties pursuant to:
   -OR- Civil Code Section 4506(1)
        Civil Code Section 4506(2)

   Dissolution of the marriage pursuant to:
   -OR- Civil Code Section 4506(1)
        Civil Code Section 4506(2)

   _____ has been a resident of this state for at least six months and of this county for at least three months immediately preceding the filing of this petition.

   > *Note:* If Respondent: May Be A Good Idea to File; If Petitioner Won't Proceed, Respondent Can.

   Nullity of the marriage pursuant to:
   Civil Code Section 4400
   Civil Code Section 4401
   Civil Code Section 4425( )

2. Statistical information:

   a. Husband's social security number: _____. Wife's social security number: _____.
   b. Date and place of marriage: _____
   c. Date of separation: _____. The number of years from date of marriage to date of separation is: _____ years, _____ months, _____ days.
   d. There are____children of this marriage including the following minor
      (Number)
      children.:

Name	Birthdate	Age	Sex

COMMENTS

Form 9.2   Petition to Dissolve Marriage (Alternative)

Another type of basic-form complaint seeking to dissolve a marriage is this printed form as used in many states.

Note that this document includes applicable sections of the state code indicating the legal authority governing the application for divorce. This makes it easier for the court to hear and render a decision.

In this instance, be sure to review your local family law codes to determine the applicability of these sections in your local jurisdiction.

Note that this form is broken down into three parts:

a) Legal separation;
b) Dissolution of marriage based on insanity or irreconcilable differences; and,
c) Nullity.

9.3 PROPERTY SETTLEMENT AGREEMENT

THIS AGREEMENT, made and entered into this ___ day of _____, 19___, by and between _____ hereinafter referred to as the ''Wife'', and _____ hereinafter referred to as the ''Husband'';

WITNESSETH:

I

This Agreement is made with reference to the following facts:

1. That the Husband and the Wife were married on the ___ day of _____, 19___, in the City of _____, State of _____, and are now and ever since have been husband and wife; that there are _____ children (child) born the issue of this marriage, namely, _____, born _____ and

2. That irreconcilable differences have arisen between the Husband and Wife, causing them to separate on or about _____, and they are not now, nor do they contemplate, living together as Husband and Wife.

3. That the Husband Wife desire by this Agreement to settle their respective property rights as well as any and all rights, duties and obligations arising out their marital relationship, (and to provide for the custody, support and maintenance of the minor children of the parties) and of the support and maintenance of the Wife.

II

1. That the Husband and the Wife are possessed of property which is held by them as community property, as joint tenants, (as tenants in common), or in any other form or manner in which either party has any rights, claims or interests of any nature, without reference to the character thereof, as follows:

a) Personal property by way of household, furniture, furnishings and applicances now in the _____ possession.
b) _____
c) As to each party hereto, the personal effects, including wearing apparel, jewelry, and luggage and other personal property in his or her possession, including cash or monies in bank accounts, in each case less than $_____ in amount.

2. That the Husband and the Wife each warrants:

a) That he or she is not in possession of any property not listed in the inventory set forth above.

b) That he or she has not transferred any property by gift or otherwise, without the consent of the other spouse at any time during the continuance of this marriage.

c) In case of a breach of either or both of the above warranties, the party who has breached shall pay to the other party one-half of the market value as of the date of this Agreement, of the property not disclosed in the inventory hereinabove, or transferred, as above stated.

III

For and in consideration of the mutual promises hereinafter set forth, the Husband and the Wife agree as follows:

1. That the property listed in Section II, Paragraph 1., is hereby sold, conveyed and transferred as follows:

a) To the Wife as her sole and separate property:

    1) _____

    2) _____

    3) _____

    4) Her personal effects, including wearing apparel, jewelry, luggage and other personal property in her possession, including cash and monies in bank accounts in an amount less that $_____.

b) To the Husband as his sole and separate property:

    1) _____

    2) _____

    3) His personal effects, including wearing apparel, jewelry, luggage and other personal property in his possession, including cash and monies in bank accounts in an amount less than $_____.

The Wife hereby relinquishes all right, title and interest to the property herein coveyed to the Husband; and the Husband hereby relinquishes all right, title and interest to the property herein conveyed to the Wife.

2. Each of the parties hereto will cooperate in executing any and all documents necessary to effectuate the provisions of this Agreement, including any consent to change of beneficiary of any life insurance policies, as necessary.

IV

That the Husband and the Wife further agree as follows:

1. That the Wife shall pay any and all of the following legal and effective debts, claims or demands heretofore incurred or created by either Husband or Wife or jointly, as the installments or balances thereof become due:

a) _____
b) Any and all current debts, incurred or created by the Wife for her own personal benefit during the separation of the parties hereto, or at any time prior to the date hereof, the existence of which may or may not be known to the Husband.

That the Wife will save and hold harmless the Husband and any and all of his property from any and all of said debts, claims and demands.

2. That the Husband shall pay any and all of the following legal and effective debts, claims or demands heretofore incurred or created by either Husband or Wife or jointly, as the installments or balances thereof become due:

a) _____
b) Any and all current debts, incurred or created by the Husband for his own personal benefit during the separation of the parties hereto, or any time prior to the date hereof, the existence of which may or may not be known to the Wife.

That the Husband will save and hold harmless the Wife and any and all of her property from any and all of said debts, claims and demands.

3. That each party hereto will pay any and all legal and effective debts, claims and demands hereafter incurred or created by either party for their personal benefit of whatever nature, and that each party will save and hold harmless the other party and any and all of his or her property from any of the said personal debts, claims and demands. That each party hereto shall not in any way incur or create hereafter any debts, claims or demands of any nature whatsoever, whereby the other party hereto becomes liable therefor in any manner.

4. That each of the parties hereto, subject only to the other provisions of this Agreement, hereby waives, relinquishes and discharges any and all rights, claims, obligations, interests and demands whatever, whether actual or potential, contingent or vested, which each party had, now has or may hereafter have as a spouse, widow or widower or heir of the other, or in any capacity or relationship whatsoever to the other, including probate homestead, family allowance or any interest in the other's estate, except that given in a Will bearing a date subsequent hereto, including any rights that he or she now has or may hereafter have against the other for alimony, support and maintenance, the payment of court costs and attorneys' fees in any action for divorce or separate maintenance that either party has now brought or may hereafter bring against the other.

V

1. This Agreement shall constitute a full and complete settlement of all of the financial affairs of the parties arising out of the marriage, or otherwise, and shall constitute a full and complete determination of their property rights and the division thereof; and that all income, increases in property and accumulations thereof acquired by either party from this date forward shall be the sole and separate property of the party acquiring the same.

2. It is expressly agreed that each party from this date forward shall refrain from molesting or interfering with the other in any manner whatsoever at all, and each party expressly agrees to at all times respect the rights or privacy of the other and that appropriate court orders may be made in connection therewith.

3. Both of the parties acknowledge that they understand the legal purports of the terms and provisions of this Agreement and have signed the same freely and voluntarily, and agree to be bound by the terms and provisions hereof, and stipulate and agree that this Agreement may be submitted to any court of competent jurisdiction in connection with the determination of the financial affairs of the parties, and stipulate that an order may be made in conformity herewith and of the executory terms and provisions hereof.

THIS AGREEMENT, shall be binding upon the parties hereto from the date of its execution.

IN WITNESS WHEREOF, the parties hereto have executed and acknowledged this instrument in triplicate, each to have the full force and effect of an original, the day and year first hereinabove written.

_____

, Wife

_____

, Husband

COMMENTS

Form 9.3   Property Settlement Agreement

This is your standard form of Property Settlement Agreement which requires no explanation.

Each section, length and content thereof depends on the amount of community and personal property involved and the number of children of the marriage, all of which can be embellished and/or reduced accordingly.

9.4   CUSTODY AND ALIMONY AGREEMENT

That the Husband and the Wife further agree as follows:

1. Subject to the orders of a court of competent jurisdiction, the Husband agrees that the sole care and custody of the _____ minor children of the parties, namely, _____, _____, shall be awarded to the Wife (Husband) with rights of reasonable visitation reserved to the Husband (Wife).

2. The Husband (Wife) hereby promises and agrees to pay direct to the Wife (Husband) for the support, maintenance and education of said minor children (child) the sum of $_____ per child per week (month) payable in a total amount of $_____ per week (per month) on _____ of each and every week (month),

commencing with the _____ following the date of the execution of this Agreement, and in addition thereto the sum of $_____ per month (week) on the first day of each and every month commencing with the month following the date of the execution of this Agreement, said sums for child support to continue during the minority of each said minor child or until further order of the court.

3. The Husband (wife) hereby promises and agrees to pay to the Wife (husband) for her (his) support and maintenance, the sum of $_____ per _____, payable on _____ of each and every _____ commencing with the _____ following the date of execution of this Agreement, for a period of time from the date hereof to and including _____ days after the Wife (husband) commences working on a full time basis, or until _____, 19__, whichever event shall first occur, in which case at that time the amount for her (his) support shall be decreased to the sum of $_____ per _____ for an additional period of _____ years thereafter, at the end of which latter period of time all alimony and support and maintenance payable to the Wife (husband) by the Husband (wife) shall cease and terminate forever. These provisions for support and maintenance of the Wife (husband) shall be subject to modification and enforcement by a court of competent jurisdiction.

4. The Wife (Husband) hereby agrees and promises to use the sum for child support set forth above of $_____ per month, to pay the premiums monthly on the family plan insurance policy during the minority of each of the said two minor children of the parties. It is agreed by the parties hereto that the beneficiaries of the insurance policies and provisions contained in this family life insurance policy as to both the Husband's life and as to the Wife's life shall immediately be changed so that the said minor children of the parties will be the sole and exclusive beneficiaries thereof during their and each of their minorities.

5. Attorneys' fees provision.

IN WITNESS WHEREOF, the parties herto have executed this Agreement on the _____ day of _____, 19__ as witnesses by their respective attorneys.

Signature lines for both parties

Witness lines for Attorneys

_____

_____

_____

COMMENTS

Form 9.4   Custody and Alimony Agreement

This is a boilerplate form of custody and alimony agreement in favor of the wife.

As herein set forth, it can be a separate and complete document, or can be made part of the Property Settlement Agreement, Form 9.3 The choice is your attorney's and/or that of the parties involved.

9.5 AGREEMENT RE ALIMONY (ALTERNATIVE)

In the event the marriage of the parties is dissolved by divorce, as a result of an action instituted by the wife, the husband agrees that he will pay to wife the total sum of _____ Dollars, the same to be hers absolutely, which sum is to be paid in _____ different installments, the first of which installments shall be in the amount of _____ Dollars and shall be due and payable immediately upon the entry of a final decree of divorce in the action; and the balance of said sum of _____ Dollars, shall be payable in _____ equal annual installments of _____ Dollars each, the first of which installments shall be payable one year from the date of the entry of the final decree of divorce, and the remainder of the installments shall become due and payable at yearly intervals until the total sum of _____ Dollars have been paid in full.

It is understood and agreed that the total sum of _____ Dollars shall be in full and complete settlement and shall be in lieu of all claims for alimony, and all rights and claims whatsoever in or to the estate or property, of whatever nature, legal or equitable, whether now owned or hereafter acquired, by the wife, and the payment of said sum by the husband, his heirs, executors, or administrators, to wife, her heirs, executors, or administrators, shall be in full and complete discharge of all duties and obligations of whatever nature owing to wife by husband.

The third installment shall bear no interest.

(This clause is optional.)

_____
Party of the First Part

_____
Party of the Second Part

WITNESSES:

_____

_____

COMMENTS

Form 9.5   Agreement Re Alimony (Alternative)

This is your normal agreement re alimony in favor of the wife which has been agreed upon prior to the filing of a divorce action by her.

This type of agreement leaves it open as to what happens to the payment of such alimony should the husband file for the divorce. You should discuss this point with your attorney. This may be the type of agreement which could be a candidate for arbitration.

9.6 DEFENDANT'S INTERROGATORIES SUBMITTED TO PLAINTIFF

IN THE CIRCUIT COURT OF THE COUNTY OF _____
STATE OF _____

_____, Plaintiff, vs. _____, Defendant.	CASE NO. _____ Domestic Relations Div.

DEFENDANT'S INTERROGATORIES SUBMITTED TO PLAINTIFF

Comes now defendant, _____, and demands that plaintiff, _____, answer the following interrogatories within the time and manner required by the rules of Civil Procedure:

1. What sums of money does plaintiff now have on deposit in any bank or financial institutions? In each case identify the institution or bank with its name and address, state the name in which the account is kept, the amount of money therein and the account type and number.

2. What property of any kind does plaintiff now own or have an interest in? In each case identify the property as to description and location, and state also the name and address of any other person or persons having any joint or common interest in the same property.

3. Does plaintiff own or have any interest, by stock ownership or otherwise, in any business? If the answer is affirmative, then state the type of business and its name and location, and state further the names and addresses of any other person or persons having any interest therein.

4. Does any other person or persons hold property in trust or in any manner for the account or benefit of plaintiff? If the answer is affirmative, give the name and address of such person or persons, the description of the property and the place or places where the same is held.

5. Is plaintiff employed by any other person, firm or organization? If the answer is affirmative, then give the name and address of such employer, the type of work done by plaintiff, the income derived by plaintiff therefrom per week and the basis or rate or method of computation of plaintiff's wages or salary or income.

6. What was plaintiff's income or receipts from all sources (identifying each source separately as to such respective portion thereof) during so much of 19___ as has already passed and for 19___?

7. Did plaintiff file a United States Income Tax Return and a _____ (or other state tax return) Tax Return for the year 19___? If the answer is affirmative, then attach a copy thereof hereto.

8. What debt or debts, if any, does plaintiff now owe to any person or persons, in each case stating the name and address:

    a. the interest transferred;

    b. to whom;

    c. the date of such transfer;

    d. the consideration received by plaintiff for plaintiff's interest.

9. Has plaintiff sold, transferred, or conveyed any interest or plaintiff in any automobiles in the last six months? If so, state the following:

    a. the interest transferred;

    b. to whom;

    c. the date of such transfer;

    d. the consideration received by plaintiff for plaintiff's interest.

BY _____
Attorneys for Defendant

PROOF OF SERVICE

The undersigned certifies that a complete copy of this instrument was served by mail, postage prepaid, upon the attorneys of record or party to the above action addressed as disclosed in the pleadings.

Date: _____ day of   _____ 19___.

COMMENTS

Form 9.6   Defendant's Interrogatories Submitted to Plaintiff

The time may come when your office will be handling a heavily contested divorce action wherein a great deal of real and personal property is involved, and the parties cannot agree as to what the assets are, let alone their value; and/or may even be of the belief that some of the assets are hidden (by either party). As a result of these types of disputes, the parties may not agree to or be willing to sign any proposed property settlement agreement until the value and whereabouts of all community property and/or personal property in which either may have an interest, has been established.

Should this occur, your attorney may want to prepare and file a set of interrogatories to discover the true value of all of the property vested in the parties, be it real or personal; and to determine the whereabouts of any property which may be hidden.

This being true, the discovery vehicle of interrogatories could be used, and if so, would be handled in the same manner as any other set of discovery questions.

9.7 POST-NUPTIAL AGREEMENT WITH MUTUAL RELEASES

THIS AGREEMENT, made this ___ day of _____, 19___, by and between Mary Smith, currently residing at _____, in the City and County of _____, State of _____, hereinafter called the Party of the First Part, and John Smith, currently residing at _____ in the City and County of _____, State of _____, hereinafter called the Party of Second Party,

WITNESSETH:

That the Party of the First Part, in consideration of One Dollar, and other valuable consideration, to her in hand paid, receipt whereof is hereby acknowledged, hereby agrees to and with the party of the Second Part as follows:

That the Party of the First Part hereby renounces and releases to the Party of the Second Part, his heirs and assigns forever, all right, title and interest, or right of dower in any property, real and personal, that the Party of the Second Part may now be seized of, or that he may hereafter acquire.

And further, she especially renounces and releases to the heirs at law, next of kin, or legatees and devisees under the Last Will and Testament of the Party of the Second Part, should the Second Party predecease the First Party, all of her right, interest and right of dower, of every name and nature, both real and personal, that the First Party might have or be entitled to in the estate of the party of the Second Part, in the event of the Second Party predeceasing her.

The purpose and intent of this Agreement is that the parties hereto have recently married, each having a child by a prior marriage, and each being desirous that their child shall inherit their property. To this end they have entered into mutual or like agreements for the purpose of insuring each to the other, that they will not claim any interest in the estate of the one dying first.

IN WITNESS WHEREOF, the parties have hereunto set their hands and seals this _____ day of _____, 19___, as first above written.

_____
PARTY OF THE FIRST PART

_____
PARTY OF THE SECOND PART

WITNESSES:

_____

_____

COMMENTS

Form 9.7 Post-Nuptial Agreement with Mutual Releases

This type of agreement permits each party to waive the right to take under the will of another party and protects any property they have, and as stated therein, insures that the property will go to whomever it is they had bequeathed their property.

9.8 SEPARATION AGREEMENT WITH PROVISIONS FOR CUSTODY, VISITATION AND SUPPORT

Paragraph #1.

THIS AGREEMENT, made and entered into this _____ day of _____, 19___, by and between _____, Party of the First Part and _____, Party of the
(Wife)   (Husband)
Second Part,

WITNESSETH

Paragraph #2.

That the parties are husband and wife, living separate and apart from each other and wish to enter into this agreement;

Paragraph #3.

That the party of the Second Part instituted a action for divorce against the Party of the First Part on the _____ day of _____, 19___ before the Superior Court (or other appropriate body) of _____ County, in the State of _____, being case number _____, asking that he be awarded the custody, care and control of the minor child of the parties hereto and the ratification of the property settlement and agreement relative to support and maintenance of said minor child.

Paragraph #4.

That the parties have heretofore reached an agreement and settlement between themselves, out of court, relative to the foregoing, including alimony.

NOW, THEREFORE in consideration of these mutual promises and agreements hereinafter contained, the parties hereto each agree with the other, as follows:

    A. (Here you should set forth the terms of the agreement applicable to the custody, care and control of the minor child of the parties as agreed between the parties, including right of visitation; the right of the moving party to determine the domicile and the condition under which the foregoing are to be done. All according to the merits and circumstances of the case.)

B. (Here you would set forth the provisions for future payments, their sources (if applicable); limitation and conditions upon which the same are to be terminated, i.e., alimony upon marriage; maintenance and support of child upon reaching legal majority, marriage etc. This paragraph could conceivably take some 2 or 3 additional pages (or paragraphs) depending on the nature of the case and the affluence of the parties involved.

C. The party of the Second Part, in consideration of the foregoing covenants and agreements hereby agrees not at any time to undertake to hold the party of the First Part liable for, or undertake to collect from the Party of the Second Part any sum or sums for alimony, court costs, attorneys fees, support or maintenance for the Party of the Second Part; and that this agreement may be pleaded in any suit as a defense to any action for alimony, court costs, attorneys fees and maintenance and support.

(*Note*: These and similar or other types of paragraphs can be added to complete the claims, contentions, needs and desires of parties.)

IN WITNESS WHEREOF, we have hereunto affixed our hands and seals this ___ day of _____, 19___, in the City of _____ County of _____, State of _____, as hereinabove first stated.

_____
(WIFE)
PARTY OF THE FIRST PART

_____
(HUSBAND)
PARTY OF THE SECOND PART

WITNESSES

_____

_____

COMMENT

Form 9.8   Separation Agreement with Provisions for Custody, Visitation and Support

This Form 9.8 Separation Agreement is different (and unique) in that it is prepared from the point of view of the Husband who is obtaining custody of the children; and the Husband who is seeking alimony payments, etc. Just the reverse of your standard separation agreement for a Wife.

As a result it can be expanded, reduced or changed to suit the merits of the case and is merely set out as a guide to how it can be done, local court rules permitting.

9.9   PETITION AND ORDER FOR DIVORCE

MINUTES OF _____   JUDICIAL DISTRICT COURT
                                 OF _____ COUNTY, _____

_____ TERM, 19___

IN THE MATTER OF THE
MARRIAGE OF:

_____   IN DISTRICT COURT

No. _____   vs.

_____County,   _____

BE IT REMEMBERED that on this the ___ day of _____, 19___, the above numbered and entitled cause came on to be heard, and then came the Plaintiff in person and by attorney and announced ready for trial and the defendant

_____

_____

_____,

and no jury having been demanded, this cause was submitted to the Court for adjudication upon the matters of fact as well as of law, and the Court having heard the pleadings, evidence and argument of Counsel, and being fully advised herein, finds the material allegations in Plaintiff's petition true, and finds for Plaintiff.

It is, therefore, considered by this Court, and so ordered, adjudged and decreed by the Court, that the Bonds of Matrimony heretofore existing between _____ Plaintiff, and _____, Defendant, be and the same are here now and forever dissolved, canceled and annulled.

It is further ordered that all costs in this behalf expended are adjudged against

_____

for which let execution issue.

SIGNED AND ENTERED this _____ day of _____, 19___.

APPROVED AND NOTICED UNDER
RULE 30 6d T.R.C.P WAIVED

_____   _____
Attorney for Plaintiff   JUDGE

_____
Attorney for Defendant

_____
Defendant's Address

COMMENTS

Form 9.9   Petition and Order for Divorce

This document is self-explanatory.

However, if you are preparing this decree for divorce, as opposed to the Court Clerk (which is done in many jurisdictions) be sure you have incorporated all of the Judge's ''notes'' relative to the property settlement agreement and/or alimony and child support/visitation rights agreement—either by reference or attachment, if applicable.

This is particularly true if the petitioner was the wife and wanted her maiden name officially re-established.

9.10   ANCILLARY PROCEEDING

NOTICE: This form to be completed and copy furnished to opposing counsel prior to show cause hearing.

ANCILLARY PROCEEDING

COURT OF DOMESTIC RELATIONS NO. _____

NO. _____

PLAINTIFF	DEFENDANT

ATTORNEY FOR PLAINTIFF	ATTORNEY FOR DEFENDANT

I certify that the following answers to the questions as listed are true and correct:

1. Date of (Marriage) _____(Separation) _____

2. Ages of children of this marriage ( )(( )( )( )( )( )( )( )
    ( )( )( )( )

3. What are your necessary monthly expenses, indicating those secured by mortgages:

(a) Rent	$____	(i) Liability Ins.	$____
(b) House payment	$____	(j) Collision Ins.	$____
(c) Food	$____	(k) Fire Insurance	$____
(d) Doctor	$____	(l) Car payment	$____
(e) Dentist	$____	(m) Gasoline & oil	$____
(f) Drugs	$____	(n) Car repair	$____
(g) Life Insurance	$____	(o) Other transportation	$____
(h) Hospitalization	$____	(p) Furniture	$____

(q) Church	$_____	(v) Haircuts	$_____
(r) Gifts	$_____	(w) Entertainment	$_____
(s) Newspapers	$_____	(x) Child Care	$_____
(t) Lunches, School	$_____	(y) Other	$_____
(u) Beauty parlor	$_____		
	TOTAL		$_____

4. Are you working? _____ Kind of work _____

5. Gross Income   Week   Month
                          $_____ $_____

   Deductions
   Withholding tax $_____
   FICA $_____
   RETIREMENT $_____
   _____ $_____
   _____ $_____
   _____ $_____
TOTAL $_____ $_____
                                   $_____ $_____

          NET INCOME

6. Other income
   Explain _____
   _____

7. Is your spouse working? _____Kind of work _____

8. Gross Income   Weekly   Semi-Monthly   Monthly
   Deductions $_____ $_____
   Withholding Tax $_____
   FICA $_____
   Retirement $_____
   _____ $_____
   _____ $_____
   _____ $_____
   TOTAL $_____ $_____ $_____
   NET INCOME $_____ $_____

9. Other Income (Spouse)
   Explain _____
   _____

10. Custody of children is at present as follows: _____
    _____

11. The following sums are reasonably necessary, or within the ability of my husband to pay, and that it will be fair and equitable to require the following:

    a. For temporary alimony $_____ $_____

    b.   For child support $_____ $_____

                   TOTAL $_____ $_____

12. Wife Net Income $_____ $_____

                   TOTAL $_____ $_____

13. Husband's Net Income $_____ $_____

    Less alimony & support $_____ $_____

    Net husband after deduction of

    child support and alimony $_____

14. (Answer only if husband) I feel that a reasonable sum for me to pay per month would be:

                                     Week   Month

    a. Temporary alimony $_____ $_____

    b. Child support $_____ $_____

                 TOTAL $_____ $_____

Witness my hand this _____ day of _____, 19___

_____

(Husband - Wife)

9.11   ORDER TO APPEAR TO SHOW CAUSE

STATE OF _____   )   In The _____ County Superior Court

COUNTY OF _____   } SS.   CAUSE NO. ____ ROOM NO. ____

)

)   ORDER TO APPEAR

)   TO SHOW CAUSE

Comes now the plaintiff, by counsel, and files herein her verified application for contempt citation from which it appears:

That the defendant, _____ on _____ was ordered by this Court to pay $_____ per week for the support and maintenance of his _____ minor child(ren), and that the defendant has refused, failed and neglected to fully comply with said order.

And the Court having examined said application, now orders that the defendant appear before him at which time the Court will hear evidence concerning said application.

IT IS THEREFORE ORDERED that the defendant, _____, be and appear in the Superior Court of _____ County, Room _____, in the City-County Building, _____, _____, on the _____, day of _____, 19___, at _____o'clock _____M., to show cause why he should not be punished for his contempt of Court.

IT IS FURTHER ORDERED that the Sheriff of Marion County serve a copy of this order upon the defendant and make due return thereof.

_____

Judge, _____ County Superior
Court, Room No. _____

9.12   STIPULATION

Stipulations must be filed with the Clerk of the Court no later than 5:00 p.m. of the date preceding Docket Call.

Cause No. _____

In the Matter of the Marriage of   In the Court of Domestic

_____   Relations No. 4

Petitioner
and   _____ County, _____

_____

Respondent

STIPULATIONS

The attorneys for the Parties in the above Cause stipulate the following facts in connection with said Cause:

I

There is (is not) a contest on the issue of divorce.

II

There is (is not) a contest on the issue of child custody and visitation. If there in no contest, set forth terms of agreement to be approved by the Court:

_____

_____

_____

_____

_____

III

There is (is not) a contest on the issue of child support. If there is no contest, set forth terms of agreememt to be approved by the Court:

_____

_____

_____

_____

_____

IV

There is (is not) a contest on the issue of the division of the property of theparties. If there is no contest, set forth terms of agreement, if any, to be approved by the Court: (need not be completed if written property settlement is to be submitted for approval)

_____

_____

_____

_____

V

There is (is not) a contest on the issue of attorneys' fees. If there is no contest, set forth terms of agreement, if any, to be approved by the Court:

_____

_____

_____

We, the undersigned attorneys for the Parties, certify that we have seriously dicussed the matters in controversy in the above Cause, and we represent to the Court that the above and foregoing, if any, are the only stipulations we have been able to agree upon.

_____
Attorney for Petitioner

_____
Attorney for Respondent

9.13 FUNCTIONAL DUTIES OF A LEGAL ASSISTANT WORKING WITH A FAMILY LAW PROBLEM*

1. Collect and organize data needed for legal actions on domestic relations.
2. Write draft of petition for dissolution of marriage.
3. Write draft of petition for separation of bed and board.
4. Write petition for annulment.
5. Write legally correct summons to appear in court.
6. Collect data for respondent's answer to a petition.
7. Write respondent's answer to a petition.
8. Collect data for petition for order to show cause.
9. Prepare petition for order to show cause.
10. Collect data to write order to show cause.
11. Write draft of citation.
12. Compile and write order to show cause.
13. Collect data needed to prepare restraining order.
14. Write legally correct restraining order.
15. Collect data for property settlement agreement.
16. Write agreement on property settlement.
17. Fill out correct record of dissolution.
18. Collect data needed for affidavit of non-military service.
19. Fill out affidavit of non-military service.
20. Assemble data needed for order of default.
21. Write order of default.
22. Prepare motion and affidavit for decree without application.
23. Assemble data to prepare decree of dissolution of marriage.
24. Prepare decree of dissolution of marriage.
25. Assemble data to prepare property settlement agreement.
26. Prepare property settlement agreement.
27. Compile petition for order to show cause regarding contempt.
28. Write court order to show cause regarding contempt.
29. Compile petition to modify child support.
30. Write petition to modify child support.
31. Write court order to modify child support.
32. Collect data for petition to change custody.
33. Write petition to change custody.
34. Write court order to change custody.
35. Prepare final decree of divorce.

---

* Source: Oregon Department of Education, Curriculum Development, Unit Career & Vocational Education.

Contents—Chapter 10
Bankruptcy

10

BANKRUPTCY

10.0   INTRODUCTION

The need to file for bankruptcy is a great financial and emotional burden to your attorney's client. It therefore goes without saying that your role as the legal assistant in offices with a heavy bankruptcy practice is one of great importance, requiring a great deal of meticulous and skillful handling.

As bankruptcy proceedings are held in the United States District Courts, in a designated district in your state, you should look to the Federal Rules of Civil Procedure for guidelines, paying particular attention to the rules relating to the Bankruptcy Act as found in Title 28, United States Code, and the new revised Bankruptcy Reform Act of 1978 to be found in the Bankruptcy Code.

In any and all events, be guided by the desires and instructions of your attorney, and once he has made the determination as to how and when the bankruptcy petition should be filed, then govern yourself accordingly in preparing the petition and in doing this, there are prescribed statutory procedures which must be followed. You are therefore cautioned to check the federal bankruptcy codes and your local state statutes.

10.1(A)   CREDITORS' PETITION FOR BANKRUPTCY

CAPTION

1. Petitioners, _____, all _____, and _____ of _____, are creditors of _____ of the City of _____, having provable claims against said bankrupt, not contingent as to liability, amounting in the aggregate, in excess of the value of the securities held by them, to $_____ or over. The nature and amount of petitioners' claims are as follows:

2. The alleged bankrupt has had his principal place of business (or has resided) within this district for the past (6) months preceding the filing of this petition.

3. The alleged bankrupt owes debts in the amount of $_____ or more and is a person who may be adjudged an involuntary bankrupt under the Bankruptcy Act.

4. Within the past four months preceding the filing of this petition, the alleged bankrupt committed an act of bankruptcy in that he did on _____.

WHEREFORE, petitioners pray that _____ be adjudged as a bankrupt under the Act.

_____

Attorney for Petitioners

_____

_____

Address

_____

_____

Petitioners

STATE OF _____
COUNTY OF _____

I, _____, one of the petitioners in the foregoing petition, do hereby swear that the statements contained therein are true according to the best of my knowledge, information and belief.

_____

Petitioner

Subscribed and sworn to before me on
_____, 19___.

_____

Notary

COMMENTS

Form 10.1(A)   Creditors' Petition for Bankruptcy

This is a modified petitioner's bankruptcy form wherein the petitioner is seeking to be adjudged bankrupt on an involuntary basis. It is used when his creditors feel that he can no longer pay his bills and wish to recoup some of their money.

In some states—California is one—the petition is at least 4 to 6 pages long, requiring more detailed information as to the petitioner's need to file bankruptcy. For this reason you should check your local laws as well as the federal regulations as to the type of petition which should be filed.

Under present law, all parties affected by a petition in bankruptcy must be notified. In some states this is done by the attorney's office and in other states it is done by the court. Your should do your research in this regard.

10.1(B)   APPLICATION TO PAY FILING FEES IN INSTALLMENTS

CAPTION

1. Applicant is filing herewith a voluntary petition in bankruptcy.

2. He is unable to pay the filing fees except in installments.

3. He proposes to pay such fees to the clerk of the District Court upon the following terms:

_____

_____

4. He has paid no money and transferred no property to his attorney for services in connection with this case or any pending case under the Bankruptcy Act, and he will make no payment or transfer to his attorney for such services until the filing fees are paid in full.

WHEREFORE, applicant prays that he be permitted to pay the filing fees in installments.

Dated: _____

_____

Applicant

_____

_____

Address

COMMENTS

Form 10.1(B)   Application to Pay Filing Fees in Installments

On occasion, an individual wishing to file a voluntary petition in bankruptcy is so deeply in debt that he cannot even afford to pay the filing fee. When this occurs, he files an application for permission to pay the fee in installments. During this interim period, filing the fee in installments, the petition is completed and filed with the court and the court holds the same, awaiting full payment of the fee before it is processed by the court unless the court order specifies to the contrary. See Form 10.1(C)

10.1(C)   ORDER FOR PAYING FILING FEES IN INSTALLMENTS

CAPTION

1. The application of the bankrupt for permission to pay the filing fees in this case in installments having been heard; IT IS ORDERED, ADJUDGED AND DECREED THAT,

The bankrupt pay the filing fees still owing as follows:

_____

_____

_____

IT IS FURTHER ORDERED THAT

All payments be made at the office of the clerk of the U.S. District Court located at _____, and that until the filing fees are paid in full, the bankrupt shall pay no money and shall transfer no property to his attorney, and his attorney shall accept no money or property from the bankrupt for services rendered in connection with this case.

Dated: _____

_____

Judge in Bankruptcy

COMMENTS

Form 10.1(C)   Order for Paying Filing Fee in Installments

This form is self-explanatory and should be prepared at the time you prepare Form 10.1(B) and filed simultaneously.

10.1(D)   APPLICATION TO STAY STATE
COURT ACTION

Attorney Information

COURT INFORMATION

In the Matter of   )   No.
)
)
)   APPLICATION TO STAY
)   STATE COURT ACTION
)
                  Bankrupt   )
_____)

The application of _____, bankrupt herein, respectfully represents and shows as follows:

1. Applicant is the above-named bankrupt, and filed a voluntary petition in bankruptcy on the ____ day of _____.

2. That on the date of the filing of said voluntary petition of bankrupty, there were pending against the applicant the following actions as indicated hereinbelow:

NAME OF PLAINTIFF: COURT   CASE NO.

(Here the legal assistant should list any and all pending litigated matters against the bankrupt, including the name of the plaintiff, the court and the case number.)

3. Each of the above actions is based upon a claim of a type provable in bankruptcy and as to which a discharge in bankruptcy would be barred. Unless said actions are stayed as to your applicant until the question of his right to a discharge is determined, your applicant will be deprived of benefits of which he is entitled under the provisions of the Bankruptcy Act.

WHEREFORE, your applicant prays that this court enter its order staying the above-referred-to actions pending determination of your applicant's right to a discharge in bankruptcy.

_____
Attorney Signature

COMMENTS

Form 10.1(D)   Application to Stay State Court Action.

This form is used when through research (and through interviews with the client) it is determined that there are lawsuits pending which might adversely affect the petition to be adjudged a bankrupt. Hence, you should file Form

10.1(d) to hold these cases in abeyance until the bankrupt petition is resolved. Bear in mind, however, you cannot file a bankruptcy petition to avoid paying the judgments or negate lawsuits unless they are the type which can be wiped out through a petition in bankruptcy. You are cautioned to check the rules and regulations in this regard.

10.1(E)   ANSWER OF RESPONDENT ..
TO APPLICATION TO STAY STATE COURT ACTION

Attorney Information

COURT INFORMATION

In the matter of	) No.
	)
	) ANSWER OF RESPONDENT_____
	) TO APPLICATION TO STAY
	) STATE COURT ACTION
Bankrupt.	)
_____	)

COMES NOW _____, and files his answer as follows:

1. With respect to that certain action now pending in the superior court in and for the county of _____, State of _____, entitled _____ v _____, and being case No. _____, this answering respondent denies that said action is based upon a claim of a type dischargeable in bankruptcy, and denies that the bankrupt is entitled to a stay of said proceedings.

WHEREFORE, this answering respondent prays that the temporary restraining order heretofore issued as to him be dissolved, and that an order be entered denying the bankrupt's application to stay state court action as to this answering respondent.

_____
Attorney Signature

COMMENTS

Form 10.1(E) Answer of Respondent to Application to Stay Court Action

This is a typical answer to contest the application to stay a court action and the petition in bankruptcy. The reason and purpose of same are self-explanatory.

However, we have found it to be a better part of valor to support the contentions in your answer that the claim cannot be disposed of in bankruptcy with specifics and accompanying legal authorities. Please discuss this with your attorney.

10.1(F) SPECIFICATION OF OBJECTIONS TO DISCHARGE

Attorney Information

UNITED STATES DISTRICT COURT
FOR THE _____ DISTRICT OF _____
_____ DIVISION

In the Matter of	)	No.
	)	
	)	SPECIFICATION OF
	)	OBJECTIONS TO
Bankrupt.	)	DISCHARGE
_____	)	

COMES NOW _____, a creditor of the above-named bankrupt, and objects to the bankrupt's discharge under Section _____ of the Bankruptcy Act as follows:

1. While engaged in the business as a sole proprietor under the name of _____, said bankrupt on or about the _____ day of _____, obtained such business property on credit by making or publishing a materially false statement and writing respecting his financial condition.

2. Attached hereto and incorporated herein by reference is a copy of said financial statement dated the _____ day of _____.

3. Said financial statement was materially raised, in that the bankrupt overstated the value of his equipment by the sum of _____ ($_____) Dollars, and in that the said bankrupt failed to reflect, as a liability, a debt in the amount

of approximately ____($____) Dollars then owing to the bankrupt's father, Mr. _____.

WHEREFORE, the objector prays that this court enter its order denying the discharge of bankruptcy of the above-named bankrupt.

COMMENTS

Form 10.1(F)   Specification of Objections to Discharge

As you know, before the hearing on a petition to be adjudged a bankrupt, creditors have a statutory time period in which to file objections to the discharge. Form 10.1(f) is an example of such document.

This pleading should be filed with the bankruptcy court clerk with copies to the petitioner and his attorney. The hearing on the specification is normally heard at the time of the hearing on the petition in bankruptcy. Please check your local court rules and regulations regarding this procedure.

Be sure that you attach all pertinent exhibits, together with a memorandum of points and authorities, to support the contentions set forth in objections.

10.2   CIVIL ACTIONS

Introduction

The district courts in the federal court system have original jurisdiction of all civil acts wherein the monetary amount exceeds $15,000.00. These are general federal questions. See Sections 1331 and Official Form 2(b) of Federal Practice and Procedure.

The federal courts are courts of limited jurisdiction, hence you must spell out with statutory specificity the authority of the court to hear the matter. Failure to spell out this authority may subject your claim to an automatic rejection at any given point of the proceedings, up to and including the appellate hearing. Therefore, as a legal assistant, you should immediately research the United States Code, Title 28, Section 1331 and 1332. These sections set forth the conditions under which a case can be filed in federal court and the statutory authority giving the federal court jurisdiction to hear and determine the claim. And further, under the Rules of Federal Practice and procedure, you will find that the 12-B motions govern how to serve and whom to serve when filing a law suit against the government. The following forms, are merely the headings to such a complaint or petition to give you an idea of how to set it up.

10.2(A)   SUMMONS
Pursuant to Rule 4 of the Federal Rules of Civil Procedure

UNITED STATES DISTRICT COURT
FOR THE SOUTHERN DISTRICT OF NEW YORK

JOHN DOE,	Civil Action, File No.
Plaintiff,	
vs.	
MARY SMITH	
Defendant.	

TO THE ABOVE-NAMED DEFENDANT:

You are hereby summoned and required to serve upon plaintiff's attorney, whose address is _____ _____, _____, an answer to the complaint which is herewith served upon you, within twenty days after service of this summons upon you, exclusive of the date it is served. If you fail to do so, judgment by default will be taken upon you for the relief demanded in the complaint.

DATED: _____

_____
Clerk of Court

(seal of the U.S.
District Court)

> *Note:* It should be noted that if the United States or an officer or agency thereof is a defendant, the time within which the answer should be filed is sixty days as opposed to twenty.

COMMENTS

Form 10.2(A)   Summons

Although Form 10.2(a) is a document which you can prepare, be aware that there is a ''printed form'' which can be used and which is more detailed as to who is being served; where; the date of service; the time of service; the place of service; and by whom. You can obtain these forms from any federal court clerk.

10.2(B) PETITION FOR REMOVAL OF CIVIL ACTION TO UNITED STATES DISTRICT COURT

Attorneys for Defendant and Petitioner

UNITED STATES DISTRICT COURT
CENTRAL DISTRICT OF CALIFORNIA

		NO. CV
Plaintiff,	)	PETITION FOR REMOVAL OF
	)	CIVIL ACTION TO UNITED
vs.	)	STATES DISTRICT COURT
	)	
, DOES I through	)	
V, inclusive	)	
	)	
Defendants.	)	
	)	

TO THE JUDGES OF THE UNITED STATES DISTRICT COURT FOR THE CENTRAL DISTRICT OF CALIFORNIA:

Defendant and Petitioner _____ respectfully petitions this Court and alleges as follows:

1. On or about September 13, 19___ there was filed in the Superior Court of the State of _____ for the County of Los Angeles the above entitled civil action, bearing Number _____ in the records and files of that Court. Petitioner first received a copy of the Summons and Complaint therein on September 14, 19___. Thirty days after such receipt by Petitioner have not expired.

2. At the commencement of this action and at all times therein mentioned, Petitioner was and now is a corporation duly organized and existing under and by virtue of the laws of the State of Illinois with its principal place of business in the State of Illinois. By reason of the foregoing, Petitioner is a resident and citizen of a state other than California.

3. The defendants identified as "DOES I through V" in plaintiff's complaint are merely fictitious parties against whom no cause of action can be validly alleged. The within controversy is based upon a policy of insurance issued by petitioner to _____ and no person or entity other than the named defendant can be liable to plaintiff on account of said policy. To the best of petitioner's information and belief, no fictitiously designated defendant has been served with process. There is no defendant who was or ia a citizen of the State of _____.

4. Petitioner is informed and believes and thereon alleges that plaintiff at the commencement of this action and at all times therein mentioned was and now is a citizen of the State of California, residing at _____ _____ _____, _____. Therefore the matter in controversy at the commencement of this action was and is one in which complete *diversity of citizenship* exists.

5. The aforesaid Superior Court action is a suit of a wholly civil nature of which the District Court of the United States, Central District of California, has original jurisdiction, and the matter in controversy between plaintiff and petitioner in this action, exclusive of interest and costs, *exceeds the sum of $15,000.00.*

6. Therefore, petitioner files this Petition for Removal, _____ of Civil Action to the United States District Court to remove this action from the aforesaid Superior Court in which it is now pending, to the District Court of the United States for the Central District of California, located in the United States Courthouse Building, _____ _____, _____, California _____.

Petitioner is filing and offers herewith a good and sufficient Bond conditioned, as the law directs, that petitioner will pay all costs and disbursements incurred by reason of the removal proceedings should it be determined that this cause was not removable or was improperly removed. There is attached to this petition marked "Exhibit A," a copy of all process, pleasings and orders received by Petitioner herein.

WHEREFORE, petitioner prays that this action be removed to the United States District Court of the Central Division of California.

Dated:

_____
Attorney for ...

COMMENTS

Form 10.2(B)   Petition for Removal of Civil Action to United States District Court.

Form 10.2(B) is an example of one type of petition for removal of a civil action to the federal courts based on the diversity of citizenship. The underlying reason for most attempts to remove a case from the State Court System to the Federal Court System is that of expediency. Moreover, filing in the Federal Court System is more simplistic than in the State Court System. For this reason, all your allegations must be succinctly and clearly stated. See Form 10.2(D).

10.2(C)   CLASS ACTION (SAMPLE)

Attorney Information

IN THE UNITED STATES DISTRICT COURT
FOR THE _____ DISTRICT OF _____
_____ DIVISION

)	CIVIL NO. _____
)	
Plaintiff,)	COMPLAINT
)	
vs)	
)	
Defendant(s))	
)	

NOW COMES Plaintiff by the undersigned counsel and respectfully alleges:

1. This action is brought pursuant to, and the jurisdiction is founded upon, Section 301 of the Labor Management Relations Act of 1947, as amended 29 U.S.C. 185 which provides in part as follows:

   a. Suits for violation of contracts between an employer and a labor organization representing employees in an industry affecting commerce as defined in this Act, or between any such labor organizations, may be brought in any district court of the United States having jurisdiction of the parties, without respect to the amount in controversy or without regard to the citizenship of the parties.

2. Plaintiff is a corporation incorporated under the laws of _____ duly admitted and qualified to do business in the state of _____ with its principal offices located at _____.

3. Plaintiff is engaged in the business of _____ and is an employer in an industry affecting commerce within the meaning of Section 301 and 2(7) of the Labor Management Relations Act of 1947, as amended, hereinafter referred to as the Act. (29 U.S.C. 152).

4. Defendant(s) _____ is (are) a labor organization representing employees of Plaintiff employed at Plaintiff's _____ plant located at _____. The Defendant was and is a labor organization within the meaning of Section 2(5) of the Act.

5. Defendants _____ and _____ are officers and/or agents of the Defendant(s) _____ and _____.

6. There is in existence a collective bargaining agreement between Plaintiff and Defendant(s), which contains a mandatory grievance and arbitration clause(s) and a no-strike clause. (A copy of said contract is attached hereto as Exhibit A).

(Insert No-Strike and Grievance and Arbitration Clause).

7. On _____, 19___, and while such agreement was in full force and effect, Defendant, its officers and agents caused, initiated and commenced a strike and work stoppage against Plaintiff at its _____ plant located at _____ in that members of Defendant who are employees of Plaintiff concertedly failed and refused to work as scheduled.

8. Defendant(s) has created a dispute with the Plaintiff which dispute is subject to and controlled by the provisions of said collective bargaining agreement between Plaintiff and Defendant Union(s) whereby such dispute is to be settled by the grievance and arbitration procedure therein without resort to any strike, work stoppage, or any other form of interference with Plaintiff's operation.

9. The Plaintiff is willing and has offered to submit the aforesaid dispute to a final decision pursuant to the mandatory grievance and arbitration provisions of the existing agreement between the parties. Notwithstanding the above, the Defendant(s) Union has refused to follow the procedure established in the Mandatory Grievance and Arbitration Clauses.

10. Plaintiff has demanded that Defendant Union (s) direct and instruct their members to return and report to work; however, Defendant Unions have not complied. Plaintiff thereby expects said work stoppage and strike to continue in violation of the collective bargaining agreement.

11. The work stoppage and strike by the Defendants is causing and will continue to cause great and irreparable damage to Plaintiff's business which cannot adequately be compensated in money damages. Plaintiff will continue to suffer such injury unless Defendants and persons acting in concert with Defendants are forthwith restrained and enjoined from continuing the illegal work stoppage and from violating the provisions of the collective bargaining agreement.

12. That unless a restraining order is entered by this Court directing the Defendants to cease from continuing to carry out the illegal work stoppage and related unlawful activity, greater injury will be inflicted on Plaintiff than could possibly result to Defendants by the granting of said relief. Defendants have an adequate remedy which may be pursued by processing their alleged claim pursuant to the mandatory grievance and arbitration procedure contained in Article(s)_____ of Exhibit A attached hereto.

13. Counsel for Plaintiff has notified the office of Defendant's legal counsel of Plaintiff's intention to request a temporary restraining order and will advise said office of the time of the hearing with the court. (If without notice, see Rule 65 of Federal Rules of Civil Procedure).

WHEREFORE, Plaintiff prays that this Court:

1. Issue a Temporary Restraining Order, forthwith (and without notice) restraining and enjoining the Defendants, each of them, their officers, agents, members, servants, employees and any and all persons acting in concert with any of them, pending further hearing and determination of this action from engaging in, ordering, authorizing, permitting, or inducing a work stoppage or strike.

2. Order the Defendants, their officers, agents, members, servants, employees and any and all persons acting in concert with any of them to exercise all of their authority, power and influence to obtain compliance with this Court's order.

3. Issue an order to show cause why a preliminary injuction should not issue restraining and enjoining the Defendants, each of them, their officers, agents, members, servants, employees and any and all persons acting in concert with any of them, pending further hearing and determination of this action from engaging in, ordering, authorizing, permitting or inducing a work stoppage or strike by and among Plaintiff's employees.

4. Upon a hearing on the merits, issue a mandatory injunction ordering the Defendants to submit their dispute to final and binding arbitration in accordance with the collective bargaining agreement between the Plaintiff and the Defendants.

5. To the extent that may be ascertainable, award damages to the Plaintiff, and enter judgment therefor against the Defendants, jointly and severally ...

6. [Then your normal ending.]

COMMENTS

Form 10.2(C)   Sample Class Action

Prerequisite to a class action:

One or more members of the class may sue or be sued as representative parties on behalf of all only if

1. The class is so numerous that joinder of all members is impractical;
2. There are questions of law or fact common to the class;
3. The claims or defenses of the representative parties are typical of the claims or defenses of the class, and
4. The representative parties will fairly and adequately protect the interests of the class.

The above and foregoing must be present in order for you to prepare and file a non-demurrable class action.

10.2(D) SAMPLE JURISDICTIONAL ALLEGATIONS BASED ON DIVERSITY OF CITIZENSHIP

A. Normal and appropriate Court caption with parties.
B. Jurisdiction founded on diversity of citizenship and amount:

   Plaintiff is a citizen of the State of _____, (or corporation incorporated under the laws of the State of _____, having its principal place of business in the State of _____), and the defendant is incorporated under the laws of the State of _____, having its principal place of business in a state other than the State of _____.

C. The matter in controversy, exclusive of interests and costs, the sum of $_____.

Dated: _____   _____

Note: Depending on the wishes of your attorney, a "WHEREFORE" prayer may be added to the above causes of action.

COMMENTS

Form 10.2(D)   Sample Jurisdictional Allegations Based on Diversity of Citizenship

The general allegation of the existence of a federal question is ineffective unless the matters constituting the claim for relief as set forth in the complaint raise the federal questions. To this end, you are cautioned to use the appropriate phrase or phrases.

See Form 10.2(b).

10.2(E) SAMPLE JURISDICTION ALLEGATIONS BASED ON CONSTITUTIONAL ISSUES

A. Normal and appropriate Court caption with parties.
B. Jurisdication founded on existence of a federal question and amount in controversy:

   The action arises under the Constitution of the United States, Article ___, §_____, (or, the ___ Amendment to the Constitution of the United States, §_____; or, the Act of _____, Statute _____; U.S.C., Title _____, §_____; or, the Treaty of the United States (here you must set out and describe the terms of the Treaty applicable to the cause of action), as hereinafter more fully appears.

   C. The matter in controversy exceeds, exclusive of interests and costs, the
      sum of $_____.

Dated: _____   _____

Note: Depending on the wishes of your attorney, a ''WHEREFORE'' prayer
      may be added to the above causes of action.

COMMENTS

Form 10.2(E)   Sample Jurisdictional Allegations Based on Constitutional Issues.

The general allegation of existence of a federal question is ineffective unless the matters constituting the claim for relief as set forth in the complaint raise a federal question. To this end, you are cautioned to use the appropriate phrase or phrases. See Form 10.2(b).

Contents—Chapter 11
Litigation

11

LITIGATION

11.0 INTRODUCTION

As there is always the possibility that your office will have to litigate a claim, regardless of the phase of law your attorney practices, this chapter capsulizes this many-faceted, highly specialized area which requires all of the special training and skill of a legal assistant.

The forms and procedures in this chapter deserve more attention than can be given in this approach. Moreover, any attempt to develop forms to be used throughout the country would not only be ludicrous, but futile, and have questionable validity since most state jurisdictions have forms based upon statutes. Furthermore, legal assistants and their attorneys have their own pet forms and formats.

Add to this the unique and out-of-the-ordinary facts and claims which sometime arise, requiring the development of a form for which there is no precedent, and you can see the dilemma one has in doing a section on litigation forms with national use.

Therefore, as to any and all of the following forms and procedures, you are cautioned to check your local state statutes for the appropriate procedures and formats to be used.

Finally, bear in mind that these capsule pleadings are to be used only as illustrations of what you should include in a document, not as "the only way" a court pleading can or should be prepared.

VERIFYING YOUR PLEADINGS

Introduction

Be advised that any and all PLEADINGS filed with the court, and served on opposing counsel (or Pro Per Defendant) must be either verified or subscribed to by the party (or parties) to the action, or his attorney.

See the following pleadings which must be verified, as a general proposition, though your state may have a different rule. If so, check your local court and code rules.

PLEADINGS WHICH MUST BE VERIFIED

1. Cross-complaint and inter-pleader.
2. Answer, which must be verified if plaintiff is the state, county, city, school district or offices thereof; and complaint or answer of said agency or officer which need not be verified.
3. An answer must be verified if the initial complaint was verified.
4. A preliminary injunction.
5. A pleading involving adverse possession.
6. An action filed to establish title in a case of destruction of records.
7. An action where title to real property is affected by public improvement or assessments. (As a general rule—and you are cautioned to check your local court rules and regulations here—all petitions must be verified.)
8. Petition for Writ of Review.
9. Petition for Writ of Prohibition.
10. Petition for Writ of Mandate.
11. Confession of Judgment.
12. Complaint Re: Unlawful Detainer.
13. Petition for Claim to Escheated Property.
14. Petition to become a Sole Trader.
15. Opposition to Sole Trader.
16. Petition to Restore by Certified Copy.
17. Petition to Perpetrate Testimony.
18. Answers to Interrogatories.

11.1   BASIC COMPLAINT FORM

Attorney Information

<table>
<tr><td></td><td>)</td><td></td></tr>
<tr><td></td><td>)</td><td>Court Information</td></tr>
<tr><td></td><td>)</td><td></td></tr>
<tr><td>Parties</td><td>)</td><td>Case No. _____</td></tr>
<tr><td></td><td>)</td><td></td></tr>
<tr><td></td><td>)</td><td>COMPLAINT FOR</td></tr>
<tr><td></td><td>)</td><td></td></tr>
<tr><td></td><td>)</td><td>(Check Your Local Code</td></tr>
<tr><td></td><td>)</td><td>Sections Applicable)</td></tr>
<tr><td>_____)</td><td></td><td></td></tr>
</table>

For cause of action, plaintiff alleges as follows:

1. Plaintiff—residency information.
2. Defendant—residency information.
3. Doe or fictitious name paragraph.
4. Doe responsibility clause of paragraph.
5. Agency clause—permission and consent of co-defendants.

ALLEGATION PARAGRAPHS:

6. On or about _____, 19__, plaintiff was [here you should set forth the facts relating to the automobile accident being sure to place the defendants in a position where the defendant breached a statutory requirement and a duty owed to the plaintiff.]

7. At said time, defendant, _____, was _____ [here again, you should set forth the status of defendant and the actions of the defendant to establish that he or she did, in fact, breach a statutory requirement and violated a duty of care to the plaintiff.]

8. [This is the paragraph where you specifically and succinctly set forth the place and locale of the accident; the defendants and each of their ownership and possession or control of the vehicle which caused the damage and the lack of relationship as between the two parties, and finally, the statute which imposes a special duty on the part of the defendant to the plaintiff.]

9. At said time and place, defendants, and each of them, so negligently _____ [show the acts or omissions of defendants and detail specifically the defendants' failure to conform to the standard of care required or their violation of a statutory regulation), as to cause (here you should set forth the damages or injury caused to plaintiff by the negligent acts of the defendant).

10. Damages: [In some states you are required to specifically set forth the fact that he broke a leg, broke his back, etc.] His general damages can be set forth in a sum of $_____. However, in some states the trend is now to leave out the monetary damage and it is no longer required that you put down $50,000, $100,000, as had been done in the past.

(Optional Paragraph)

Plaintiff is informed and believes, and based upon such information and belief, alleges that said injuries will result in some permanent disability to him. [*Note:* This last statement is optional since in some states it is not required.]

11. As a further proximate result of the negligence of the defendants, and each of them, plaintiff has incurred (and will continue to incur) medical and related expenses in the approximate amount of $50,000, or as may be proved at time of trial.

WHEREFORE, [This is where you pray for your judgment and damages according to the allegations in your complaint and for costs of suit]

_____
Attorney for Plaintiff

COMMENTS

Form 11.1   Basic Complaint Form

This is the first pleading prepared to set a litigated matter in motion.

The skeleton pleading herein is designed to show what should be incorporated in a complaint to eliminate the opposing counsel's demurrer.

This document, along with the Summons (and in some states a "Notice of Commencement of Action") should be filed with the court and thereafter served on all party-defendants.

11.2   COMPLAINT FOR DAMAGES, BREACH OF CONTRACT, FIDUCIARY RELATIONSHIP....

Attorney's Name

SUPERIOR COURT OF THE STATE OF _____
FOR THE COUNTY OF _____

_____	)
_____,	) CASE NO.
	)
Plaintiffs,	) COMPLAINT FOR DAMAGES:
	)
vs.	) 1) Breach of Contract
	) 2) Breach of Fiduciary
_____, DOES I through	) Relationship
X, inclusive,	) 3) Conversion
	) 4) Inducing Not to Deal
Defendants.	)
_____	)

COMES NOW, the plaintiff, _____
_____, and for cause of action, alleges as follows:

FIRST CAUSE OF ACTION

I

Plaintiff is now, and at all times herein mentioned, was a corporation duly organized and existing under and by virtue of the law of the State of California, and doing business in the County of _____, County of _____, State of _____.

II

Plaintiff is informed and believes, and based on such information and belief, alleges that defendant _____ was at all times herein mentioned, and now is, a resident of the County of _____, State of _____.

III

That the true names or capacities, whether individual corporate, associate or otherwise of defendants DOES I through X, inclusive, are unknown to plaintiff, who therefore sues said defendants by such fictitious names and will ask leave of court to amend its complaint to show their true names and capacities when the same have been ascertained.

IV

At all times herein mentioned, defendants, and each of them, were the agents and employees of the remaining defendants and each of them, and in doing the things herein alleged, were acting in the scope of such agency and employment.

V

Plaintiff is, and since 19__ has been, actively and continuously engaged in the service business which consists of supplying service to various customers at various intervals.

VI

Pursuant to the conduct of said business, plaintiff established value and extensive trade in said business and acquired a large number of customers including insurance companies and law firms. Plaintiff regularly provided said customers with their service requirements by the establishment of services in locating missing persons, locating assets, general criminal investigations, sub-rosa (undercover work) investigation for insurance companies and law firms and casualty insurance adjusting.

VII

Customers of a service business ordinarily patronize one concern and obtain their service requirements from one concern and the business relationship is such that it will normally continue until interfered with.

VIII

That on or about January 11, 19___, in the County of _____, State of
_____, plaintiff and defendant entered into a written employment a-
greement, by the terms of which defendant agreed to be employed by plaintiff
as manager of plaintiff's _____ County office and that in consideration
of defendant's written agreement to perform the conditions, convenants and
promises as set forth therein, plaintiff agreed to compensate defendant for said
services pursuant to and in the manner outlined in said written employment
agreement dated January 11, 19___, a copy of which is attached hereto, marked
Exhibit ''A,'' and made a part hereof as though fully set forth in haec verba.

IX

That plaintiff has performed all conditions, convenants and promises under
the written employment agreement dated January 11, 19___, on its part to be
performed.

X

That on or about January, 19___, in breach of the terms of the above referred
to written employment agreement, defendant _____, voluntarily terminated his employment with plaintiff without giving the required notice as set
forth in said written employment agreement attached hereto as Exhibit ''A.''

XI

Plaintiff is informed and believes, and based on such information and belief,
alleges that immediately after terminating his employment with plaintiff, defendants, and each of them, established, and ever since have operated, a
competing business in the _____ County area, which said business is of
the same type and operated in the same manner as that of the plaintiff, all in
violation and in breach of the written employment agreement dated January 11,
19___, entered into by said plaintiff and defendants, and each of them, herein.

XII

That as a direct and proximate result of the breach of said contract on the part
of the defendants, and each of them, as hereinabove alleged, plaintiff has
suffered irreparable injury to its business, all to its damages in the sum of
$300,000.00.

FOR A SECOND, SEPARATE AND DISTINCT CAUSE OF ACTION,
PLAINTIFF COMPLAINS OF DEFENDANTS, AND EACH OF THEM,
AS FOLLOWS:

I

Plaintiff re-alleges all of the allegations contained in paragraphs I through
VII, inclusive, of its First Cause of Action, and by this reference incorporates
the same herein as though fully set forth.

II

On or about January 11, 19__, defendant _____ became the manager of plaintiff's _____ County office. In the course of said employment as a manager, said defendant was given access to and did acquire knowledge of the names and addresses of all of plaintiff's customers, as well as their requirements, peculiar likes and dislikes, and the degree of difficulty in meeting their requirements. All of said information were confidential and trade secrets and were acquired and developed over many years and at the expenditure of large sums of money, time and labor on the part of plaintiff. Part of defendant's duties consisted of soliciting new customers for plaintiff, establishing and maintaining the needs of its customers and receiving and adjusting the complaints of customers and, as a consequence thereof, defendant developed friendly contacts with the customers of plaintiff.

III

All said information relating to plaintiff's customers acquired by defendant in the course of his employment was confidential and a trade secret not accessible to others for their benefit.

IV

Plaintiff is informed and believes, and based on such information and belief alleges, that immediately after terminating his employment with plaintiff, the defendants, and each of them, established their own business in direct competition with plaintiff's; plaintiff is informed and believes, and based on such information and belief, alleges that thereafter defendants, and each of them, called on various customers of plaintiff, solicited their patronage and advised them that they were in business for themselves, with the intent that said customer would cease patronizing plaintiff. Said customers solicited by defendants, and each of them, had long been customers of plaintiff for many years.

V

That defendants, and each of them, obtained access to said trade secrets through a relationship of trust and confidence; that defendants, and each of them, breached the obligation of such fiduciary relationship by fraudulently appropriating said trade secrets to their own use and benefit, without permission and authority from plaintiff and to the detriment of plaintiff.

VI

In doing the things herein-above alleged, defendants, and each of them, acted maliciously and oppressively, and with wanton disregard for the rights of plaintiff who is therefore entitled to punitive and exemplary damages in the sum of $300,000.00.

FOR A THIRD, SEPARATE AND DISTINCT CAUSE OF ACTION, PLAINTIFF COMPLAINS OF DEFENDANTS, AND EACH OF THEM, AS FOLLOWS:

I

Plaintiff re-alleges all of the allegations contained in paragraphs I through VII, inclusive, of its First Cause of Action, and paragraphs II and III of its Second Cause of Action, and by this reference incorporates the same herein as though fully set forth.

II

Plaintiff is informed and believes, and based upon such information and belief, alleges that defendants, and each of them, without authorization or permission of plaintiff, converted for their own use and benefit, and are continuing to use for their own use and benefit, plaintiff's compiled, confidential customer data and trade secrets in their competing business.

III

Plaintiff is further informed and believes, and based on such information and belief, alleges that defendants, and each of them, did the things above referred to and are continuing to do the things complained of herein with the knowledge and intent to injure plaintiff in its business.

IV

Plaintiff is informed and believes, and based upon such information and belief, alleges that the acts of defendants, and each of them, as herein alleged did in fact and continue to cause irreparable harm and injury to plaintiff in its business, all to plaintiff's damage in the sum of $300,000.00.

FOR A SEPARATE, DISTINCT AND FOURTH CAUSE OF ACTION, PLAINTIFF COMPLAINS OF DEFENDANTS, AND EACH OF THEM, AS FOLLOWS:

I

Plaintiff re-alleges and re-affirms each and all of the allegations contained in paragraphs I through VII, inclusive, of its First Cause of Action and paragraphs II and III of its Second Cause of Action, and by this reference incorporates the same herein with the same force and effect as though expressly set forth in haec verba.

II

Plaintiff is informed and believes, and based upon such information and belief, alleges that defendants, and each of them, used the aforementioned trade secrets, including the customer data to entice away and solicit plaintiff's customers without the permission or authority of plaintiff.

III

Plaintiff is further informed and believes, and based upon such information and belief, alleges that defendants, and each of them, in so soliciting plaintiff's customers, falsely represented and continue to represent to said customers, that plaintiff mistreated defendant, _____, during his employment with plaintiff.

IV

Plaintiff is informed and believes, and based upon such information and belief, alleges that for the above reasons its customers have indicated that they will not further assign, and have not further assigned, cases to plaintiff. Plaintiff is informed and believes, and based upon such information and belief, alleges that by such false and malicious representation, defendants, and each of them, did induce, have induced and are continuing to induce, a refusal to deal or continue a business relationship on the part of said customers with plaintiff, all to plaintiff's damages in the sum of $300,000.00

WHEREFORE, plaintiff prays for judgment as follows:

FIRST CAUSE OF ACTION:

1. For general damages in the sum of $300,000.00;

SECOND CAUSE OF ACTION:

2. For punitive and exemplary damages in the amount of $300,000.00;

THIRD CAUSE OF ACTION:

3. For general damages in the sum of $300,000.00;

FOURTH CAUSE OF ACTION:

4. For general damages in the sum of $300,000.00;

AS TO ALL ACTIONS:

5. For costs of suit herein incurred; and

6. For such other and further relief as the Court deems just and proper.

By _____
Attorneys for Plaintiff

COMMENTS

Form 11.2   Complaint for Damages: Breach of Contract, Fiduciary Relationship...

This type of complaint for damages is prepared when there is evidence of a business infringement based on a contract of employment or business relationship, such as employer-employee; and as a result of such breach, there has been a conversion of property to the detriment of the plaintiff.

To establish this type of lawsuit, you must show that the defendant had an employment contract; that the contract was breached as to its terms; that the defendant had converted for his own use said property, that he had privity to the converted material; and that as a result of the foregoing, plaintiff and his business were damaged and irreparably harmed thereby.

Failure to state these facts on the fact of the complaint will make it susceptible to a demurrer. These allegations should be set out in separate paragraphs as described in Form 11.1.

11.3   COMPLAINT FOR NEGLIGENCE (...)

Attorney Information

COURT INFORMATION

	Plaintiff,	Complaint for Negligence
vs.		(Where the Culpable Party
	Defendant.	is in Question)

1. (Set forth your allegation of jurisdiction.)
2. On the ____ day of _____ 19__, on a public highway called Bolster Street in the City and County of _____, State of _____, defendant _____ or defendant _____, or each of them, willfully and recklessly and/or negligently drove or caused to be driven a motor vehicle against plaintiff who was then crossing said highway.
3. As a result plaintiff was thrown down and had his leg broken, and was otherwise injured, was prevented from transacting his business, suffered great pain of body and mind, and incurred expenses for medical attention and hospitalization in the sum of $1,000.00.

WHEREFORE plaintiff demands judgment against defendant _____ or against defendant _____ or against both of them in the sum of _____ Dollars including costs.

DATED: _____

_____
Attorney for Plaintiff

COMMENTS

Form 11.3   Complaint for Negligence (...)

This complaint is self-explanatory.

Just be sure you set forth the authority of the court to hear and determine the matter as to the defendant, as well as the plaintiff.

11.4   DECLARATION OF (ATTORNEY'S NAME) TO ACCOMPANY COMPLAINT...

County of _____

State of _____

I, _____, declare as follows:

1. That I am an attorney at law, duly licensed to practice in all of the Courts of the State of _____, I am presently one of the attorneys of record for the moving defendant _____ herein.

2. That if called upon as a witness, I could and would testify as to the following facts based upon my own personal knowledge in that I have been assigned this file and I am familiar with all of the documents and records contained therein.

3. (Personal statements of facts to which attorney would testify (1—8 paragraphs).

4. Argument for and in support of change of venue.

It is further submitted to the Court that allowing this action to continue in California merely because the plaintiff resides here would not be in the furtherance of justice; that allowing said action to continue in California will only cause extreme hardship, delay and frustration of these proceedings in that the site of the accident is in Tampa, Florida and the witnesses to be called, notwithstanding the plaintiff, will be located in Tampa, Florida.

It is further submitted to the Court that this action should be dismissed without prejudice and filed in the proper Court in Tampa, Florida or Memphis, Tennessee or in the alternative, abated until such time as the plaintiff files her action in the proper court.

I declare under penalty of perjury that the foregoing is true and correct.

Executed this _____ day of October, 19__, at _____, _____.

_____

COMMENTS

Form 11.4   Declaration of .... to Accompany Complaint

This is the type of declaration which should be prepared to accompany a complaint to support your attorney's position and allegations in any given matter.

This example is for a change of venue, but any subject would be treated just as thoroughly and with the same "personal knowledge" incorporated therein at Paragraph 3.

In some cases you might want to include a declaration by the client. This of course, would be determined by your attorney.

11.5   AMENDING YOUR PLEÅDINGS

Introduction

The occasion may arise when you will find it necessary to amend your complaint or answer, or pleading relating to the prosecution of a client's claim. This may be done to include information or new evidence not heretofore included. Or it may be that your attorney wants to modify an answer or complaint resulting from the sustaining of a demurrer by the court.

The two most-often used methods of amending a pleading are by way of a stipulation between the parties; or upon Notice of Motion to the court for leave to amend.

11.5(A)   AMENDMENT TO COMPLAINT

Attorney statistics

	COURT CAPTION
)	
)	
)	
Parties)	Same Court Case No.
)	
)	AMENDMENT TO COMPLAINT

TO THE CLERK OF THE SUPERIOR COURT, _____ defendant and his attorneys of record, and all other parties interested:

Request is herein made to amend the complaint filed herein on July 17, 19__ in connection with the above named parties, being Superior Court Case No. _____ for the following reason:

Since the filing of the original complaint plaintiff has become aware through on-going investigation that the defendant herein designated and served as ''DOE I,'' is in truth and fact JOHN CATLIN of 12056 _____, _____, California 90045, and he has been served accordingly with a copy of the subject summons and complaint, proof of service being filed concurrently with this court.

Dated: _____

_____
Attorney for plaintiff

COMMENTS

Form 11.5(A)   Amendment to Complaint

This can be any complaint wherein you have, subsequent to filing, discovered the name of a defendant previously described and designated as a ''Doe.''

Or,

Where you incorrectly spelled the name of a defendant, such as S.T. Schmidt when it should have been S.J. Smith. Or a corporation has been termed ''incorporated'' but you had listed it on the summons and complaint as not being incorporated.

11.5(B)   AMENDED ANSWER TO AMENDED COMPLAINT

Attorney for _____

SUPERIOR COURT OF THE STATE OF _____
FOR THE COUNTY OF _____

_____)	No. _____
a corporation,)	
)	
Plaintiff,)	AMENDED ANSWER TO
)	
vs.)	AMENDED COMPLAINT
)	
_____, DOE I,)	
DOE II, DOE III, DOE IV, DOE V,)	
DOE VI,)	
)	
Defendants.)	
_____)	

COMES NOW defendant _____, and severing itself from the other defendants, and for an answer to plaintiff's verified complaint, for itself and itself alone, admits, denies and alleges as follows:

1. Answering paragraphs 1, 2 and 3 of the First Cause of Action of plaintiff's verified complaint, this answering defendant does not possess sufficient information or belief to admit or deny the allegations therein contained, and basing its denial upon such lack of information and belief this answering defendant denies, generally and specifically each, all and every allegation therein contained.

2. Answering paragraph 4 of the First Cause of Action of plaintiff's verified complaint, this answering defendant denies, generally and specifically each, all and every allegation therein contained, except that the documents attached as Exhibits A and B to plaintiff's verified complaint do not in fact appear in the _____ County Recorders records at the book and page numbers therein set forth.

3. Answering paragraph 5 of the First Cause of Action of plaintiff's verified complaint, this answering defendant does not possess sufficient information or belief to admit or deny the allegations therein contained, and basing its denial upon such lack of information and belief, this answering defendant denies, generally and specifically that the plaintiff herein is the successor in interest through merger of the interest of The _____ Company and _____ Company.

4. Answering paragraph 6 of the First Cause of Action of plaintiff's verified complaint this answering defendant denies, generally and specifically each, all and every allegation therein contained.

ANSWER TO SECOND CAUSE OF ACTION

5. Answering paragraph 7 of the Second Cause of Action of plaintiff's verified complaint, this answering defendant incorporates the same herein, as though specifically set forth at length, each and all of the admissions, denials and allegations contained in its answers to paragraphs 1, 2, 3, 4 and 5 of the First Cause of Action hereinabove set forth.

6. Answering paragraphs 11, 14, 15, 16 and 17 of the Second Cause of Action of plaintiff's verified complaint, this answering defendant denies, generally and specifically each, all and every allegation therein contained.

7. Answering paragraph 9 of the Second Cause of Action of plaintiff's verified complaint, this answering defendant denies, generally and specifically each, all and every allegation therein contained, except that a portion of the property of _____ is subject to the right of way easement described in Exhibit B to plaintiff's verified complaint.

8. Answering paragraphs 10 and 12 of the Second Cause of Action of plaintiff's verified complaint, this answering defendant does not possess sufficient information or belief to admit or deny the allegations therein contained, and basing its denial upon such lack of information and belief, this answering defendant denies, generally and specifically each, all and every allegation therein contained.

9. Answering paragraph 13 of the Second Cause of Action of plaintiff's verified complaint, this answering defendant denies that the wall described in said paragraph 13 is an "encroaching wall."

ANSWER TO THIRD CAUSE OF ACTION

10. Answering paragraph 18 of the Third Cause of Action of plaintiff's verified complaint, this answering defendant incorporates the same herein, as though specifically set forth at length, each and all of the admissions, denials and allegations contained in its answers to paragraphs 1, 2, 3, 4, ,5, 7, 8, 9, 10, 11, 12 and 13 of plaintiff's verified complaint.

11. Answering paragraph 19 of the Third Cause of Action of plaintiff's verified complaint this answering defendant denies that the wall is an encroachment.

12. Answering paragraph 20 of the Third Cause of Action of plaintiff's verified complaint, this answering defendant denies, generally and specifically each, all and every allegation therein contained.

WHEREFORE, this answering defendant prays judgment as follows:
1. That plaintiff take nothing by virtue of its complaint herein;
2. That all relief and judgments asked by plaintiff be denied;
3. For defendant's cost of suit incurred herein;
4. For attorneys' fees; and
5. For such other and further relief as to this Court seems just and proper.

DATED: June 20, 19__.

_____
Attorney for Defendant

COMMENTS

Form 11.5(B)   Amended Answer to Amended Complaint

This document merely amends answers to those paragraphs which are to be corrected, changed or modified in the original complaint. In this instance, the court has required or allowed the plaintiff to amend the original complaint, either via the sustaining of a demurrer filed by defendant or a motion to dismiss for some inadequacy in the complaint.

11.5(C)   AMENDMENT TO THE COMPLAINT

Come now the plaintiffs, _____ and _____, and move to amend the complaint on file as follows:

1.

As a proximate result thereof, this plaintiff sustained bodily injuries, a portion of which are permanent. As a result of said injuries, plaintiff has had, and in the future will have pain, suffering, worry and anxiety. By reason of said injuries and consequences, plaintiff has sustained general monetary damages.

FOR A SECOND SEPARATE AND DISTINCT CAUSE OF ACTION, PLAINTIFF _____, ALLEGES:

2.

As a proximate result thereof, this plaintiff sustained bodily injuries, a portion of which are permanent. As a result of said injuries, plaintiff has had, and in the future will have, pain, suffering, worry and anxiety. By reason of said injuries and consequences, plaintiff has sustained general monetary damages.

WHEREFORE, judgment against the defendants, and each of them, as follows, is prayed for by plaintiff, _____:
1. Costs of suit;
2. Such other and further relief as to this Court may deem proper;
3. General money damages for personal injury;
4. Medical and related expenses according to proof;
5. Loss of earnings and impaired earning capacity according to proof.

WHEREFORE, judgment against the defendants, and each of them, as follows, is prayed for by plaintiff, _____:
1. Costs of suit;
2. Such other and further relief as to this Court may deem proper;
3. General money damages for personal injury;
4. Medical and related expenses according to proof;
5. Loss of earnings and impaired earning capacity according to proof.

DATED: December 8, 19__.

BY: _____
Attorneys for plaintiff

11.6   AFFIRMATIVE DEFENSES

Introduction

An affirmative defense is new matter and the defendant must raise this defense concurrently when pleading or filing the answer to a complaint. IT IS NOT A SEPARATE DOCUMENT. Failure to show or plead an affirmative defense will preclude the introduction of the new evidence inherent therein at the time of the trial.

New matter or new evidence defenses can be raised by asserting the following (examples only):

(a) In personal injury cases, you can assert contributory negligence; assumption of risk, etc.

(b) In defamation or slander cases, you can assert affirmative defense as to the truth of the allegations contained in such a complaint;

(c) In conversion cases, you can assert the defense of consent or lack of consent of the plaintiff; in contract transactions and complaints, you can assert lack of consideration, fraud, statute of limitations.

(*Note*: The above sample of affirmative defenses which can be pleaded and the following sample paragraphs of affirmative defenses are those used in the State of California. You should look to your local codes for applicable affirmative defenses).

(Sample Form of Paragraphs)

1. (On or about _____), and prior to the commencement of this action, for value received, the plaintiff acknowledged in writing that it had been paid for all labor, materials and services provided to that date. Some or all amounts claimed by the plaintiff were extinguished by such written release.

2. That the _____ Cause of Action, of plaintiff's verified complaint, is barred by the provisions of Section 3097 of the California Civil Code by virtue of the fact that plaintiff failed to provide the owner, or reputed owner, of the subject real property with the required preliminary notice in writing within twenty days (20) after plaintiff first allegedly finished labor, services, equipment or materials.

3. On or about _____ and prior to the commencement of the instant action, this answering defendant satisfied and extinguished the alleged payment by payment of a full sum claimed by said cause of action. (See Exhibit "A").

4. Upon the termination of plaintiff's employment by defendant, plaintiff had a duty to mitigate damages by seeking other employment elsewhere. By the

exercise of reasonable effort, plaintiff could have obtained employment elsewhere, of a substantially similar character, properly following his termination of employment by defendant; but plaintiff failed and refused to exercise such effort, and failed and refused to seek or accept such employment elsewhere.

5. Defendant refers to and re-alleges all of the allegations contained in Paragraphs 1 through 7, inclusive, of its _____ Affirmative Defense to the _____ CAUSE OF ACTION, as though fully set forth.

6. _____ Cause of Action of plaintiff's complaint fails to state facts sufficient to constitute a cause of action against these (this) answering defendant(s) in that plaintiff has failed to comply with the pleading requirements of Section 7031 of the Business and Professionals Code.

11.6(A) ANSWER TO COMPLAINT
(WITH AFFIRMATIVE DEFENSES)

Attorney for Defendant

IN THE SUPERIOR COURT OF THE STATE OF _____
IN AND FOR THE COUNTY OF _____

Plaintiff,	Case No. _____
	ANSWER TO COMPLAINT
vs.	
Defendants.	

COMES NOW Defendant, _____ individually and doing business as _____, for himself and no other and answers the Plaintiff's unverified Complaint as follows: under section _____ of the Code of Civil Procedure, Defendants and each of them deny each and every allegation of the Plaintiff's Complaint, more specifically and generally and demand that Plaintiff take nothing by said Complaint.

FIRST AFFIRMATIVE DEFENSE

As to each and every cause of action in the Plaintiff's Complaint, Defendants, and each of them allege that there never was a contract, either oral or in writing between Plaintiff and Defendants, and each of them. That at all times,

Defendants, and each of them, were employees of Plaintiff _____ and at all times were working under his direction, supervision, advice and control and that any decisions, actions or failures to act were directly as a result of the supervision, direction and control of the employer, _____, to his employees, _____ and _____.

SECOND AFFIRMATIVE DEFENSE

That if any contract existed, it would be invalid under the Statute of Frauds as a contract for services and/or goods over the maximum of Five Hundred ($500.00) Dollars* and said contract was not in writing.

THIRD AFFIRMATIVE DEFENSE

That whatever damage may or might have occurred was due in total to the elements and rain which were at all times beyond the control of Defendants, and each of them and that said elements were brought to the attention of the employer, _____, and he ordered the work to continue even in the face of the inclement elements.

WHEREFORE, Defendants and each of them pray that Plaintiff take nothing by his Complaint, for costs of suit incurred herein, and for whatever relief the Court deems just and proper.

DATED: _____

_____
Attorney for Defendants

COMMENTS

Form 11.6(A)   Answer to Complaint (With Affirmative Defenses)

Affirmative defenses are (part of) used in an answer and are in essence allegations to offset, negate or counteract the claim of the plaintiff.

These allegations are on the part of the defense, and based on a violation of a city, state, federal or other governmental agency code, rule or regulation;

Or, the violation of the terms of the contract by the plaintiff, or to show contributory negligence on the part of the plaintiff.

Affirmative defenses can be used to strike, dismiss or obtain partial judgment as to a cause or causes of actions within the complaint.

You are advised and cautioned to discuss the use of affirmative defenses with your attorney BEFORE incorporating them in your answer. (This procedure is advocated since there might be sufficient grounds for a cross-complaint which would negate the alleging of affirmative defenses.)

---

* Statutory amount may be different in your state.

11.7   ANSWERS

Introduction

The answer plays the vital role of raising "issues" of fact in a pending litigated claim. If you are the defendant, this is done either by:

A. Denying the truth of the material allegations of the complaint in part or wholly;

B. By pleading an affirmative defense to the allegations as contained in the complaint;

C. By filing a demurrer to the complaint; or

D. By filing a cross-complaint or cross-claim (if applicable in your state).

It should be noted that as a defendant you are not required to defend evidentiary facts or conclusions of law.

The following samples are the types and formats of responsive pleadings which can be utilized by a defending office. (You will find examples of forms used in the State of California; and the forms governed by the Federal Rules of Civil Practice and Procedure. You are advised to look to your local codes to determine whether or not these formats and Rules of Civil Practice are applicable in your state).

11.7(A)   ANSWER BASED ON LACK OF INFORMATION AND BRIEF

Attorney for _____

MUNICIPAL COURT FOR THE _____
COUNTY JUDICIAL DISTRICT
COUNTY OF _____,
STATE OF _____

	Plaintiff,)	NO.
	)	
vs.	)	
	)	
	)	ANSWER TO COMPLAINT
	)	
	)	
	Defendant.)	
_____	)	

COMES NOW defendant _____, and severing itself from the other defendants, and for an answer to plaintiff's verified complaint, for itself and itself alone, admits, denies and alleges as follows:

1. Answering paragraph I of the First Cause of Action of plaintiff's verified complaint, this answering defendant does not possess sufficient information or belief to admit or deny the allegations therein contained, and basing its denial upon such lack of information and belief, this answering defendant, denies, generally and specifically each, all and every allegation therein contained.

2. Answering paragraph II of the First Cause of Action of plaintiff's verified complaint, this answering defendant....

WHEREFORE.....

COMMENTS

Form 11.7(A)   Answer Based on Lack of Information and Belief

This form 11-7(A) shows you how to use the expression "lack of information and belief" which can be used throughout the denial paragraphs.

It is a form of general denial which does not commit the defendant or acknowledge his guilt or innocence. It is merely stating that he does not have *sufficient* knowledge to make a determination one way or the other.

Remember when using this form of denial, that interrogatories can later be served on the defendant and the answers submitted to the questions could be in conflict with his statement "lack of information" or "insufficient information or knowledge."

11.7(B)   SUPPLEMENT TO ANSWER

SUPERIOR COURT OF THE STATE OF _____
FOR THE COUNTY OF _____

Plaintiff,	) NO.
	)
	) SUPPLEMENT TO ANSWER
	)
Defendants.	)
	)
_____)	

DEFENDANT _____ and, _____ dba _____
herewith file a Supplement to his Answer:

FOURTH AFFIRMATIVE DEFENSE

As a separate affirmative defense, defendant alleges that the said contract, Exhibit ''A,'' is illegal and void and there should be no damages accruing therefrom in that said contract is in violation of Business and Professions Code, Section _____, since Paragraph II of said contract prevents and reduces competition by not allowing defendant to lease equipment from persons or parties other than plaintiff.

FIFTH AFFIRMATIVE DEFENSE

As a separate affirmative defense, defendant alleges that if there was a breach of said contract by defendant, plaintiff failed to take reasonable action to mitigate, minimize or reduce damages which he could have foreseen and avoided by reasonable effort and without undue expense, namely, by, *inter alia*, picking up said equipment from plaintiff's place of business and selling or leasing the said equipment to others. On November 20, __, plaintiff received written notice that the equipment will be available for its removal.

SIXTH AFFIRMATIVE DEFENSE

As a separate affirmative defense, defendant alleges that defendant shall be entitled to attorneys fees and costs incurred in the defense of the allegations of the plaintiff under Paragraph V of said contract, Exhibit ''A,'' and Civil Code Section _____.

WHEREFORE, defendant prays judgment that plaintiff take nothing by his action, and defendant be awarded reasonable attorneys fees if defendant prevails, and for cost of suit and just relief.

DATED: _____

COMMENTS

Form 11.7(B)   Supplement to Answer

Both party-litigants may, on motion, make a supplemental complaint or answer, as long as they are submitting new, material facts to the case at bar. These facts must have come to light AFTER the initial complaint or answer was filed.

Thereafter, the court has to approve the request to file the supplemental answer, and your attorney must prove that it is substantially new material, going to the heart of the claim.

11.8(A)   DENIAL (GENERAL) ANSWER TO COMPLAINT

Attorney data

COURT CAPTION

	)	
	)	
	)	Case No.
PARTIES	)	ANSWER TO COMPLAINT
	)	
_____	)	

Defendant, JOHN DOE answers the Complaint on file herein as follows:

1. In answer to the unverified Complaint on file herein, and by virtue of the provisions of _____ Code of Civil Procedure, Section _____, defendant JOHN DOE, files his *general denial* to said *unverified Complaint*, and further answering all of the allegations contained in plaintiff's unverified Complaint, denies each and every, and all of the allegations contained therein, and the whole thereof.

WHEREFORE, defendant prays that plaintiff take nothing by his Complaint, for costs of suit, and for such other and further relief as the court deems just and proper.

_____

Attorney for defendant

Note: No verification is required by the party-defendant to an "unverified" complaint. Please confirm this policy in your local court rules.

COMMENTS

Form 11.8(A)   Denial (General) Answer to Complaint

This form appears to be self-explanatory.

You are cautioned to include the legal authority upon which you base your "general denial" within the body of the complaint as shown.

11.8(B)   QUALIFIED GENERAL DENIAL
WITH A PRAYER

The combination of admission of a particular allegation and a general denial is termed a qualified general denial and is permissible even when the complaint is verified.

FORMS

A. "Admits each and every allegation contained in paragraphs 1 through 10, and paragraph 14." "Denies each and every allegation not specifically admitted."

B. "In answer to the allegations in paragraph 14, defendants admit the allegations commencing at line 2 with the word for and ending with the word Massachusetts at line 28, and denies each and every other allegation as contained in said paragraph."
OR, you could state with more specificity as follows:

C. "In answer to allegations in paragraph 3, defendant admits the allegation that it is a corporation doing business within the City and County of Los Angeles, State of California, and denies each and every other allegation contained in said paragraph."

11.8(C)   SPECIFIC DENIAL WITH PRAYER

A specific denial is based upon personal knowledge, such as:

Form and Content

""Defendant denies that he owes the plaintiff $300.00, or any other sum or sums whatsoever."

Failure to state that he does not owe any sum or sums whatsoever, raises the question that he might own plaintiff $301.02, which would be an admission of debt, hence it is very important that you state that he denies that he owes plaintiff $300.00, or any sum or sums whatsoever.

11.8(D)   SPECIAL DEMURRER

A special demurrer is directed to the substance of plaintiff's case and if this specificity is lacking, the same may be disregarded.

Grounds and Samples

1. Another action is pending between the same parties for the same cause of action as the within action.

2. There is a non-joinder of parties.

Example:

"There is a defect or non-joinder in that Mary Smith has not been joined as either a plaintiff or a defendant."

Or,

"There is a defect or non-joinder of parties in that said action is brought by plaintiff as holder of legal title, and the defendant is holder of a beneficial interest and is not joined as a plaintiff or defendant."

3. Then there is the right to file a Special demurrer where there has been a misjoinder of parties. In this particular demurrer, the misjoinder or non-joinder must appear on the face of the complaint. If not, a motion to order a joinder or a material witness or party to the action should be made.

Example:

"There is a misjoinder of parties in that Mary Smith is improperly joined as a defendant or plaintiff."

4. Causes of action are not separately stated.
5. The pleading is uncertain.

Example:

"Several causes of action are alleged in the Complaint, and not separately stated (Here you should identify the causes of action and explain)."

Example (Uncertainty)

"It cannot be ascertained from Paragraph 5, Page 4 through 12, whether the plaintiff was within the course and scope of his employment at the time he suffered injuries."

6. In an action based on a contract where it cannot be ascertained whether or not the contract was written or oral.

Example (Oral or written contract):

"It cannot be ascertained from the Complaint on file herein whether the contract on which the alleged cause of action is founded and referred to therein, is written or oral."

Caution: If should be noted that this demurrer should be filed in the same time period as you would file an answer to complaint.

7. The court has no jurisdiction over the subject matter.
8. One of the parties has no legal capacity to sue.

Example (No jurisdiction):

"The court has no jurisdiction over the subject matter in that the plaintiff seeks to exercise general equitable relief in the nature of quieting title to real property."

Example (Lack of capacity to sue):

"Plaintiff does not have legal capacity to sue (being a minor, incompetent, lack of privity to the transaction)."

11.8(E)   GENERAL DEMURRER TO COMPLAINT....

Attorney Information

COURT INFORMATION

Parties	) Case No. _____)) GENERAL DEMURRER TO) COMPLAINT; POINTS AND) AUTHORITIES IN _____) SUPPORT THEREOF

Defendants _____, demur to the Complaint on file herein on the following grounds:

1. That the complaint does not state facts sufficient to constitute a cause of action against these answering defendants in that plaintiffs have failed to comply with the pleading requirements of Section _____ of the Business and Professions Code of the State of _____.

DATED: _____

_____

I hereby certify that this demurrer is filed in good faith, is not filed for the purpose of delay, and in my opinion the ground are well taken.

_____

(Attach your Memorandum of Points and Authorities and appropriate declaration(s)).

GENERAL DEMURRER*

"The complaint does not state facts sufficient to constitute a cause of action."

Or,

"The first cause of action does not state facts sufficient to state a cause of action."

Or,

"The complaint does not state facts sufficient to constitute a cause of action in that the alleged cause of action is barred by the Statute of Limitations (or you can state any other defenses appearing on the fact of the Complaint.)"

---

* Demurrers are not used in some states: under the Federal Rules of Civil Procedure this has become a Motion to Dismiss.

COMMENTS

Form 11.8(E)   General Demurrer

The general demurrer attacks the whole complaint, or some alleged cause of action or count, on the basis that a cause of action has not been stated.

Some of the defenses to a cause of action leading to the filing of a general demurrer are as follows:

1. Statute of Limitations
2. Laches
3. Standing to Sue
4. Res Judicata
5. Illegality in a Contract Action
6. Contributory Negligence or Assumption of Risk in a Tort Action.

Note: A general demurrer shall set forth succinctly and with clarity the grounds upon which any of the above objections to the Complaint (or other) are taken. Failure to do so will cause the Demurrer to be disregarded and not sustained.

11.8(F)   OPPOSITION TO DEMURRER OF DEFENDANT...

NAME AND ADDRESS OF ATTORNEY

COURT CAPTION

PARTIES		CASE NO.
	)	
	)	OPPOSITION TO DEMURRER
	)	OF DEFENDANT;
	)	MEMORANDUM OF POINTS
	)	AND AUTHORITIES;
	)	DECLARATION
	)	OF _____
	)	
	)	Hearing Date:
	)	Department No.:
	)	Time:
_____	)	

TO ALL PARTIES AND TO THEIR ATTORNEYS OF RECORD:

Plaintiff _____ opposes the demurrer of defendant _____ on the grounds that:

1. A cause of action is stated against said defendant;
2. Declaratory Relief is proper in this case, and
3. The demurrer for uncertainty is disfavored, is premature and should be overruled.

Said opposition is based on the attached Memorandum of Points and Authorities; Declaration of _____, and on the pleadings, records and files herein.

Dated:

_____
Attorney for Plaintiff

11.8(G)   CROSS-COMPLAINT

A cross-complaint is a *separate document* in a separate cover (in some states) separately captioned and designated as a "Cross-Complaint for...."

In some jurisdictions, it is part of the Answer, and therefore may be entitled "Answer and Cross-Complaint for ...." You are cautioned to check your local courts for this procedure.

In any event, it is considered a separate independent action and may join new and additional parties; and may be filed with or without the Answer—*and in an extreme case—whether an Answer is filed or not.* Talk to your attorney about this latter procedure.

Caution: The foregoing is a dangerous procedure in that a Cross-Complaint in and of itself does not raise any of the issues in the plaintiff's complaint. This failure would automatically deem admitted all of the allegations set forth in plaintiff's complaint. As a practical matter, and a general rule, cross-complaints are usually filed and served with the Answer to the Complaint; but may be filed and served after the time for filing the answer has expired. We do not recommend this procedure since it is possible that you may overlook the answering period and end up in default.

11.8(H)   COUNTERCLAIM

A *counterclaim* is a part of a defendant's answer and may be raised even though there is no privity of a relationship or direct tie-in with the plaintiff's complaint; however, it must go to the diminishing or defeat of a plaintiff's recovery.

Should you use this section be sure to set forth any claim against the plaintiff which has not been pleaded in the complaint. It is not necessary to re-establish jurisdiction of the court to hear the matter. You should check with your attorney if there is any question in your mind as to the necessity of setting forth independent grounds of jurisdiction for the counterclaim. In any event, this counterclaim should be filed and served within 20 days of receipt of complaint.

11.9   RESPONSIVE PLEADINGS UNDER FEDERAL RULES OF CIVIL PROCEDURE

Counterclaim. This type of responsive pleading is no longer used in some states; however under Federal Rules of Civil Procedure it is utilized, and broken down into two (2) types: Compulsory and Permissive.

A counterclaim is part of a defendant's answer and may be raised even though there is no privity of relationship or direct tie-in with plaintiff's complaint; however, it must go to the diminishing or defeat of a plaintiff's recovery.

In utilizing the counterclaim allegation, you should set forth any claim against the plaintiff which has not been pleaded in the complaint. It is not necessary to reestablish the jurisdiction of the court to hear the matter. (You are cautioned to check with your attorney if there is any question in your mind as to the necessity of setting forth independent grounds of jurisdiction for the counterclaim.)

If your state has adopted the Federal Rules of Civil Procedure, you should check them before you follow any procedure outlined above.

Cross-claim. This type of document is pleaded primarily under the Federal Rules of Civil Procedure. It would behoove you therefore, to check your local code or with your attorney to determine if your state has adopted these rules.

Should you decide to go the cross-claim route, you merely set forth the grounds for the cross-claim utilizing the same court and jurisdictional procedures applicable.

COMMENTS

11.9   Answer (Under Federal Rule 12(b)

Some of the defenses which can be used in answering a complaint filed in the federal court system are as follows:

1. The complaint fails to state a claim against defendant upon which the court can grant relief.
2. The right to bring the action, as set forth in the complaint, did not accrue within the statutory period allowed by law.

3. There is a lack of diversity of citizenship as between the parties to this action.

11.10   INTERROGATORIES

By way of example only, the following will set forth the procedure and statutory limitation relating to the filing and serving of interrogatories as adhered to under California Rules of Discovery.

The California Code of Civil Procedure Section 2030(a), *et. seq.* provides that a party (as distinguished from a witness) is required to furnish written answers under oath to interrogatories as and when propounded by the adverse party. The purposes of these interrogatories may vary from obtaining basic information as to the name and address of the parties or party who may or may not have knowledge of the facts pertaining to this case, and whose deposition may or may not be taken at a later date, to ascertaining other relevant facts.

Under this rule, (C.C.P. §2030(a)), interrogatories unlike depositions may be directed to any party to the action and be concerned with any matter of facts that are pertinent to the facts in issue. C.C.P. §2030(b) further provides that written interrogatories shall not be filed unless the court, on motion of notice, and for good cause shown, so states and orders. This does not mean that these documents may not be filed; it merely means that the originals can be lodged with the court (or a copy thereof) but not filed unless the court has determined that the contents have become relevant to an issue in the course of a trial or other proceedings.

Step-by-Step Procedure

1. These sets of interrogatories may be served upon the adverse party without leave of court, any time after service of the summons or the appearance of the adverse party. Be advised that the number of sets of interrogatories propounded to any party is not limited. However, the court upon motion, may issue a protective order to prevent unnecessary oppression and harassment.

2. The answers to these questions should be answered separately and fully under oath, to the best of the knowledge and belief of either the plaintiff or defendant; and dated and signed by them. In California, it is not necessary for the attorney to sign these answers unless, for whatever reason, the plaintiff or defendant is out of the state or without the jurisdiction of the court. If this is the case, then the attorney can sign the verification setting forth the fact that the plaintiff or defendant is unavailable and that the attorney has the power of attorney to sign said answers.

3. The prevailing party should file and serve a copy of the answers on the party submitting the interrogatories within the statutory limitation.*

11.10(A)   INTERROGATORIES PROPOUNDED
BY DEFENDANT (WRONGFUL DEATH)

Attorney for Defendant.

)	NO. _____
)	
)	Interrogatories Propounded
)	By Defendant
)	(Wrongful Death)
)	

Defendant, pursuant to Sections _____ and _____, Code of Civil Procedure,** requests that the following interrogatories be answered under oath, separately and fully, within 20 days by _____.

_____
Attorney for Defendant.

Scope: It is intended by these interrogatories to elicit information not only within your own personal knowledge but obtainable by you, including information in possession of your attorney, investigators, insurance carriers and their representatives. Whenever the term "accident" is used, it refers to the accident or incident which is the subject matter of your lawsuit.

If you cannot answer the following interrogatories in full, after exercising due diligence to secure the information to do so, so state, and answer the remainder, and stating whatever information or knowledge you have concerning the unanswered portions.

A. FUNERAL AND BURIAL EXPENSES....

B. ILLNESSES, INJURIES AND USE OF TOBACCO, LIQUOR AND DRUGS BEFORE THE ACCIDENT SUED UPON....

---

* Rule 33 of the Federal Rules of Civil Procedure states that,

"The party upon whom the interrogatories have been served shall serve a copy of answers, and objections, if any, within 30 days after the service of the interrogatories, except that a defendant may serve answers or objections within 45 days after service of the summons and complaint . . . The party submitting the interrogatories may move for an order under Rule 37(a) with respect to any objections to or other failure to answer an interrogatory."

** Your applicable Code Sections.

C. EMPLOYMENT OF DECEDENT, PAST AND AT THE TIME OF DEATH....

D. INJURIES AND MEDICAL EXPENSES OF DECEDENT AT OR NEAR THE TIME OF DEATH...

E. DAMAGES CLAIMED BY SURVIVOR, INCLUDING ANTICI-PATED FUTURE BENEFITS FROM THE DECEDENT AND SERVICES TO SURVIVORS...

F. COSTS OF SUPPORT REGARDING THE DECEDENT, THE DECEDENT'S NET WORTH AND LIFE EXPECTANCY OF THE DECE-DENT...

G. INSURANCE....

COMMENTS

Form 11.10(A) Interrogatories Propounded by Defendant (Wrongful Death)

This form is a skeleton of what should be the scope and content of your questions regarding a wrongful death action.

Just be sure that they are short and to the point and are stated in such a way as to obtain the answer you want. Use as many paragraphs and subsections as you feel are necessary to get the information required.

The example sections herein are optional and others may be added based on the circumstances of the death.

11.10(B) INTERROGATORIES PROPOUNDED BY DEFENDANT TO A MINOR PLAINTIFF

Attorney for

COURT INFORMATION

) No.
)
) Interrogatories Propounded
) By Defendant to Minor
) Plaintiff
)

Defendant, pursuant to Sections _____ and _____, Code of Civil Procedure,* requests that the following interrogatories be answered under oath, separately and fully, within twenty days by the Guaradian ad Litem for the minor plaintiff.

By _____

Attorney for Defendant

Scope: It is intended by these interrogatories to elicit information not only within your own personal knowledge but obtainable by you, including information in possession of your attorney, investigators, insurance carriers and their representatives. Whenever the term ''accident'' is used, it refers to the accident or incident which is the subject matter of your lawsuit.

If you cannot answer the following interrogatories in full, after exercising due diligence to secure the information to do so, so state, and answer to the extent possible, specifying your inability to answer the remainder, and stating whatever information or knowledge you have concerning the unanswered portions.

1. State the full name and birth date of the minor child.
2. With whom does the minor plaintiff reside?
3. State his/her present address and telephone number.
4. State the names and addresses of all persons who witnessed the accident or any events relating thereto.
5. State whether or not you or your attorney have any photographs of the scene of the accident, the cars involved, or the parties involved. If your answer is yes,

   (a) How many such photographs?
   (b) Where are said photographs?
   (c) Give names and addresses of persons who have custody of such photographs.

6. State whether you, or anyone acting in your behalf, have obtained statements in any form of any person regarding any of the events or happenings that occurred at the scene of the accident referred to in your complaint, immediately before, at the time of, or after said accident, or regarding injuries claimed to have been suffered by the minor child as a result of said accident.

   (a) State the names and addresses of the persons giving such statements and the date such statements were given.
   (b) State whether said statements were written or oral.
   (c) Were said statements signed or unsigned?
   (d) Do you or your attorney have a copy of said statements?

---

* Your applicable Code Sections.

7. To your knowledge, was the minor plaintiff unconscious at any time as a result of the accident?

   (a) Where was he at the time?
   (b) How long did it last?

8. List, based upon your own knowledge, what injuries the minor plaintiff sustained in the accident herein sued upon.

   (a) State any additional injuries that you were advised the minor plaintiff had.
   (b) Who so advised you?

• • • •

COMMENTS

Form 11.10(B)   Interrogatories Propounded by Defendant to a Minor Plaintiff

This form of questions propounded specifically to a minor is important in that most interrogatories are boilerplate and geared to adult plaintiffs.

Depending on the age of the minor, you can embellish or shorten the questions; and it may be that a *guardian ad litem* would have to answer some of them if the child is under 14 (or other appropriate minor age in your state). Please check your local code for this process.

11.10(C)   TWELVE SAMPLE OBJECTIONS TO INTERROGATORIES

1. RELEVANCE (Basic)

   Objection: The question is not calculated to lead to the discovery of information relevant to the subject matter of is action.

2. RELEVANCE (Broad and Remote)

   Objection: The question is overly broad and remote and as such is not calculated to lead to the discovery of information which is relevant to the subject matter of this action.

3. RELEVANCE (Indefinite Time)

   Objection: The question is remote and indefinite as to time and consequently is not calculated to lead to the discovery of information which is relevant to the subject matter of this action.

4. OPPRESSION   *Objection:* To answer this question would result in an-
    (Indefinite   noyance, embarrassment, or oppression to plaintiff in that
    Time)   the question is overly broad, indefinite as to time and
                         without reasonable limitation in its scope.

5. WORK PRODUCT   *Objection:* Attorney's work product privilege. Plaintiff
    (I.D. of Ex-   has not yet decided on which, if any, expert witnesses may
    pert Witness)   be called at trial. Any experts utilized by plaintiff to date
                         are for purposes of consultation and case preparation.

6. OPPRESSION   *Objection:* Oppressive, harassing and burdensome; the
    (Legal   information sought requests plaintiff's counsel to provide
    Analysis)   legal analysis and review for defendant when the laws,
                         ordinances, safety orders, etc. are equally available to the
                         parties.

7. OPPRESSIVE   *Objection:* The question is boilerplate in form, requiring
    (Boilerplate)   reference back to the preceding questions or introduc-
                         tions, thus making the questions oppressive, burdensome,
                         ambiguous and unintelligible.

8. OPPRESSIVE   *Objection:* The question is oppressive and burdensome
    (Ambiguous-   because it is vague, ambiguous, and unintelligible so as to
    Speculation)   make a response impossible without speculation as to the
                         meaning of the question.

9. OPPRESSIVE   *Objection:* The question calls for information which is not
    (Equally   in plaintiff's possession, and which is available to all
    available   parties equally, and is therefore oppressive and burden-
    information)   some.

10. ASKED AND   *Objection:* Asked and answered in prior interrogatories; to
    ANSWERED   wit:

11. ATTY-CLIENT   *Objection:* Attorney-client privilege protects disclosure of
    PRIVILEGE   the information sought.
    (General)

12. WORK   *Objection:* The question seeks disclosure of trial witnes-
    PRODUCT   ses (other than experts) and is therefore violative of the
    (Trial Witnesses)   attorney work product privilege.

11.11   DEPOSITIONS

Introduction

What distinguishes a deposition from any other type of discovery is the fact that it is the only vehicle of discovery which permits you to take the testimony of an individual who is not a part of the action.

This form of discovery is often referred to as a ''mini-trial'' since all party-litigants are present and their testimony is being recorded by a certified court reporter; the transcript of this testimony is filed with the court and made a part of the court record.

SETTING A DEPOSITION:

1. The deposition of an individual can be taken either:
   (a) Upon oral examination; or
   (b) By way of written interrogatories.
2. A deposition may be held either:
   (a) By any party in the action;
   (b) At any time after the service of summons;
   (c) Without leave of court.

-AND-

3. The deposition of a witness (non-party) may be taken:
   (a) By issuance and service of a subpoena re deposition;
   (b) By issuance and services of a subpoena duces tecum for production of documents at the time of the taking of the deposition.

11.11(A)   SUMMARY DEPOSITION WITH PAGE AND LINE

SUMMARY DEPOSITION OF _____
Thursday, July 31, 19__

STATISTICS

Home Address _____   Telephone No. _____
Business Address _____   Telephone No. _____

BACKGROUND

Originally 915 Internat'l, which is now   P.8, 1. 14-25
bankrupt, manufactured the line referred
to as inflatable balls, in 1967; and in
the early part of 1968, began   P.8, 1. 14.
manufacturing the line of balloons.

_____ who had formerly worked for 915 Internat'l came to _____ and introduced the line of inflatable balls to _____.	P.9, 1. 19 and P.10, 1. 16.
The identical formula for making the subject balls was used by 915 Internat'l and is used by _____.	P.10, 1.25
_____ is the sole and exclusive distributor of these products in the United States.	P.29, 1. 9-13

COMMENTS

Form 11.11(A)   Summary Deposition with Page and Line

This is a form of digesting a deposition in summary form which includes page and line. It speaks for itself.

11.11(B)   DEPOSITION SUMMARY (ALTERNATIVE)

DEPOSITION SUMMARY OF MARGARET HEIDT TAKEN ON OCTOBER 16, 19__

She has resided in Oakland, N.J. for fourteen years. She lives with her husband and has three children. None of the children live with her. She is 48 years old on the date of deposition. (70: 2-15).

In the accident she broke her left hip. She broke her leg between the knee and the foot. She broke three lower vertebrae in her back. She has numerous broken ribs on both sides of her body. She had some trouble with her bladder, in that she had a bleeding which lasted for about three months. She fractured her pelvis. It was broken in four or five places. She had lacerations on her forehead in the upper left portion. Stitches were taken, approximately 3 or 4. She knocked a tooth loose in the accident, and she had problems with her neck. (70: 25-72:15).

The problems in the neck caused Mrs. Heidt to black out if she turned her head in a certain position, even when she was lying down. It started in the hospital in California. The doctor did not tell Mrs. Heidt she had a neck injury, but they X-rayed the neck to find out if there was something wrong which caused the blackout. They couldn't determine whether or not there was. When she turned her head to the right and back she would black out completely. She doesn't know how long she stayed out, probably for minutes. Her blood pressure would drop. She had the problem until June of 19__. From that time until the time of the deposition she had no recurrence of that. (72: 17-73:22) she also had problems with her eyes; if she was seeing something white, there would be a black speck in front of it. (73: 25-75:1).

COMMENTS

Form 11.11(B)   Deposition Summary (Alternative)

This is an alternative way of digesting a deposition in summary form. Note that it is more narrative than Form 11.11(A); and it also includes a cross-reference to other volumes and pages, of either the same witness or it could be cross-reference to another witness on the same subject matter.

11.11(C)   NARRATIVE DEPOSITION
WITH CROSS REFERENCE

DEPOSITION OF *********

Page

7   On October 8, 19___ in the evening, he had about three bourbon and soda drinks. He paid for those drinks in cash. (Cross-reference to deposition in _____ case: At page 20, he appears to have paid for drinks on credit. Also, in daily summary sheets of the bar, he had tab of three drinks.)

13   He stopped for a red traffic light at Parthenia and Reseda Boulevard when he was going northbound on Reseda Boulevard. (Cross-reference: Page 26 of his deposition in _____ case states that he does not remember if he stopped at any lights from the intersection of Roscoe and Reseda to the place of the accident.)

15   He does not know whether or not the vehicle his truck hit was moving or stopped at the time of the impact.

16   He changed to the Number 1 lane from the Number 2 lane of Reseda Boulevard somewhere in the neighborhood of approximately a half a block before the intersection of Prairie and Reseda. When he changed from the Number 2 lane to the Number 1 lane, he was going about 35 miles per hour.

17   (Contradicts statement on page 16). He was traveling very slowly, say 15 to 20 miles per hour, when he changed lanes. He clarified by stating that when

he did get into the Number 1 lane he traveled at
about 35 miles per hour. He changed from the
Number 2 lane into the Number 1 lane to get
around the slow vehicle in front of him in
the Number 2 lane.

18   Once he got into the Number 1 land, he accelerated
to approximately 35 miles per hour.

He does not know whether or not the vehicle he hit
was in the intersection or south of the intersection, or whether it was moving or stopped.

DEPOSITION OF ************

No information in her deposition was of any significance to our case. Her
statements related mostly to her personal injuries as a result of the accident.

COMMENTS

Form 11.11(C)   Narrative Deposition with Cross-Reference

As indicated from its title, this is a narrative type of digesting a deposition
with reference to where similar language can be found in another volume, with
page and line.

This second type of narrative deposition sets up a different format, in that
the page numbers are placed in the margin, with the cross-reference incorporated
within each paragraph.

11.12   PRODUCTION OF DOCUMENTS (NOTICE AND MOTION)

If discovery is to be used at all and your attorney is to be successful in the
trial of the action, he must be aware of the existence of any pertinent documentation relevant to the subject matter of the lawsuit. He must also have physical
copies of the documentation.

The Notice and Motion will specify what documents are required for
production and inspection (and/or copying), and will specify the time and place
at which the same are to be accomplished. This notice and motion should be
accompanied by a supporting declaration which spells out, with specificity,
good cause supporting the discovery requested, together with a memorandum of
Points and Authorities in Support Thereof.

11.12(A)   REQUEST FOR PRODUCTION OF DOCUMENTS, ... UNDER RULE 34

CAPTIONS AND INTRODUCTION

Plaintiff requests defendant to respond within _____ days to the following requests:

1. That defendant produce and permit plaintiff to inspect and to copy each of the following documents:

(Here should be listed the documents, either individually or by category, with a succinct, clear description of each.)

(Also here should be stated the time, place and manner of making the inspection and other related acts.)

2. That defendant produce and permit plaintiff to inspect and to copy, test or sample each of the following objects:

(Here should be listed the objects, either individually or by category with a clear, succinct description of each object.)

(Here, again, you should state the time, place and manner of making the inspection and other related acts.)

3. That defendant permit plaintiff to enter (describe property to be entered) and to inspect and photograph, test or sample (briefly describe that portion of the real property and objects to be inspected).

(Here, again, you should set forth the time, the place and the manner of making the inspection and any other related acts.)

_____ (Signature)

Attorney for Plaintiff
Address

11.12(B)   NOTICE TO ATTEND TRIAL AND TO PRODUCE DOCUMENTS ...

Attorneys for _____

SUPERIOR COURT OF THE _____

FOR THE COUNTY OF _____

	)	NO.
	)	
Plaintiffs,	)	Notice to Attend Trial and
	)	
	)	To Produce Documents
vs.	)	At Trial
	)	
Defendants.	)	
	)	
_____	)	

TO DEFENDANTS _____
AND TO ITS ATTORNEYS OF RECORD:

PLEASE TAKE NOTICE that pursuant to the provisions of Code of Civil Procedure Sections _____ and _____, plaintiff requests the attendance of the person hereinafter named as an officer of defendant _____ at the trial of the above-entitled action which is set for August 4, 19__, at 9:00 a.m. in Department 1 of the above-entitled court, and the said person is directed and requested to bring to the said trial at said time and place the original of each of the records, documents, memoranda and other writings hereinafter described which are in the possession of, or under the control of, defendants. In the event that the original of any of the said items is not available for production at the said trial, the said person is directed to produce accurate copies of the said items.

1. Name of person requested to attend:

_____

Secretary of _____

2. Records, documents and other writings to be producted at the time of trial.

     a. Contract between Plaintiff and Defendant for work of improvement in _____ County, _____.

     b. Preliminary notices sent by Plaintiff to Defendant, or to any of them, on or about the following dates:

1. September 7, 19__.
2. September 29, 19__.
3. December 3, 19__.

11.12(C)   OBJECTIONS TO NOTICE TO PRODUCE

Attorney Information

COURT INFORMATION

	)	Case No. _____
	)	
Parties	)	OBJECTION TO
	)	NOTICE TO PRODUCE
	)	
_____	)	

TO: PLAINTIFFS, AND TO THEIR ATTORNEYS OF RECORD HEREIN:

Defendant objects to plaintiffs Notice to Produce (attached hereto as Exhibit "A" and incorporated herein as though set forth in full) served on or about _____, 19__, on the following grounds:

1. *The items to be inspected and/or produced are not specified as required by* _____ *Code of Civil Procedure* _____.

This defendant objects to plaintiffs' Notice to Produce on the grounds that it does not conform to the requirements of _____ Code of Civil Procedure _____ and more specifically _____ wherein it states:

"(b) . . . The request shall set forth the items to be inspected whether by individual item or by category and describe each item to be inspected whether by individual item or by category and describe each item and category with reasonable particularity. . . ." ....

Plaintiffs, in their Notice to Produce, do not specify what documents they desire produced but merely state ". . . all documents identified in response to the interrogatories." Defendant therefore has no knowledge as to what documents plaintiffs refer or which documents they desire to have produced.

2. *Pursuant to the attached Notice to Produce, this defendant's last day to produce documents is five (5) days prior to the date that responses to the Interrogatories to Defendant are due, referred to in said Notice to Produce. It is therefore impossible for defendant to know what items or documents will or should be produced according to said Notice.*

This defendant further objects to plaintiffs' Notice to Produce on the grounds that according to plaintiffs' Notice to Produce, this defendant's last day to produce documents is _____, 19__.

Defendant's responses to said Interrogatories are not due until _____, 19__, five (5) days subsequent to the due date for defendant's response to plaintiffs' Notice to Produce. This defendant cannot possibly respond to such a Notice to Produce in that at the time said documents are to be produced, this defendant will have not yet responded to plaintiffs' Interrogatories. Without having the responses to said Interrogatories, this defendant has no way of knowing what documentation to produce as requested by plaintiffs.

Dated: _____

_____
Attorneys for Defendant

Note: A copy of the "Notice to Produce" should be attached as Exhibit "A.")

11.13   REQUEST FOR ADMISSIONS

As you progress through the discovery procedures it will become increasingly apparent that certain items in the litigation are not disputed and other items will need documentation prior to the trial of the action. These undisputed facts could conceivably be grounds for either a partial summary or final judgment; or a summary judgment on the pleadings.

This vehicle of discovery, like the summary judgment, is considered to be one of the most devastating in the litigation procedure since the opposing counsel has only four choices:

1. Admit the matter;
2. Deny the matter;
3. Refuse to admit or deny the matter; and,
4. Object.

If he admits the matter, it is a judicial admission and admissible into evidence; if he denies the matter, the moving party can make a motion requiring opposing counsel to pay the costs of proving the same if it is not in fact proved at the time of trial; if opposing counsel refuses to admit or deny the matter, he is required by law to have made a reasonable investigation before making such a response and to prove that he has done so. If he objects, he has to prove the objection is based on lack of personal knowledge and this is hard to do if he has raised it in the complaint.

11.13(A)   REQUEST FOR ADMISSIONS OF GENUINENESS OF DOCUMENTS

```
                                  )
                                  )    NO. _____
                                  )
_____,            )    REQUEST FOR ADMISSION
                                  )    OF GENUINENESS
              Plaintiff,          )    OF DOCUMENT
                                  )
                                  )
vs.                               )
                                  )
_____,            )
                                  )
              Defendant.          )
                                  )
_____   )
```

TO THE DEFENDANT, _____, AND TO THE ATTORNEYS OF RECORD _____:

Plaintiff requests the defendant within twenty (20) days after the filing and service of this Request, to make the following admissions for the purpose of this action only, and subject to all pertinent objections as to admissibility which may be interposed at the trial:

That the original of each of the following described documents, copies of which are annexed hereto and exhibited with this Request and described hereinafter, is genuine, namely:

1. That certain document, a copy of which is annexed hereto and marked Exhibit "A," being Agency and Servicing Agreement, Loan No. _____, signed by Plaintiff, as the borrower, on February 11, 19__, and by _____ for defendant.

2. That certain document, a copy of which is annexed hereto and marked Exhibit "B," being Disclosure Statement of Loan, Loan No. _____, signed by the Plaintiff and dated February 11, 19__.

3. That certain document, a copy of which is annexed hereto and marked Exhibit "C," called a Broker's Loan Statement, signed by plaintiff on February 11, 19__ and by _____, _____, as a designated representative of defendant on Loan No. _____.

Dated _____

_____
Attorney for Plaintiff

11.13(B)   REQUEST FOR ADMISSIONS
(UNDER RULE 36)

Attorney Information

COURT INFORMATION

Plaintiff,	Case No. _____
vs.	REQUESTS FOR ADMISSIONS (Under Rule 36)
Defendant.	

Plaintiff requests that defendant, within _____ days after service of this request, make the following admissions for the purpose of this action only, and subject to all pertinent objections as to admissibility which may be interjected at the trial:

1. That each of the following documents, exhibited with this request, is genuine (here, indented, you should list all the documents and describe them with clarity).

2. That each of the following statements is true (here should be listed the following statements you want admitted and they should be stated in such a way that you can get a clear no or yes answer).

DATED: _____

_____
Attorney

11.13(C)   ANSWERS TO REQUESTS FOR ADMISSIONS

MUNICIPAL COURT FOR THE _____ JUDICIAL DISTRICT
COUNTY OF _____, STATE OF _____

_____,	NO.
Plaintiffs,	ANSWERS TO REQUESTS
vs.	FOR ADMISSIONS
_____,	
Defendants.	

_____, a _____ corporation, pursuant to Code of Civil Procedure, Section _____, answers the Requests for Admissions heretofore mailed and submitted by plaintiff as follows:

Answer to Request No. 1: We admit we entered into a contract with defendant; we do not know whether it is a sole proprietorship and we did not intend to enter into an agreement with John Doe or enter into a contract with John Doe doing business as _____ or any other additional party.

Answer to Request No. 2: We admit that we received the document referred to as Exhibit "3" but deny that it was given by plaintiff John Doe, but rather by _____.

Answer to Request No. 3: Admitted.

Answer to Request No. 4: Admitted.

Answer to Request No. 5: Admitted.

Answer to Request No. 6: Admit that the same was recorded on July 15, 19__.

Answer to Request No. 7: Admitted.

Answer to Request No. 8: Denied.

Dated: May 21, 19__.

11.14(A)   MOTION FOR SUMMARY JUDGMENT

Attorneys for Plaintiff.

SUPERIOR COURT OF THE STATE OF _____
FOR THE COUNTY OF _____

Plaintiff,	)	No.
	)	
vs.	)	(NOTICE FOR) MOTION FOR
	)	SUMMARY JUDGMENT
	)	FOR PLAINTIFF:
	)	DECLARATION AND POINTS
	)	AND AUTHORITIES IN
	)	SUPPORT THEREOF.
	)	
Defendants.	)	Hearing Date: May 30, 19__
	)	
	)	Department 18, 9:30 a.m.
	)	

TO DEFENDANTS, AND EACH OF THEM, AND TO THEIR RESPEC-
TIVE ATTORNEYS OF RECORD:

NOTICE is hereby given that on May 30, 19___, at 9:30 a.m. or as soon
thereafter as the matter may be heard in the courtroom of Department 18, of the
above entitled court located at _____, _____ the plaintiff,
_____ will move the court for an order striking the answers of defendants _____, and _____ and for entry of summary judgment in
favor of plaintiff against said defendants as prayed in the complaint on file
herein.

Said motion will be made on the ground that there is no defense on the action
on the bond.

Said motion will be based upon this notice, the pleadings, records, the files
herein, upon the declaration and memorandum of Points and Authorities served
and filed in support of this motion for summary judgment.

Dated _____

COMMENTS

Form 11.14(A)   Summary Judgment—Motion for
Summary Judgment

These forms are used only when you are sure that you can win the case by
such a motion.

Note that the filing of this motion does not toll or extend the time within
which opposing counsel is required to file a responsive pleading. For this reason,
be sure to flag the Statute of Limitations on your file and your follow-up
procedure to avoid the taking of default against your attorney; or, should you
desire, to take a default against the opposing counsel.

Remember that under Rule 56 of the Federal Rules of Civil Practice, the
parties making and opposing a Motion for Summary Judgment are permitted to
file affidavits in support of their arguments.

11.14(B)   SUMMARY JUDGMENT

Attorney for Plaintiff

_____

_____

_____,   )   No.
)
                    Plaintiff,   )   SUMMARY JUDGMENT
)
vs.   )   pursuant to Section 437c*
)   of the Code of Civil
)   Procedure
)
)
                    Defendant.)
_____)

This cause having come on regularly to be heard in Department _____ of the above entitled Court, the Honorable _____, Judge presiding, on August 6, 19__, pursuant to duly noticed motion for summary judgment. _____ appearing for the moving party, and _____ appearing for the responding party; and the Court having considered the pleadings, the documents presented and filed with respect to the motion and particularly the affidavits or declarations, and having heard and considered the contentions of counsel; and the Court having heretofore granted the said motion on the statutory ground that there is no defense to the action and that no triable issue of fact is presented:

IT IS ORDERED that the answer of defendant, _____, be, and it is, stricken;

IT IS FURTHER ADJUDGED AND DECREED that plaintiff, _____, have judgment against the defendant, _____, in the sum of _____ as principal, and the sum of _____ as interest, and the sum of _____ as and for attorney's fees, for a total sum of _____, together with costs in the sum of _____.

Dated this _____ day of _____, 19__.

_____

_____
JUDGE OF SUPERIOR COURT

*California Law.

COMMENTS

Form 11.14(B)   Summary Judgment

This form speaks for itself and is the result of the Notice and Motion for Summary Judgment as set forth in Form 11.14(A).

11.14(C)   MOTION TO DISMISS, PRESENTING THE INSTANCE OF FAILURE TO STATE A CLAIM, OF LACK OF SERVICE OF PROCESS, ... UNDER RULE 12(b)

CAPTIONS AND INTRODUCTION

The defendant moves the court as follows:

1. To dismiss the action because the complaint fails to state a claim against defendant upon which relief can be granted.

2. To dismiss the action or in lieu thereof to quash the return of service of summons on the grounds (a) that the defendant is not a corporation organized under the laws of _____ and was not and is not subject to service of process within the _____ district of _____, and (b) that the defendant has not been properly served with process in this action, all of which more clearly appear in the affidavits hereto annexed as Exhibit ''A'' and ''B'' respectively.

3. To dismiss the action on the ground that it is in the wrong district because (a) the jurisdiction of this court is invoked solely on the ground that the action arises under the Constitution and laws of the United States and (b) the defendant is a corporation incorporated under the laws of the State of _____ and is not licensed to do or doing business in the _____ district of _____, all of which more clearly appear in the affidavits hereto annexed as Exhibits ''C'' and ''D'' respectively.

4. To dismiss the action on the ground that the court lacks jurisdiction because the amount actually in controversy is less than $_____, exclusive of interest and costs.

_____(Signature)

Attorney for Defendant
Address

NOTICE OF MOTION

See motion under Form 11.14(A).

11.14(D) MOTION TO INTERVENE AS DEFENDANT UNDER RULE 24

United States District Court for the _____ District of _____
Civil Action, File No. _____

_____,	)	
	)	
Plaintiff,	)	MOTION TO INTEVENE
vs.	)	AS A DEFENDANT
	)	
_____,	)	
	)	
Defendant.	)	
Applicant for Intervention.	)	
_____	)	

Plaintiff moves to be intervened as a defendant in this action, in order to assert the defenses set forth in his proposed answer, a copy of which is attached hereto, on the gorunds that he is the manufacturer and vendor to the defendant, as well as to others, of the articles alleged in the complaint to be an infringement of plaintiff's patent, and as such has a defense to plaintiff's claim presenting both questions of law and of facts which are common to the main action.

_____(Signature)
Applicant for Intervention

Notice of Motion

TO: Attorney for Plaintiff

PLEASE TAKE NOTICE, that the undersigned will bring the above motion on hearing before this court at Room _____, United States Courthouse, _____ (here you place the address of the Court) on the _____ day of _____, 19__, at the hour of _____, or as soon thereafter as counsel can be heard.

_____(Signature)
Address of the Attorney

Contents—Chapter 12
Mechanics' Liens

12

MECHANICS' LIENS

12.0   INTRODUCTION

If you find yourself working in the legal department of a corporation, or in a law office which handles corporate clients in the construction business, meticulous scrutiny of the stop notices, notice of completion, mechanics' liens, etc. is mandatory in defending a complaint to foreclose a mechanic's lien. This is to insure the accuracy of dates in compliance with laws governing mechanics' liens, the terms of the original contract, the timely filing and recordation of the various notices and service of these documents upon parties culpable.

You are cautioned to check with your local state statutes and office of recorder to comply with the time table for the filing of these stop notices, completions, certifications and so forth since they vary from state to state.

DEFINITION

A lien is a charge upon the property of another which is not dependent upon possession and is created by statute. The two most prevalent Mechanic's Lien systems are New York and Pennsylvania.

The New York system states that the right to file a mechanic's lien is dependent upon the indebtedness of the owner of the property to the general contractor, after service of notice that labor, material and so forth have been furnished. This is commonly called a derivative lien.

The Pennsylvania system states that the laborer, subcontractor or other such individual has a direct lien which is not dependent on the indebtedness of the owner of the property to the general contractor. It is suggested therefore that you look to your local statutes to determine which ''system'' governs your state.

12.1   NOTICE OF FILING LIEN FOR MECHANIC'S LIEN

Attorney Information

COURT INFORMATION

)	Case No. _____
)	
Parties)	NOTICE OF FILING LIEN FOR
)	MECHANIC'S LIEN...
)	(Oklahoma City, Oklahoma)
_____)	

TO: _____
ADDRESS: _____

You are hereby notified, that the undersigned _____ of _____, State of _____, did on the ___ day of _____, 19___, file its claim for a Mechanic's Lien and materialman's statements as a subcontractor, in the office of the _____ in and for the County of _____, State of _____, upon and against the following described real property located in the County of _____, State of _____ to wit:

(Here you should set forth succinctly and completely the description of the real property involved.)

That the undersigned claimant asserts a lien on the property by reason of the _____ contract with one _____ contractor, and this claimant asserts a lien upon the real property in the sum of _____ Dollars by reason thereof, being the balance due this claimant on the account, and this notice is for the purpose of informing you of the filing of the statement and claim for the lien.

_____
CONTRACTOR

COMMENTS

Form 12.1   Notice of Filing Lien for Mechanic's Lien

This is the document you would prepare after all other attempts to obtain payment from the owner or general contractor have failed;

And after you have requested of the owner, via a Stop Notice, to withhold from any funds due and payable to the general contractor (or requested of the lending institution to withhold from the owner), the amount of funds due and owing to the claimant according to contract and/or agreement.

Please research the time schedule in this regard, as under certain state statutes you have a statutory time period in which to file Form 12.1 from the date of service (or filing) of your Stop Notice (See Form 12.4).

12.2   CLAIM OF LIEN

ATTORNEY INFORMATION

COURT INFORMATION

Parties

)
)
)
)
)
)
)
)
)

Case No. _____

CLAIM OF LIEN
(Florida)

STATE OF _____)
COUNTY OF _____ } SS.

_____ (name of lienor), _____ (residence or business address of lienor), being duly sworn states that pursuant to a contract with _____ (name of lienor's employer or person with whom he contracted) he (performed, furnished) the following (labor and services and materials):

(Here describe the labor or services performed or material furnished in detail. You should describe specifically and specially the fabricated materials separately).

_____ to the value of _____ (which is the contract price) on the following described real property [describe the real property succinctly and clearly for identification, being sure to give the access street and number, if known[owned by _____ (name of owner against whose interest the lien is claimed) whose interest in such real property is (state owner's interest in the property if known).

And further states that the last item of _____ (such as labor, services, material, etc.) was (furnished, performed, etc.) on the day of ___, 19___, and of the contract price (here state the amount unpaid) for which amount he claims a lien on the real property described.

_____
Signature of Lienor

Subscribed and sworn to before me this ___ day of _____, 19___.

_____
Notary Public in and for said
County and State

Expiration Date of Commission

COMMENTS

Form 12.2   Claim of Lien

Form 12.2 is another form of a mechanic's Lien which sets forth a claim for services rendered or materials furnished.

Once again, because mechanics' liens are governed by state statute, you should check your local codes for processing Form 12.2 and be guided thereby.

12.3   MECHANIC'S LIEN FORM (CORPORATION)

Attorney Information

COURT INFORMATION

	) Case No. _____
	)
	) MECHANIC'S LIEN FORM—
Parties	) CORPORATION
	) (Michigan)
	)
_____	)

That it is the intention of _____, a corporation under the laws of the State of _____ with its address at _____, to claim and hold a lien upon the tract of land lying in the County of _____, State of _____ described as follows, to wit:

[(Here set forth the complete description of the property.)]

for the sum of _____ Dollars, with interest thereon from the ____ day of _____, 19___.

That said amount is due and owing to said claimant for _____ furnished and performed in that certain improvement of said land described as follows, to wit:

[Here again set forth the property being improved].

That the name of the person for whom and at whose request said material was furnished and said labor performed is as follows, to wit

[here set forth the persons for whom the the lien claimant worked.]

That the date of the first item of said claimant's contribution to said improvement was the ____ day of _____, 19___, and the date of the last item thereof, the _____ day of _____, 19___.

That a description of the property to be charged with and to the best of the claimant's ability to ascertain the same above given.

That the name of the owner of said land and premises at the date of making this statement, according to the best information said claimant now has or is able to ascertain, is/are _____ (put the name of the owner).

Dated this ___ day of _____, 19___.

_____

Corporation

By: _____

COMMENTS

Form 12.3   Mechanic's Lien Form (Corporation)

This is the type of mechanic's lien form you would use if the client was a corporation as opposed to an individual contractor or subcontractor.

The essential elements are the same and the processing of this claim would be according to state statutes applicable.

12.4   STOP NOTICE TO OWNER

Attorney Information

COURT INFORMATION

	) Case No. _____
	)
	)
Parties	) STOP NOTICE TO OWNER
	) (California)
_____	)

TO: _____

YOU ARE HEREBY NOTIFIED that on the ___ day of _____, 19___ (or between the dates of _____, 19___, and _____, 19___, I, _____, the undersigned performed (or agreed to perform) labor for you (or furnished or agreed to furnish material to you) at the request of (general contractor or other party) on (or used in the work of improvement or building constructed on the property) located at (give address or legal description) of which you are (reputed) owner.

The following labor (or materials furnished has (have) been performed (or furnished:

[Here state the labor or materials furnished by the client].

The amount and value of that (already) performed (or already furnished) is _____ Dollars, and the amount in value of the whole agreed to be performed (or furnished) is _____ Dollars.

_____(general contractor or the person having authority) promised and agreed to pay the undersigned as follows:

> (Here you should set forth the arrangements or the installment payments due; or whatever arrangements were made for the man to be paid; but the general contractor has failed and refused and continues to fail and refuse to pay any part thereof); (or if the contractor was paid a certain sum of money then state what he was paid and what the balance is left unpaid that is still due and owing).

Therefore, the undersigned hereby requests and demands that you withhold from said _____ (this would be the general contractor or other person in authority) the sum of _____ Dollars.

DATED: _____

_____
Claimant
Address

COMMENTS

Form 12.4   Stop Notice to Owner

This is the initial document prepared to put the owner and general contractor on notice that the subcontractor has not been paid according to agreement and/or contract; and/or schedule or other installment arrangement as agreed upon.

Form 12.4 should be served on the owner and the general contractor via registered or certified mail. (We have found it a good practice to also notify the bank or other lending institution of this breakdown in communication and payment.)

12.5   NOTICE OF CESSATION OF WORK ON IMPROVEMENT

NOTICE IS HEREBY GIVEN THAT:

1. The undersigned is the owner of the property hereinafter described.
2. That the full name of the undersigned is.
3. That the full address of the owner is as follows:

(Here you should give the complete street address of the property so vacated and even here you might put in the legal description.)

4. (This paragraph (and the following paragraphs

5, 6, or 7, whatever you want to make it) in some states sets forth the nature of the interest in the property such as vendee in the contract of purchase or lessee, or similar description; and further, they may require that you name any other persons with title to the property such as joint tenants or tenants in common.

And further, in some states they may require the names of predecessors in interest, if the property was transferred prior to the commencement of the work. You should check with your local state rules on this inclusion.)

8. After the commencement of a work of improvement on the property, there has been a cessation from labor thereon, as of the ___ day of _____, 19___, and such cessation has continued until the giving of this Notice of Cessation.

9. The name of original (general) contractor for such work of improvements was/is (if under the conditions there was no original or general contract for the work of improvement, check with your attorney to determine if you should place in this section the word ''none'').

10. The property on which the work of improvement was commenced is located in the City of _____, County of _____, State of _____, and the legal description therefor is as follows:

(Here please set forth the complete legal description of the property including title, page, tract, lot, and block, etc.)

(However, if there is no common or street address at the time of the commencement of the work, please put the word ''none'')

_____   _____
Date   Signature of owner

Verification
Notarization/Acknowledgment

COMMENTS

Form 12.5   Notice of Cessation of Work on Improvement

In some states this may be called Notice of Cessation of Labor. It is a statutory document and you should check your local building and contractors' rules and regulations to determine the applicability and purpose.

In any event, if Form 12.5 (or counterpart) if filed by the owners, it is only after work on a building project has ceased for a continuous period, i.e., 30 days etc. Thereafter, the following statutory time limitations may be applicable:

In the beginning: 30 days or more, depending on applicable statutes;
Then 60 days after filing of notice by original contractor; and/or 30
days after filing of notice by every person, *other* than the original
contractor.

Caution: If Notice of Cessation of labor *is not filed*; then, within 90
days from the expiration of cessation of labor, for a continuous
period of 60 days.

These procedures and time limitations are important to establish and
maintain a lien on the property or project to insure payment of your client's fee
for services and/or labor and materials furnished.

12.6   BUILDER'S & MECHANIC'S LIEN NOTE

$ __160,000_____   _____, Texas, _____

For value received, I, We, or either of us, as principals, promise to pay to the
order of _____

_____

_____

in the City of _____,
_____ County, Texas, the sum of _____ Dollars ($160,000.00), in legal
and lawful money of the United States of America, with interest thereon from
date hereof until maturity at the rate of _____ per cent (_____%) per annum; the
interest payable _____; matured unpaid principal and interest shall bear
interest at the rate of ___ per cent (___%) per annum from date of maturity until
paid.

This note is due and payable as follows, to-wit:

It is expressly provided that upon default in the punctual payment of this note
or any part thereof, principal or interest, as the same shall become due and
payable, the entire indebtedness secured by the hereinafter mentioned liens
shall be matured, at the option of the holder; and in the event default is made in
the prompt payment of this note when due or declared due, and the same is
placed in the hands of an attorney for collection, or suit is brought on same, or
the same is collected through Probate, Bankruptcy or other judicial proceedings, then the makers agree and promise to pay ten per cent (10%) additional on
the amount of principal and interest then owing, as attorney's fees.

Each maker, surety and endorser of this note expressly waives all notices,
demands for payment, presentations for payment, notices of intention to accel-

erate the maturity, protest and notice of protest, as to this note and as to each, every and all installments hereof.

Payment of this note is secured by a Builder's Mechanic's, Materialman's and Laborer's Lien created in a contract of even date herewith between the Makers hereof, Owners, and the Payee herein, Contractor, and is also secured by a Deed of Trust of even date herewith to _____, Trustee, and is subject to and governed by said contract and Deed of Trust, which are hereby expressly referred to, incorporated herein and made a part hereof, upon the following described real property situated in _____ County, Texas:

COMMENTS

Form 12.6   Builder's and Mechanic's Lien Note

This printed form 12.5 is basically self-explanatory. However, at Figure #1 you should place the terms and conditions of payment.

For example:

"$20,000.00 in cash upon the signing of this note and the balance of $140,000.00 to be paid as follows:

1) On the ___ day of _____, 19___, the initial payment on principal in the amount of $_____.

2) On the ___ day of _____, 19___ the initial payment on interest in the amount of $_____

3) On the ___ day of _____, 19___, and on the same date, in the same amount hereinafter stated, until (here you would set forth whether it is interest or principal is paid in full or such other conditions applicable.)

4) The balance to be due and payable within ten (10) days (or such other time period) of the completion of the contract of improvement unless otherwise agreed upon, in writing, by all parties to this note."

Bear in mind that this Form 12.5 is merely a guide as no boilderplate form can meet all requirements of such an agreement upon which this note is based.

12.7   MECHANIC'S LIEN—RELEASE OF LIEN

KNOW ALL MEN BY THESE PRESENTS:

That in consideration of full payment, the receipt of which is hereby acknowledged, the undersigned (here put in the name of the person signing the document), does hereby remise, release, and discharge the following described land and premises, to wit: (give both legal and commonly known address and description of property), together with the improvements thereon, from all claim to or interest in the same, or any part thereof, which _____ (lienholder's name) may have under and by virtue of that certain contract which was entered into between (lienholder) and filed for record in the Office of the County Recorder of the County of _____, State of _____, on the _____ day of _____, 19___, and recorded therein, in Volume ___ at page ___ of Official Records of _____ County.

DATED: _____

_____
(Signature of Lienholder)

COMMENTS

Form 12.7 Mechanic's Lien—Release of Lien

This Form 12.7 is self-explanatory.

You are cautioned to check all conditions and terms of the contract to determine if they have been satisfied; and the lienholder (your client) has been paid all monies due and owing to him.

Thereafter, make an original and three copies of this Release to be served to all interested parties; then have it recorded and/or filed with the appropriate agencies.

12.8 NOTICE OF COMPLETION OF IMPROVEMENT

Attorney Information

COURT INFORMATION

	) Case No. _____
	)
Parties	) NOTICE OF COMPLETION OF
	) IMPROVEMENT
	) (Baltimore, Md.)
_____	)

NOTICE IS HEREBY GIVEN THAT:

1. The undersigned is the owner of the interest or estate stated below in the property herinafter described.
2. The full name of the undersigned is _____.
3. The full address of the undersigned is _____.
4. Nature of the title of the undersigned is _____.

(Show the title of the undersigned such as contractor, lessee, purchaser, etc.)

5. The full names and addresses of persons who hold title with the undersigned as joint tenants or as tenants in common are:

[insert the parties in interest].

6. The names of the predecessor in interest of the undersigned, if the property was transferred subsequent to the commencement of the work and improvement herein referred to:

[Insert the names applicable].

7. A work of improvement on the property hereinafter described was completed on _____ (this should be the date of actual completion).

8. The name of the contractor for such work of improvement was _____

[if, there is no contractor for work of improvement as a whole, insert the word none].

9. The property on which the improvement was completed was located in the city and county of _____, state of _____, and is described as follows: [here set forth the legal description of the property as well as the common address of the property].

10. The street address of the property [if there is no such address, then you should mark it none].

DATED: _____

_____

OWNER

(Verification)

COMMENTS

Form 12.8   Notice of Completion of Improvement

This form 12.8 also is self-explanatory.

The comments to Form 12.7 apply here.

Additionally, you should have some vehicle for verifying that the work has, in fact, been completed to protect your client before this document is signed by him; and filed or recorded with the proper authorities.

Remember, money changes hands as a result of this completed work, and you should therefore, not leave anything to "assumption." Therefore, check to determine what improvement(s) was contracted to be done under the terms of the contract and "walk list it," or "walk through it" to be sure all improvements were done as agreed upon.

Contents—Chapter 13
Real Estate

13

REAL ESTATE

13.0   INTRODUCTION

As a legal assistant working in a law office with a heavy real estate practice, your duties may vary from collecting data and information needed to complete instruments of conveyances, to preparing draft complaints and answers and other such documentation dealing with unlawful detainer proceedings.

In some jurisdictions you will be preparing various types of leases, land sale contracts and secured transaction agreements, and monitoring foreclosure proceedings as well as real estate closings.

This section will give you some forms and formats which you will find useful in performing your duties in this area.

13.1   BASIC DEED

A. (Opening Wording and Date)

This indenture, made in the City of _____, State of _____, on the ___ day of _____, 19___,

B. (Parties)

By and between _____, residing at _____, in the City of _____, State of _____, herein called the Party of the First Part, and _____, residing at _____, in the City of _____, State of _____, herein called the Party of the Second Part.

C. (Consideration)

That in consideration of _____ Dollars ($____), in lawful money of the United States, in hand paid by the Party of the Second Part, the Party of the First Part does hereby grant and convey unto said Party of the Second Part, his heirs and assigns forever.

D. (Description)

> Here, you should set out the complete legal description, as well as the commonly known description of said parcel of land being deeded, including any buildings and improvements thereon. Some states they require that you also include the tract and block numbers.

E. (Nature of the Transfer)

To have and to hold the premises herein granted, together with the appurtenances, unto the Party of the Second Part, his heirs and assigns, to and for his and their own use, benefit and advantage forever.

F. (Encumbrances)

That the premises herein being pleaded are free from all encumbrances as except herein otherwise stated:

> Here should be set forth any outstanding mortgages or taxations or conditions, restrictions, zonings, things of that nature. It is suggested that you check with the title company to get clearance in this regard.

G. (Restrictions/Easements...)

The Party of the Second Part, his heirs and assigns, shall not erect or permit to be erected any building other than a single family dwelling not more than two stories in heighth.

> The above is an example of a restriction that could be utilized, but it is not necessarily the only one.

H. (The Right to Convey)

That the Party of the First Part has good, absolute and *indispensable estate* in fee simple, and has good right, full power and lawful authority to convey the property herein being deeded.

I. (Warranties)

That the Party of the First Part shall execute or procure any further necessary assurances of the title to said premises and that he will forever warrant and defend the title to said premises.

J. (Grantor's Signature with Witnesses)

IN WITNESS WHEREOF, ...

COMMENTS

Form 13.1 Basic Deed

This basic deed contains most of the essential elements required to make it a valid transfer of title to real property from one person to another. However, other items can be added depending on the nature, circumstances, and the property being conveyed. This decision would be made by you and/or your attorney after having discussed the transfer of real property with your client. There could be other things that he would want to include in the deed. In any event, Form 13.1 sets up the basic outline and phraseology for drafting a deed.

13.2 QUITCLAIM DEED*

THIS INDENTURE WITNESSETH, That _____ (''Grantor'') of _____ County in the State of _____, QUITCLAIM(S) to _____ of _____ County in the State of _____, for the sum of _____ Dollars ($_____) and other valuable consideration, the receipt of which is hereby acknowledged, the following described real estate in _____ County, Indiana:

IN WITNESS WHEREOF, the Grantor has executed this deed, this _____ day of _____, 19___.

Signature _____   Signature _____
Printed _____   Printed _____
Signature _____   Signature _____
Printed _____   Printed _____

STATE OF
COUNTY OF

Before me, a Notary Public in and for said County and State, personally appeared _____ _____ _____, who acknowledged the execution of the foregoing Quitclaim Deed, and who, having been duly sworn, stated that any representations therein contained are true.

Witness my and and Notarial Seal this ____ day of _____, 19___

My commissions expires   Signature _____

_____   Printed _____, Notary Public

This instrument was prepared by _____, attorney at law.

_____

*Note: This form approved by Indiana State Bar Association for use in Indiana. Use of this form constitutes practice of law and is limited to practicing lawyers.

COMMENTS

Form 13.2   Quitclaim Deed

This is a deed of conveyance operating by way of release. Its purpose is to clear a possible defective title to land. This intended use is to pass any title, interest or claim which the grantor may have in the property. It can be used in an easement situation or a break in the chain of title.

Note that in giving a quitclaim deed, the grantor is not giving any implied warranty to the grantee as to title in the property. The grantor is merely giving whatever interest, if any, he possesses in the property. It could be nothing, but the grantor thinks he may have an interest, and wants to give the title.

Simply put, a quitclaim deed is generally used by a person who has an interest and wants to clear the title.

13.3   BASIC LEASE

A. (Date)

This lease agreement, entered into on this ___ day of _____, 19___,

B. (Parties)

By and between _____, hereinafter referred to as the lessor, and _____, hereinafter referred to as the lessee.

C. (Premises)

In consideration of the rental below-described and of the covenants stipulated, the lessor agrees to lease the following-described premises located at _____ Avenue, _____ City, _____ County, State of _____, and legally described as follows:

> (Here should be set forth the full legal description, the commonly described rental purposes above.)

D. (Term)

To have and to hold the premises unto the leasee, its successors and assigns, for the term of _____ (year, days), commencing on the ___ day of _____, 19___, and ending on the _____ day of _____, 19___.

E. (Rent)

That the rent for the term of this lease is _____ Dollars ($___), payable without demand or notice in monthly installments of _____, on the _____ day of each and every month of the term beginning on the ___ day of _____, 19___.

> (Here again, you can incorporate the acknowledgment of the first and last month's rent in advance as well as a security deposit. In some instances, this is optional and/or negotiable, as between the parties.)

F. (Use)

The use of the premises shall be for _____
_____, and for no other purpose except with the written consent of lessor.

G. (Assignment)

The lessee may not assign this lease or sublease any part of said premises without the written consent of the lessor.

H. (Lessor's Maintenance Responsibilities)

The lessor hereby agrees to keep the entire exterior portion of the premises in good repair and maintenance.

> (Here is an opportunity for you to insert any other responsibilities of the lessor which your client may wish to have spelled out to avoid confusion in the future.)

I. (Lessee's Maintenance Responsibilities)

The lessee hereby agrees to maintain the interior portion of the premises in good repair at all times.

> (Here you insert any other responsibilities of the lessee which your client may wish to have spelled out to avoid confusion in the future.)

J. (Default Remedies)

Said lessee hereby covenants and agrees that if a default shall be made in the payment of rent or if the lessee shall violate any of the covenants of this lease, then the lessee shall become a tenant at sufferance, waiving all right of notice, and the lessor shall be entitled to re-enter and take possession of the demised premises.

> (This is tantamount to your three-day or thirty-day notice which leads to an unlawful detainer action.)

K. (Termination)

The lessee agrees to quit and deliver up said premises at the end of the term of this lease in good condition, ordinary wear and tear accepted.

L. (Option)

The lessee has the option to renew the lease for a further term of ___ years (days, months), beginning with the ___ day of _____, and ending with the ___ day of _____, for a total rent of _____, payable _____ Dollars ($___) per month. All other terms and conditions of the lease agreement shall remain in full force and effect.

M. (Signatures and Witnesses)

IN WITNESS WHEREOF, ...

COMMENTS

Form 13.3   Basic Lease

As you know, most leases are contracts for the temporary use and occupancy of land, and/or the improvements thereon. These leases can be on a month-to-month tenancy; or from day to day(s) up to one year.

However, if the occupancy is to be for more than one year, it must be in writing in accordance with the provisions of the Statute of Frauds.

Further, if there is a possibility that the lease will be disputed at a future time, we have found it a practical move to have the lease recorded for the protection of the client.

13.4   BASIC MORTGAGE

A. (Date)

This indenture made and entered into this _____ day of _____, 19___.

B. (Parties)

By and between John Smith, hereinafter called the mortgagor, and Mary Jones, hereinafter called the mortgagee.

C. (Amount of indebtedness, interest rate, manner of payment)

WHEREAS,

The mortgagor is indebted to the mortgagee in the sum of _____ dollars, being lawful money of the United States, with interest thereon computed from the ___ day of _____, 19___, at the rate of _____ percent per annum, and is to be paid under the following terms and conditions:

_____

_____,

according to a certain bond, note, or other obligation bearing the date as hereinabove set forth.

D. (Description of property)

(Here should be set forth with clarity, and succinctly as possible, the entire legal description of the property being mortgaged.)

E. (Conveyance of property)

NOW, THEREFORE, for and in consideration of the sum of $1.00, paid by the mortgagee, receipt of which is hereby acknowledged by the mortgagor, and for the matter of security of the performance of the covenants and agreements hereinafter contained, the mortgagor has granted, bargained, sold and conveyed, and does hereby grant, bargain, sell and convey unto the said mortgagee, that said lot, piece or parcel of land as described above.

F. (Signed, sealed, witnessed) (notarization optional)

IN WITNESS WHEREOF, ...

G. (Acknowledgment)

COMMENTS

Form 13.4   Basic Mortgage

As you know, a mortgage is an instrument that pledges property as security for the payment of a debt for performance of an obligation.

The law is in a state of flux as to who retains legal title when property is mortgaged There is the lien theory which holds that title remains with mortgagor and that the mortgage only creates a lien upon the property. On the other side of the coin, you have the common law theory, or title theory, which holds that the mortgage acts as a deed conveying the entire estate to the mortgagee. You should, therefore, check with your local code sections to see which of the foregoing is applicable in your state. Additionally, there is a variance in the state jurisdictions as to the type of evidence of debt which should accompany the mortgage. For example, in New York a bond form is used, while in the state of Florida a promissory note is the evidence used therein.

13.5   BASIC SALES CONTRACT

A. (Parties)

This contract, made and entered into this ___ day of _____, 19___, by and between JOHN DOE, hereinafter referred to as seller, and MARY SMITH, hereinafter referred to as purchaser,

B. (Offer and Acceptance)

That the seller agrees to sell and convey and that the purchaser agrees to purchase,

C. (Description of Property)

All that certain plot, piece or parcel of land, buildings and improvements thereon erected, situated and being in the County of _____, State of _____, and legally described as follows:

(Here should be included the entire legal description as well as the commonly known street address.)

D. (Consideration)

In consideration thereof, the purchaser agrees to pay to seller the sum of ___ Dollars ($___) in the following manner and on the following terms:

E. (Terms and Conditions)

(Here you set out succinctly and with clarity such things as the down payment, whether cash or promissory note, or other means; whether or not there will be a first or second mortgage; whether or not it is going to be a *purchase money mortgage* and the terms thereof. In other words, this is the paragraph where you set forth all of the terms and conditions of the sale of the property in detail.)

F. (Type of Deed)

Seller agrees to convey title free and clear of all encumbrances, except as herein set forth by a good and sufficient _____ deed.

(Such as a Deed of Trust, where a third party acts as escrow agent by holding the deed until the obligation of a mortgage is satisfied.)

G. (Closing Date)

H. (Signature of Seller and Purchaser, and Witnesses)

(In some cases, and perhaps in some jurisdictions, notarization of these signatures may be required.)

COMMENTS

Form 13.5   Basic Sales Contract

There are certain essential elements which must be included in any contract, regardless of the form, to make it legally binding. The following lists these requirements:

1. That the parties to the agreement must be competent to enter into a contract.
2. That the contract contain a statement of consideration.
3. That a valid contract must contain an offer and an acceptance.
4. That the purpose for, and the subject matter of, the contract be a lawful one.
5. That under the Statute of Frauds, a contract involving real property must be in writing and signed by all parties to be enforceable.

13.6 CONDOMINIUM CONTRACT AND PURCHASE AGREEMENT
(Basic Form and Outline)

WHEREAS, _____, the Seller of the unit, known as
_____, and located at _____.

AND WHEREAS, the said unit or apartment is proposed to be converted into a condominium complex;

AND WHEREAS, it will be necessary to establish an association of owners for the operation and regulation of the common areas and facilities of the Condominium complex,

IT IS AGREED AS FOLLOWS:

1. *Subscription and purchase amount.* [Here set forth the amount of the purchase and the terms of payment.]
2. *Plan and Purpose.* [Here set up the rules and regulations and bylaws by which the condominium complex is to be governed.]
3. *Conveyance of Title.* [Here set up the manner in which title passes to the subscription owner.]
4. *Location of project.* [Self-explanatory]
5. *Priority of Mortgage Lien.* [Self-explanatory]
6. *Cancellation rights.* [Set up the conditions, terms, and time periods for cancellation and refunds]
7. Function and/or participation of lending institution in connection with operation of complex (optional).
8. *Type of Dwelling Units Available.* (Self-explanatory)
9. *All Agreements and understandings to be in writing.* (Self-explanatory)
10. *Interim occupancy On Rental Basis.* [Set up the terms and conditions for this occupancy; as well as the restrictions and penalties for decorating and improvements while waiting for condominium to be completed.]

WITNESS: _____

SUBSCRIBER

_____

SUBSCRIBER

_____

ADDRESS

_____

TELEPHONE NUMBER

CORPORATION

BY _____

NAME AND TITLE

_____

ADDRESS

_____

TELEPHONE NUMBER

COMMENTS

Form 13.6   Condominium Contract and Purchase Agreement

This form speaks for itself. It sets forth the basic clauses and sections that should be included in any Condominium Contract and Purchase Agreement.

It is not completed fully in that each Condo Agreement varies according to the owner and type of complex it is planned to be and the type of subscribers being sought to purchase the same.

This is because of the restricted nature, rules and regulations placed on potential purchasers; type of community dwelling being constructed; security and value of each Condo unit.

13.7   CONDOMINIUM DEED

RECORDING REQUESTED BY

AND WHEN RECORDED MAIL TO

MAIL TAX STATEMENTS TO

THIS FORM FURNISHED BY TITLE INSURANCE AND TRUST COMPANY

FOR A VALUABLE CONSIDERATION, receipt of which is hereby acknowledged, XYZ CORPORATION a corporation organized under the laws of the state of _____ hereby GRANTS to JOHN DOE AND JANE DOE, husband and wife the following described property in the County of Los Angeles, State of California:

A condominium comprised of:

(a) An undivided 1/56th interest in and to Lot 1 of Tract _____ City of _____, county of Los Angeles, state of California, as per map recorded in book _____ page _____, of Maps, in the office of the county recorder of said county.

(b) The unit consisting of Parcels 5, 5A, and 60A as shown on the map of said Tract _____,

the Certificate (as required under California Civil Code Section 1351) being recorded in book _____, page _____, of said Official Records.

This deed is made and accepted upon the covenants, conditions and restrictions and other matters set forth in that certain Declaration of Covenants, Conditions and Restrictions recorded (Date) _____, as Document No. _____, in Book _____ Page _____, of Official Records of Los Angeles County, State of California, all of which said covenants, conditions and restrictions and other matters are incorporated herein by reference to said Declaration of Covenants, Conditions and Restrictions with the same force and effect as though fully set forth herein.

In Witness Whereof, said corporation has caused its corporate name and seal to be affixed hereto and this instrument to be executed by its _____ President and _____ Secretary thereunto duly authorized.

Dated: _____   _____

STATE OF CALIFORNIA   By _____

                                                 President

COUNTY OF _____   By _____

                                               Secretary

On _____ before me, the undersigned, a Notary Public in and for said State, personally appeared _____, known to me to be the _____ President, and _____ known to me to be _____ Secretary of the Corporation that executed the within Instrument, known to me to be the persons who executed the within Instrument on behalf of the Corporation therein named, and acknowledged to me that such Corporation executed the within Instrument pursuant to its bylaws or a resolution of its board of directors.

WITNESS my hand and official seal.

Signature _____,

_____
Named (Typed or Printed)

(This area for official notarial seal)

Title Order No. _____   Escrow or Loan No. _____

MAIL TAX STATEMENTS AS DIRECTED ABOVE

13.8   INTRODUCTION TO EASEMENTS

Another possible interest or right in the use of land is the easement. Though the theory and laws relating to easements vary from state to state, generally, an easement is a right or interest in land of another, existing apart from the ownership of the land and considered as an incorporeal, non-possessory interest in land. It can be a positive or negative right and/or interest in land, such as the right of egress and ingress, which is created by a conveyance with limited use and/or enjoyment.

13.8(A)   EASEMENT, BASIC FORM

This agreement made in the City and County of _____ on this ___ day of _____, by JOHN DOE who lives at _____ in the City, County and State of _____, hereinafter called the party of the first part and JOHN SMITH, residing at _____, in the City, County and State of _____, hereinafter called party of the second part,

WITNESS AS FOLLOWS:

That the party of the first part represents and warrants that he owns and has fee simple title to that parcel of real property located in the City of _____, County of _____, and State of _____, bounded and described as follows:

Note: Here you should set out the complete legal description of the property, including the tract, block and boundary lines.

That the party of the second part desires to use said property for:

Here you should describe completely, and with clarity, the exact nature and type of easement desired, i.e., walkway, to build a fence, etc.

It is mutually agreed as between the parties under the following conditions as follows:

The party of the first part does hereby grant, assign and set over to the party of the second part:

Describe the nature and type of easement granted, with any and all restrictions that your client may deem necessary.

Except as herein granted, the party of the first part shall continue to have the full use and enjoyment of the property.

The party of the second part shall bear full responsibility for the use and enjoyment of the property and shall hold the party of the first part harmless from any claim of damages to person or premises resulting from the use, occupancy and possession of said property by the party of the second part.

Further, to have and to hold said easement unto the party of the second part and to his successors and assigns forever.

IN WITNESS WHEREOF, the parties hereto have executed this agreement on the date above first written.

_____

_____

COMMENTS

Form 13.8(A)   Easements, General Form

This is a general form designed so that you can incorporate the phraseology pertinent to the circumstances. But more important, there is really no wording which can be specifically prescribed when preparing an easement agreement. All you really need to do, is to state with clarity, and succinctly, the intent of the parties with an accurate description of the real property involved. If you have that, any "form or format" of an agreement will suffice.

However, you should always record an easement to protect future ownership of the property and as a way of a way of putting them on notice of the existence of an easement involving the land.

13.9   EASEMENT—CREATING A RIGHT OF WAY

1. This agreement made in the City and County of _____ on this ___ day of _____, by JOHN DOE who lives at _____, in the City, County and State of _____, hereinafter called the party of the first part and JOHN SMITH, residing at _____, in the City, County and State of _____, hereinafter called the party of the second part,

WITNESSES AS FOLLOWS:

2. That the party of the first part, and his heirs and assigns, grants and conveys unto the party of the second part and to his heirs and assigns, an

easement in , to, upon and over all that paved portion of a certain roadway situated at:

> *Note*: Once again, give a fully detailed legal description of the property to be conveyed.

3. It is understood that said easement is for the sole purpose of ingress and egress, and it is agreed and understood that it is not to be construed as an easement given to the exclusion of the party of the first part or his heirs and assigns; or to others later granted a similar right.

4. That the party of the second part, and his heirs and assigns, covenants with the party of the first part, and with his heirs and assigns, to at all times maintain and repair, at his or their expense, said easement for its proper upkeep and maintenance.

5. That the party of the second part is to hold the said right of way easement for a period of _____ years.

[Here put a time limitation such as 5 years, 12 years].

6. The usual closing paragraph.

COMMENTS

Form 13.9   Easement—Creating a Right of Way

This form appears to be self-explanatory. Just be sure that the property for the right of way, the liability for maintaining the right of way and the time limitations placed on the right of way are described according to the intent of the parties and clearly understood by both.

Please note that in creating a right of way, title to the property, as a general rule, remains with the grantor.

13.10   EASEMENT DEED

THIS DEED Made and entered into this _____ day of _____ nineteen hundred and _____, by and between

_____

_____

of the _____ of _____ State of _____ party(ies) of the first part, and _____

_____

of the _____ of _____ State of _____
party(ies) of the second part.

WITNESSETH, that the said party(ies) of the first part, for and in consideration of the sum of _____ paid by the said party(ies) of the second part, the receipt of which is hereby acknowledged, do by these presents grant unto the said party(ies) of the second part, _____

An EASEMENT for the following purposes:

over the following described Real Estate, situated in the _____ of _____ and State of Missouri, to-wit:

TO HAVE AND TO HOLD the said EASEMENT, together with all rights and appurtenances to the same belonging, unto the said party of the second part, and to _____

heirs and assigns   forever.

IN WITNESS WHEREOF, the said part _____ of the first part has executed these presents the day and year first above written.

_____

_____

_____

STATE OF MISSOURI } SS.
___ of ___

On this _____ day of _____ 19___, before me personally appeared to me known to be the person described in and who executed the foregoing instrument, and acknolwedged that _____ executed the same as _____ free act and deed.

IN TESTIMONY WHEREOF, I have hereunto set my hand and affixed my official seal in _____ the _____ and State aforesaid, the day and year first above written.

_____

Notary Public

My term expires:

_____

STATE OF MISSOURI } SS.
___ of ___

before me appeared to me personally known, who, being by my duly sworn, did say that he is the _____ of _____

a Corporation of the State of _____, and that the seal affixed to the foregoing instrument is the corporate seal of said corporation and that said instrument was signed and sealed in behalf of said corporation, by authority of its Board of Directors; and said _____
acknowledged said instrument to be the free act and deed of said corporation.

IN TESTIMONY WHEREOF, I have hereunto set my hand and affixed my official seal in _____ the _____ and State aforesaid, the day and year first above written.

_____
Notary Public

My term expires:

13.11   DEED OF RELEASE

IN CONSIDERATION of the payment of the indebtedness mentioned in a certain Deed of Trust executed by _____,
dated _____ and recorded in the Recorder's Office of the _____ of St. Louis in Book No. _____ Page No. _____, the undersigned owner of the note or notes described in said Deed of Trust, does hereby release and reconvey the property described in the said Deed of Trust to the grantors therein, their heirs or assigns, forever discharged from the lien of said Deed of Trust.

WITNESS the execution hereof this _____ day of _____, 19___.

_____

_____

_____

STATE OF MISSOURI ⎰
____ of ____　　　 ⎱

personally appeared to me known to be the person or persons described in and who executed the foregoing instrument, and acknowledged that _____ executed the same as _____ free act and deed.

IN TESTIMONY WHEREOF, I have hereunto set may hand and affixed my official seal in the State aforesaid, the day and year first above written.

_____

My term expires

_____
Notary Public

STATE OF MISSOURI)
____ of ____   )

On this _____ day of _____ 19___ before me appeared _____
to me personally known, who, being by me duly sworn, did say that he is the
_____ of _____
a Corporation of the State of _____, and that the seal affixed to the foregoing
instrument is the corporate seal of said corporation, and that said instrument
was signed and sealed in behalf of said corporation, by authority of its Board of
Directors; and said _____ acknowledged said instrument to be the free act
and deed of said corporation.

IN TESTIMONY WHEREOF, I have hereunto set my hand and affixed my
official seal in the State aforesaid, the day and year first above written.

_____
Notary Public

My term expires

COMMENTS

Form 13.11   Deed of Release

Form 13.11 is self-explanatory. It is a document which should be recorded
in the same manner as the Deed of Trust to which it refers.

This document is evidence of payment in full of the indebtedness on the
property encumbered.

It is a good idea to make a copy of the release form for your files.

13.12   APPOINTMENT OF SUBSTITUTE TRUSTEE

THE STATE OF ____)
)
)   KNOW ALL MEN BY
)   THESE PRESENTS:
COUNTY OF ____   )
)

WHEREAS, by Deed of Trust dated _____, _____ as Grantors,
conveyed to _____, Trustee, certain real property situated in _____ County,
_____, to secure the payment of one certain Note therein described, which
Deed of Trust is [recorded in Volume _____, Page _____ of the _____] [filed
under File Number _____ and recorded at Film Code Reference Number _____
of the Official Public] Records of _____ County, _____, to which and the
record thereof reference is here made for all purposes; and

WHEREAS, default has been made in the payment of said Note described in said Deed of Trust and the sale provided for therein should be made; and

WHEREAS, the owner and holder of said Note described therein and the beneficiary in said Deed of Trust desires to appoint a Substitute Trustee:

NOW, THEREFORE, I _____, the owner and holder of such Note and Deed of Trust, have named and appointed, and by these presents do name and appoint, _____, of _____ County, _____, Substitute Trustee to act under and by virtue of said Deed of Trust, and hereby request said Substitute Trustee to sell the property in said Deed of Trust described and as provided therein.

EXECUTED this _____ day of _____.

_____

Proper Acknowledgment will be added.

13.13   SUBSTITUTE TRUSTEE'S DEED

THE STATE OF _____)
)
)   KNOW ALL MEN BY
)
COUNTY OF _____)   THESE PRESENTS:
)

WHEREAS, by a certain Deed of Trust dated _____ _____, [recorded in Volume _____, Page _____ of the _____] [filed under File Number _____ and recorded at Film Code Reference Number _____ of the Official Public] Records of _____ County, _____,

_____,
as Grantors, conveyed to _____,
Trustee, certain real property hereinafter described, for the purposes of securing and enforcing payment of a certain note described in said Deed of Trust, of even date therewith and in the original principal sum of $_____; and

WHEREAS, _____, the present owner and holder of said note and Deed of Trust, as authorized by and provided in said Deed of Trust, appointed the undersigned to serve as Substitute Trustee and to enforce the trust, the said Grantors, having made default in the payment of said note when due and there being due thereon the principal sum of $_____, plus interest and attorney's fees as provided in said note; and

WHEREAS, I the duly named Substitute Trustee, did on the _____ day of _____, after having posted written notices of the time, place and terms of a public sale of the hereinafter described property, which written notices were posted at three public places in _____ County, _____, the County in which said real estate is situated, one of which notices was posted at the courthouse door of said County, and which said notices were posted for three (3) consecutive weeks prior to the day of sale, sell the hereinafter described property at public vendue, at the courthouse door of _____ County, _____, to _____, the highest bidder, for the sum of $_____.

NOW, THEREFORE, in consideration of the premises and of the payment to me of the sum of $_____ by said _____, I, as Substitute Trustee, by virtue of the authority conferred upon me in writing by the said beneficiary of said Deed of Trust, have GRANTED, SOLD and CONVEYED, and by these presents do GRANT, SELL and CONVEY, unto the said _____, his heirs and assigns, all of the [following described real property situated in _____ County, _____:] [property located in _____ County, _____, more fully described on Exhibit "A" attached hereto and by this reference incorporated herein.]

TO HAVE AND TO HOLD the above described premises and property, together with the rights, privileges and appurtenances thereto belonging, unto the said _____, his heirs, and assigns forever; and I, as said Substitute Trustee, do hereby bind the said _____, their heirs, executors and administrators, to warrant and forever defend the said premises unto the said _____, his heirs and assigns forever, against the claim or claims of all persons claiming or to claim the same or any part thereof.

EXECUTED this _____ day of _____.

_____

13.14   COMPLAINT TO FORECLOSE JUDGMENT LIEN

Attorneys for Plaintiff

SUPERIOR COURT OF THE STATE OF _____
FOR THE COUNTY OF _____

Plaintiff,)	Case No. _____
)	
vs.)	COMPLAINT TO FORECLOSE
_____as Administrator)	JUDGMENT LIEN
of the Estate of _____,)	
Administratrix of the Estate)	
of _____, Deceased;)	
STATE OF _____;)	
COUNTY OF _____;)	
THE FRANCHISE TAX BOARD)	
OF THE STATE OF _____;)	
THE DIVISION OF LABOR LAW)	
ENFORCEMENT, DEPARTMENT)	
OF INDUSTRIAL RELATIONS,)	
STATE OF _____; _____ in his)	
Official capacity as Tax)	
Collector for the County)	
of ___, State of)	
_____; and DOES 1 THROUGH 5,)	
Inclusive,)	
)	
Defendants.)	
)	

Plaintiff alleges:

1. At all times herein mentioned, plaintiff was and is a resident of the County of _____, State of _____.

2. At all times herein mentioned, defendant _____ Public Administrator, has been and is the duly appointed Administrator of the Estate of _____, Deceased, pursuant to the order of the Superior Court of _____ County, Case No. _____ Probate.

3. At all times mentioned herein, defendant _____ has been and is the duly appointed special Administratrix of the Estate of _____, Deceased, pursuant to the order of the Superior Court of _____ County, Case No. _____ Probate.

4. Plaintiff is informed and believes and thereupon alleges that at all times mentioned herein, defendants _____ and _____ were and are husband and wife.

5. The true names and capacities, whether individual, associate, corporate or otherwise, of defendants DOES 1 through 50, inclusive, are unknown to plaintiff who therefore sues said defendants by such ficititious names. Plaintiff will seek leave of this court to amend this complaint when their true names and capacities have been ascertained.

6. Each of the defendants named herein has some claim to or interest in the subject property as hereinafter described.

7. At all times mentioned herein the heirs or devisees of _____, Deceased, are or claim to be the record owners of an undivided one-half interest in the following described real property (hereinafter the "subject property"), subject to the administration of the Estate of said Decedent:

"Parcels _____ and _____ in the unincorporated area of the County of _____, State of _____, according to the map thereof filed for record in Book ___ Page ___ of Record Surveys, in the office of the County Recorder of said county on June 4, 19___."

8. At all times mentioned herein, the heirs or devisees of _____, Deceased, are or claim to be the record owners of the subject property, subject to the administration of the Estate of said Decedent.

9. Plaintiff is a judgment creditor under an Abstract of Judgment which has become a lien on the subject property; said judgment was entered in the Municipal Court of the State of _____, for the County of _____, Case No. _____, on April 14, 19___, and recorded on April 21, 19___, in Book _____, Page _____, Official Records in the Offices of the County Recorder of _____ County, State of _____. A true and correct copy of said Abstract of Judgment is marked Exhibit "A", attached hereto and incorporated by reference as though fully set forth at length herein.

10. The State of _____ claims lien rights against such named parcel of the subject property for general and special taxes in the amount of $465.26.

11. The Franchise Tax Board of the State of _____ claims lien rights against the subject property under the Personal Income Act in the amount of $154.39 pursuant to certificate number ___ recorded December 9, 19___ in Book ___, at Page___, in the Official Records of the County Recorder of _____ County, State of _____.

12. The Division of Labor Law Enforcement, Department of Industrial Relations, State of _____, claims lien rights against the subject property in the amount of $871.00 pursuant to an Abstract of Judgment; said judgment was entered in the Municipal Court of the State of _____ for the County of _____, Case Number _____, on December 20, 19___, and recorded on January 12, 19___, in Book _____, Page _____, Official Records in the office of the County Recorder of _____ County, _____.

13. _____, in his official capacity as Tax Collector for the County of _____, State of _____, claims liens against the subject property for general and special taxes not yet payable for fiscal year 19___-19___ in a sum not yet ascertained.

14. Defendants _____ and _____ claim lien rights in the subject property under an Abstract of Judgment; said judgment was entered in the Superior Court

of the State of _____, for the County of _____, Case Number _____ on February 16, 19___ and recorded on March 16, 19___, in Book _____, Page _____, Official Records in the office of the County Recorder of _____ County, State of _____.

15. Plaintiff's lien as hereinabove alleged is prior to and superior to all other liens or interests or claimed liens or interest of defendants, and each of them, and any and all other encumbrances on the subject property.

WHEREFORE, plaintiff prays for the following relief:

1. For a declaration adjudging that the rights, claims, ownership, liens, titles and demands of defendants, and each of them, are subsequent to and subject to the lien of plaintiff under plaintiff's Abstract of Judgment;

2. For a declaration as follows:

A. Adjudging that plaintiff's lien as hereinabove alleged be foreclosed, and that the usual judgment be made for the sale of the subject property according to law by a commissioner to be appointed by the court;

B. Directing that the proceeds of the sale be applied in payment of the amount due to plaintiff;

C. Adjudging that each of the defendants and all persons claiming under any of them, subsequent to the recordation of plaintiff's Abstract of Judgment, whether as lien claimants, judgment creditors, claimants under a deed of trust, purchasers, encumbrancers or otherwise, be barred and foreclosed from all rights, claims, interests or equity or redemption in the subject property and every part of the subject property when the time for redemption has elapsed;

D. Determining the order of sale of the various parcels of the subject property;

3. For an order permitting plaintiff or any parties to this action to become a purchaser at the foreclosure sale.

4. For an order directing the commissioner to execute a deed to the purchasers of the subject property at the sale after the time for redemption has elapsed and authorizing the purchasers to be let into possession of the subject property on production of the commissioner's deed;

5. For costs of suit incurred herein; and

6. For such other and further relief as the court deems just and proper.

DATED: December _____, 19___.

_____
Attorneys for Plaintiff

COMMENTS

Form 13.14   Complaint to Foreclose Judgment Lien

This is a typical complaint not only to foreclose on a judgment lien, but also an attempt to set up "priority" of liens payable when more than one "lien creditor" is involved.

In this instance, the public administrator may win since he was duly appointed by the court to administer the estate of decedent as the decedent apparently did not name an executor in his will, and someone (in this case the decedent's spouse) volunteered to be the "special administrator" of the estate, though a public administrator had been appointed.

The public administrator has a duty to collect all assets of the estate in order to satisfy all the fees, gifts, devisees, etc. This procedure may vary from state to state; you are therefore cautioned to check your local codes before proceeding.

13.15   GLOSSARY

Common Law Mortgage

1. A conditional conveyance of land. (See *Mitchell v. Burnham*, 44 Me. 299.)

2. A transfer of property passing conditionally as security for a debt. (See *Potter v. Vernon*, 129 Okl. 251, 264 P. 611, 613.)

The foregoing definitions are applicable in the common-law conception of a mortgage. But in many states, today, it is regarded as a mere lien, and not as creating a title or estate.

Equity of Redemption

This is a real property interest; and a right that the buyer has in the property. It is a real property right which must be redeemed within a reasonable time, provided the mortgagee had no control over the cause of default.

Foreclosure

The process by which all further rights existing in the mortgagor are defeated and lost. These proceedings are regulated by statute. Such as:

1. Strict foreclosure;
2. Action and sale;
3. Power of sale.

As to Strict Foreclosure: A decree of strict foreclosure of a mortgage determines the amount due under the mortgage, orders its payment within a specified time period; and further, if there is a default in payment, that the debtor's right and equity or redemption be barred and foreclosed.

As to Action and Sale: A lawsuit must be brought; all who have an interest in the property must be made party-defendants; case must be tried; judgment must be entered and the property sold. Proceeds of the sale are applied to the debt and the surplus given to the mortgagor (a default judgment is entered against the mortgagee.)

As to Power of Sale: Must be expressly conferred on the mortgagee by the terms of the mortgage. No court action is required. But a notice of sale must be given to the mortgagor and the sale advertised. The sale must be at an auction and conducted fairly and an effort made to sell the property at the highest price obtainable with the right of redemption.

General Contractor

The general contractor is the person who has contracted for the job. A subcontractor is the person who has contracted with the general contractor to do a stipulated portion of a job. The materialman is the person who has contracted the material for the job.

Guarantor

This person does not join in making a promise. His liability arises on the happening of an event: a stipulated event, such as the failure of the principal to perform; or the insolvency of the principal. It is collateral to the promise and *unenforceable unless, it is in writing*. This too is created by contract.

Land Contract

Seller agrees to sell, and the buyer agrees to buy and pay a stipulated and/or agreed purchase price which is set out in a contract. Note that the purchaser is the equitable owner; the seller holds the legal title and does not deed the property to the purchaser until the full purchase price has been paid. In case of default, if there is a voluntary surrender of the property, the seller takes absolute title and possession of the property and the buyer's equity will be cut off.

Mortgage

Conveys an interest in real property and is executed with the same formality as a deed. Otherwise, it cannot be recorded. An unrecorded mortgage is invalid against a bona fide purchaser or a mortgagee's full value when they have no notice or knowledge of the mortgage; or against creditors who acquire a lien on the property.

Mortgagor: (Owner)

May sell the property without the consent of the mortgagee (lender); has the right to any surplus land or property if sold at a foreclosure proceeding; cannot assign his or her liability.

Right of Contribution

When there are two or more sureties for the same principal and for the same obligation, and one pays the entire obligation or more than his share, he becomes entitled to reimbursement from co-sureties for the amount paid over and above his share.

Right of Subrogation, Surety's

The acquiring, the operation in law, of all the rights of the creditors against the principal, if he, the surety, is compelled to perform the obligations of the principal. This right does not arise until the creditor has been paid in full.

Surety

A person who is liable for the payment of another's debt; or for the performance of another's duty.

If required to perform, he is entitled to reimbursement from his principal for any loss. Surety and principal together become the obligees to pay or perform. This is normally created by contract.

Contents—Chapter 14
Enforcements of Judgments (Money)

14

ENFORCEMENT OF

JUDGMENTS (MONEY)

14.0   INTRODUCTION

The purpose of laws relating to proceedings in aid of execution of judgments is to create an economic and orderly procedure for the collection of debts and to create priority of debt collection.

In most states this procedure is controlled by statute. You are therefore cautioned to check your local statutes before utilizing any of the following forms to be sure that you are complying with your state procedure in completing the forms and processing them through the courts and law enforcement agencies.

Once this has been accomplished, then check to be sure that the following items have been completed before you attempt to enforce the collection of a money judgment:

1. Your Findings of Fact have been prepared;
2. Conclusions of Law have been prepared;
3. The Judgment has been prepared for the signature of a judge hearing the action; and
4. The Memorandum of Costs has been prepared. Once all of these have been prepared and the court has rendered a decision in the matter, assuming that it is in your favor, then you can proceed to prepare the necessary and appropriate documents for enforcing the judgment. The following forms are an example of what can be utilized in this regard.

14.1 COVENANT NOT TO EXECUTE ON JUDGMENT IN PENDING LAWSUIT

This Agreement, made and entered on this ___ day of _____, by and between the party of the first part and the party of the second part witnesses as follows:

That a certain lawsuit has been filed being Case No. _____ in the _____ Court of _____, wherein the first party, hereinafter called plaintiff, and the second party, hereinafter called defendant, has been on trial for the past ____ days and has now been submitted to the jury and the jury has not yet returned its verdict;

It has now been agreed between the parties that notwithstanding any judgment that may be rendered in the cause, the first party enters into the following covenants hereinafter named:

That in consideration and payment to the first party of _____ dollars by the second party, the receipt of which is hereby acknowledged, and the further payment of _____ percent of the costs accrued in the suit in the event that the first party shall be liable therefor, the first party hereby covenants and agrees that he will not at any time, nor shall anyone on his behalf seek or attempt to execute against the party of the second part on a judgment hereinafter rendered by a jury.

And the first party hereby covenants and agrees that he will indemnify and hold harmless the party of the second part against any and all such executions, against any and all contribution by reason of such judgment, and against any and all liability for indemnity by reason of any such judgment.

It is the intent of this Agreement that the second party, its (his) representatives and assigns, shall never at any time be liable, beyond the consideration set forth in this instrument, by reason of the heretofore alleged injuries, or suit, or judgment rendered therein; or any suit or suits filed by reason thereof.

_____

_____

COMMENTS

Form 14.1   Covenant Not to Execute on Judgment Pending Lawsuit

This document may or may not be placed on Court pleading paper; and may or may not be filed with the Court. It can be an out-of-court settlement document as between the parties and kept in the file. You should use your judgment in this regard or rely on the determination of your attorney.

However, we have found it to be a better part of valor to file this document (prepared on Court pleading paper) with the Court once the Court has jurisdiction over the dispute.

14.2   JUDGMENT ON DECISION BY THE COURT

Attorney Information

UNITED STATES DISTRICT COURT
SOUTHERN DISTRICT OF NEW YORK

Plaintiff,	)	Civil Action
	)	
vs.	)	Case No. _____
	)	
Defendant.	)	JUDGMENT
_____	)	

This action came on for trial (herein) before the court, the honorable _____, district judge presiding, and the issues having been duly tried (heard) and a *decision* having been duly rendered.

IT IS ORDERED, ADJUDGED AND DECREED AS FOLLOWS:

That the plaintiff recover of the defendant the sum of $_____ with interest thereon at the rate of ___% as provided by law with costs.

(Optional paragraph)

That the plaintiff take nothing, that the action be dismissed on the merits and that the defendant recover of the plaintiff his costs incurred.

DATED at New York, New York, this ___ day of _____.

_____
Clerk of the Court

COMMENTS

Form 14.2   Judgment on Decision by the Court

The key to Form 14.2 is that trial of the issues was before a court without a jury present. The resulting decision and award therefore were made by the judge presiding. You would prepare this judgment from the court minutes if this is the procedure in your state.

14.3 JUDGMENT ON JURY VERDICT

Attorney Information

UNITED STATES DISTRICT COURT
SOUTHERN DISTRICT OF NEW YORK

Plaintiff,	)	Civil Action
vs.	)	File No. _____
Defendant,	)	JUDGMENT

This action came on for trial before the court and jury, the Honorable _____, District Judge, presiding, and the issues having been duly tried and the *jury* having duly rendered its verdict.

IT IS ORDERED AND ADJUDGED AS FOLLOWS:

That the plaintiff recover from the defendant the sum of _____ dollars with interest thereon at the rate of _____% as provided by law with his costs incurred.

(Optional paragraph)

That the plaintiff take nothing, that the action be dismissed on the merits and that the defendant recover of the plaintiff the costs incurred.

DATED at New York, New York, this _____ day of _____.

_____
Clerk of the Court

COMMENTS

Form 14.3 Judgment, Jury Verdict

The key to Form 14.3 is that the trial of the issues was heard before the court with a jury present. The resulting decision and award in this instance were rendered by the peers of the litigant.

In some states this judgment would be prepared by the court clerk. You are therefore cautioned to check your local rules as to who prepares the judgment and order in this instance.

14.4 ABSTRACT OF JUDGMENT

ATTORNEY OR PARTY WITHOUT ATTORNEY (name and address). TELEPHONE NO.:

☐ Recording requested by and return to:

ATTORNEY FOR (Name):

NAME OF COURT AND BRANCH, IF ANY:

STREET ADDRESS:
MAILING ADDRESS:
CITY, ZIP CODE:

PLAINTIFF:

DEFENDANT:

FOR RECORDER'S USE ONLY

CASE NUMBER:

FOR COURT USE ONLY

ABSTRACT OF JUDGMENT*

1. The judgment creditor applies for an abstract of judgment and represents
   a. Judgment debtor's

   Name and address

   ☐ Address unknown

   Driver's license state and number: .... ☐ unknown.
   Social Security number: .... ☐ unknown.
   b. Summons was personally served at or mailed to (address):

☐ Information regarding additional judgment debtors is shown on the reverse.
Dated: _____

(Type or print name)

_____
(Signature of Judgment Creditor or Attorney)

*Form Adopted by the Judicial Council of California Revised Effective January 1, 1981.

2. **I certify that the following is a true and correct abstract of the judgment entered in this action.**

3. Judgment creditor (name):

    Plaintiff

4. Judgment debtor (full name as
    it appears in judgment)

            Defendant

5. Total amount of judgment as entered
   a. Principal $ 50,000.00
   b. Attorney fees: $ 5,000.00
   c. Interest $ 600.00
   d. Costs: $ 495.00
   e.   Total: $ 56,095.00

6. Judgment was entered
   a. on (date):
   b. ☐ in judgment book, minute book or docket
       (1) Volume no.:   (2) Page no.:

7. A lien in favor of a judgment creditor pursuant to
   CCP 688.1 is
   a. ☐ not endorsed on the judgment
   b. ☐ endorsed on the judgment as follows:
       (1) amount $56,095.00
       (2) in favor of (name):
       Judgment-Creditor

8. A stay of execution has
   a. ☐ not been ordered by the court
   b. ☐ been ordered by the court effective until
       (date);

This abstract issued on (date): .... Clerk, By ——, Deputy

ABSTRACT OF JUDGMENT
(CIVIL)

PLAINTIFF (name):

DEFENDANT (name):

CASE NUMBER:

ABSTRACT OF JUDGMENT (CIVIL) Reverse Side

Information regarding additional judgment debtors:

9.

Name and address

☐ Address unknown

Driver's license number is: _____ unknown.
Social Security number is: _____ unknown.
Summons was personally served at or mailed to (address):

10.

Name and address

☐ Address unknown

Driver's license number is: _____ unknown.
Social Security number is: _____ unknown.
Summons was personally served at or mailed to (address):

11.

Name and address

☐ Address unknown

Driver's license number is: _____ unknown.
Social Security number is: _____ unknown.
Summons was personally served at or mailed to (address):

12.

Name and address

☐ Address unknown

Driver's license number is: _____ unknown.
Social Security number is: _____ unknown.
Summons was personally served at or mailed to (address):

ABSTRACT OF JUDGMENT (CIVIL) Reverse Side

13.

Name and address

☐ Address unknown

Driver's license number is: _____ unknown.
Social Security number is: _____ unknown.
Summons was personally served at or mailed to (address):

14.

Name and address

☐ Address unknown

Driver's license number is: _____ unknown.
Social Security number is: _____ unknown.
Summons was personally served at or mailed to (address):

15.

Name and address

☐ Address unknown

Driver's license number is: _____ unknown.
Social Security number is: _____ unknown.
Summons was personally served at or mailed to (address):

16.

Name and address

☐ Address unknown

Driver's license number is: _____ unknown.
Social Security number is: _____ unknown.
Summons was personally served at or mailed to (address):

17. ☐ Continued on attachment 17.

COMMENTS

Form 14.4   Abstract of Judgment

This document is prepared after judgment has been rendered.

You should make a copy and file same with the Court, have the same recorded in the County where the defendant or said property is located; while at the same time giving the instructions to the Marshal or Sheriff to execute on the judgment to have the same satisfied in the total amount prescribed thereon. This latter procedure is done provided there has not been a stay of execution order by the Court. See Paragraph 8.

The completion of Paragraph 6 is mandatory.

Note: This Abstract of Judgment can be prepared for more than one judgment creditor. If this is applicable in your case, be sure that the names and addresses of the additional judgment debtors are correct and that separate instructions are given to the Marshal for execution on the judgment.

14.5   ASSIGNMENT OF JUDGMENT

(CAPTION OF THE CASE)

For value received, I hereby sell, assign, transfer and set over unto _____, his executors, administrators, heirs and assigns, the judgment

> Here you must describe the Judgment by date, by the document, amount, and any other pertinent information.

I hereby covenant that said judgment is in full force and effect, and that the sum of _____ dollars with interest thereon at the rate of ____, from the ___ day of _____, 19___, is now due and payable thereon.

I further covenant that I am the lawful and sole owner of said judgment, and that the same is free from all liens and encumbrances, including my attorney (or otherwise) except as follows:

> *Note*: Should there be any other debts due and owing under this judgment, this is the place where you Set them out.

IN WITNESS WHEREOF, etc.

_____

COMMENTS

Form 14.5   Assignment of Judgment

This document is self-explanatory. The pertinent and mandatory information is noted on the document. Please study it carefully following the directions without exception, unless otherwise determined by your attorney.

14.6   GENERAL RELEASE AND ACKNOWLEDGMENT OF SATISFACTION OF JUDGMENT

Attorney Information

COURT INFORMATION

Plaintiff,	)	No. _____
	)	
vs.	)	IN THE DISTRICT COURT OF
	)	_____ COUNTY, _____
Defendant	)	_____ JUDICIAL DISTRICT
_____	)	

This cause came on to be heard in its regular order and the parties appeared in person and through their respective attorneys of record, and waived a jury and stated to the jury that all claims and causes of action which were, or could have been asserted by and between them, had been compromised and settled and the consideration therefor paid in full, and that judgment should be entered that Plaintiff take nothing and that court costs should be taxed against the Defendants; therefore, in accordance with such compromise settlement agreement:

IT IS ORDERED, ADJUDGED AND DECREED that Plaintiff _____ pay nothing by reason of this suit and that the Defendant _____, go hence without delay except as to the payment of court costs.

All relief sought herein which is not expressly granted is denied.

ENTERED this the _____ day of _____, 19___.

_____

JUDGE PRESIDING

APPROVED AND CONSENTED TO:

_____

PLAINTIFF

_____

ATTORNEY FOR PLAINTIFF

_____

ATTORNEY FOR DEFENDANT

COMMENTS

Form 14.6   General Release and Acknowledgment of Satisfaction of Judgment.

Form 14.6 generally is prepared by the litigants, who having started a litigated proceeding in the court system, have decided not to have the matter settled by a judge and jury, preferring to settle and/or compromise the matter out of court.

The court having jurisdiction of the matter because of the initial filing of pleadings, must be notified of this decision and thus make the final decree in order to have the same binding on all party litigants.

Once again, this procedure may vary from state to state. Please do your research in this regard.

14.7   NOTICE OF MOTION TO RENEW JUDGMENT

Attorney Information

COURT INFORMATION

Plaintiff,	)	No. _____
	)	
vs.	)	NOTICE OF MOTION TO
	)	RENEW JUDGMENT;
	)	DECLARATION OF ____;
	)	(Could be more than on
	)	declaration); MEMORANDUM
	)	OF POINTS AND
	)	AUTHORITIES
	)	(Add your code authority)
	)	
	)	Hearing Date:
	)	Department:
	)	Time:
Defendant.	)	
	)	

TO: THE ADMINISTRATOR OF THE ESTATE OF DEFENDANT
_____.

PLEASE TAKE NOTICE that on ____, 19__, at the hour of _____ or as soon thereafter as counsel can be heard, in Department (Division) _____ of the above-entitled court, Plainitff _____ will move the court for an order renewing his judgment in this action and allowing said judgment to be enforced or carried into execution.

Said motion will be made upon the grounds that Plaintiff has been unable to secure payment on said judgment since the same was rendered, despite diligent efforts to do so, and on the further grounds that since the death of Defendant, the Administrator of Defendant's estate has actively sought to preclude Plaintiff from obtaining payment on said judgment.

Said motion will be based upon this notice of motion, the declaration of _____ and _____ (then your usual endings with signatures by the attorneys).

COMMENTS

Form 14.7   Notice of Motion to Renew Judgment

The purpose of Form 14.7 is self-explanatory.

However, to avoid misunderstanding, you are cautioned that the memorandum of points and authorities in support of this motion should accompany the Notice of Motion when filing the same with the court, with copies to all parties.

Since this instant form deals with an estate matter, all legal heirs, legatees, devisees, beneficiaries, etc. should be notified of the motion. This because the result of the hearing may affect the assets received by them or to be received by them from the estate.

14.8   APPLICATION FOR COLLECTION OF MONEY JUDGMENT UNDER THE UNIFORM RECIPROCAL ENFORCEMENT OF STATE LAW ACT.

COURT CAPTION AND PARTIES

Paragraph 1. This should be a statement that an action in this State on a Sister State judgment is not barred by the applicable statute of limitations.

Paragraph 2. This should be a statement based on the applicant's information and belief that no stay of enforcement of the Sister State judgment is currently in effect in the Sister State (this would require research on your part as the legal assistant.)

Paragraph 3. This should be a statement that the amount remains unpaid under the Sister State judgment.

Paragraph 4. This should be a statement that no action based on the Sister State judgment is currently pending in any Court in the State and that no judgment based on the Sister State judgment has previously been entered in any proceeding in the State.

Paragraph 5. Where the judgment debtor is an individual, there should be a statement setting forth the name and last known residence address of the judgment debtor. (The statements required in this paragraph may be made on the basis of the judgment creditor's information and belief).

Paragraph 6. This should be a statement setting forth the name and address of the judgment creditor.

Note: Then the normal closing paragraph in any application follows and we suggest that it be under penalty of perjury, or if applicable in your State, have the same notarized.

COMMENTS

Form 14.8 Application for Collection of Money Judgment Under Uniform Reciprocal Enforcement of State Judgment Law Procedure

This Application must be executed under oath and a properly authenticated copy of the judgment as rendered must be attached to the Application when forwarded to the Sister State or Country.

14.9 UNIFORM RECIPROCAL ENFORCEMENT OF STATE LAW

Introduction

The Uniform Reciprocal Enforcement of State Law Act provides a vehicle to enforce duties of support where the petitioning party and the respondent are in different but reciprocating jurisdictions.

A petition is filed in the state where the petitioner lives, but is heard in the jurisdiction where the respondent or his property is found. Duty of support is based upon a foreign court order and judgment may be enforced by registration. The county prosecutor is required to represent the petitioner.

All of the 50 states and the District of Columbia are reciprocating states. Additionally, the following foreign countries are reciprocating jurisdictions:

1. American Samoa.
2. The Canadian Provinces of:
   Alberta, British Columbia, Manitoba, New Brunswick, Northwest Territories, Ontario, Saskatchewan and The Yukon.

3. The Commonwealth of Australia.
4. Guam.
5. Puerto Rico
6. Republic of South Africa.
7. The Virgin Islands.

This ability to reciprocate by foreign countries where applicable is based upon the constitutional doctrine of "treaty supremacy" as provided in Article VI, Clause 2, of United States Constitution.

14.9(A) COMPLAINT TO ESTABLISH SISTER STATE JUDGMENT RE DIVORCE OR SEPARATE MAINTENANCE.

CAPTION OF COURT AND PARTIES

1. Establish residence of plaintiff.
2. Establish residence of defendant.
3. Establish marriage of the parties (when, where, that is, city, county and state and/or country).
4. Establish the existence or non-existence of children, name and ages, and where born.
5. Establish divorce proceedings by setting forth who filed; the date on which they were filed; the court of jurisdiction and the number of the action. (Attach a copy of this divorce action as authenticated.)
6. Establish custody of children (if applicable).
7. If number 6 is applicable, then you should state the arrearages; or abandonment, or whatever the cause for this Complaint.
8. If your office is representing the petitioner, state the willingness of petitioner to assume the responsibility of the care and custody of the children involved; as well as the ability of the defendant to pay and how much petitioner feels the defendant should pay for the care, custody and maintenance and support of said children.
9. In regard to number 8, you should set forth that the best interests of the children would be served by the petitioner having custody of same.

WHEREFORE, (the usual prayers which are pertinent to your allegations.)

_____

_____

Contents—Chapter 15
Workmen's Compensation

15

WORKMEN'S COMPENSATION

15.0   INTRODUCTION

Nowhere in the area of law is there more personalized suffering sustained by an entire family. The misery and pain inflicted upon the family of the injured employee when he or she becomes unemployable because of an industrial accident or occupational disease cannot be measured in damages for ''Pain and suffering'' as in a personal injury case. These individuals may be maimed for life; or at the very least unable to secure gainful employment in the same or similar job activity. In most cases the adverse residual effects of an industrial injury or occupational disease will remain with the applicant throughout his or her lifetime.

As a legal assistant working for an attorney with a busy practice in the area of Worker's Compensation laws both on the state and federal levels, you should be an expert in the process of an industrial claim, from the interview through and including the appeal, on behalf of a worker's compensation incident.

Note that the practice and procedure for filing or making a claim under federal law may be found in the federal codes or in the appropriate rules and regulations of an administrative agency.

15.1   APPLICATION FOR AWARD FOR SERIOUS AND WILLFUL MISCONDUCT OF EMPLOYER

Attorney Information

STATE OF _____
AGRICULTURE AND SERVICES AGENCY
DEPARTMENT OF INDUSTRIAL RELATIONS
DIVISION OF INDUSTRIAL ACCIDENTS
WORKMEN'S COMPENSATION APPEALS BOARD

	)	CASE NO.
	)	
	)	
Applicant,	)	APPLICATION FOR AWARD
	)	FOR SERIOUS AND WILLFUL
vs.	)	MISCONDUCT OF EMPLOYER
	)	
_____	)	
	)	
a corporation, _____	)	
INSURANCE COMPANY,	)	
	)	
Defendants.	)	
_____	)	

Pursuant to Section _____ of the Workmen's Compensation Appeals Board's Rules of Practice and Procedure, applicant alleges serious and willful misconduct of the employer based on the following theories:

FIRST THEORY
(Failure to Provide Safe Place to Work)

I

Each of the defendants _____ and _____ Insurance Company (hereafter both and each referred to as defendant), was and is at all times herein mentioned a corporation duly organized and existing by and under the laws of the State of _____ with its principal place of business at _____, _____.

II

On May 21, 19___, applicant was employed by defendant as a construction worker and was engaged in the performance of his duties within the scope of his employment on the property of _____ _____, County, _____, California, under the immediate supervision and direction of one _____ and one _____.

II

On said date, at about 1:25 P.M., applicant was directed by _____ who was acting as general foreman to operate a skiploader.

III

With knowledge of the requirements of Labor Code Sections ___-___, defendant intentionally and willfully and with knowledge that serious injury to applicant was a probable result, failed to furnish and use safety devices and safeguards for the benefit of applicant, failed to adopt and use methods and processes reasonably adequate to render applicant's employment and place of employment safe, and failed to do those things reasonably necessary to protect the life and safety of applicant in that

A. Defendant furnished to applicant and directed applicant to operate a skiploader which had defective brakes, had a defective rear drag buckset, had a defective power transmission system, and each of these things, each and all of which rendered said skiploader likely to go out of control and to crash;

B. With knowledge of the foregoing tendencies of said skiploader, defendant failed to provide proper or any warning to applicant of said tendencies.

IV

As a proximate result of said serious and willful misconduct of defendant, applicant was stricken with great force and violence when the said skiploader went out of control and crashed into nearby vehicles and other objects and sustained injuries resulting in both temporary and permanent disability, causing applicant to be out of work from May 21, 19___, to the present and continuing indefinitely into the future, and to receive medical treatment at various times between May 21, 19___, and the present and continuing indefinitely into the future.

SECOND THEORY
(Violation of Industrial Safety Order)

I

Paragraphs I, II, III, and IV of the first theory are incorporated herein by reference.

II

Title ___, _____ Administrative Code, General Industry Safety Order, Sections ___, _____, _____, were each applicable to work being performed by applicant on May 21, 19___, in that said skiploader and its associated parts were each within the meaning of one or more of said safety order.

III

The existence and terms of said safety order and the conditions making it applicable to applicant's work at the time of the injury were known by _____, _____ and each of them.

IV

Said safety orders were each violated in that:

A. Defendant furnished to applicant and directed applicant to operate a skiploader which had defective brakes, had a defective rear drag buckset, had a defective power transmission system, and each of these things, each and all of which rendered said skiploader likely to go out of control and to crash;

B. With knowledge of the foregoing tendencies of said skiploader, defendant failed to provide proper or any warning to applicant of said tendencies.

V

The violation of said safety orders proximately caused applicant's injury in that applicant was stricken with great force and violence when said skiploader went out of control and crashed into nearby vehicles and other objects while applicant was aboard said maching and sustained injuries resulting in both temporary and permanent disability, causing applicant to be out of work from May 21, 19___, to the present and continuing indefinitely into the future, and to receive medical treatment at various times between May 21, 19___, and the present and continuing indefinitely into the future.

WHEREFORE, applicant requests that he be awarded additional benefits consisting of an increase of one-half in compensation otherwise recoverable, together with costs and expenses.

Executed on _____, 19___, at _____, _____.

_____

_____
ATTORNEY FOR APPLICANT

COMMENTS

Form 15.1 Application for Award for Serious and Willful Misconduct of Employer

This is a formal procedure pleading utilized in a worker's compensation claim, which is filed on behalf of the employee when the attorney feels (through investigation) that the on-the-job injury was the result of some gross misconduct of the employer; and it is normally based on the theory that the applicant's injury would not have happened had the employer or the employer's supervisors or other agents in charge of the applicant had been more competent and aware of faulty and unsafe equipment or working conditions, or just plain negligent in remedying the hazards proximately causing the accident and subsequent injury to the applicant.

This document is filed against the employer per se, *Not* the worker's compensation insurance carrier of the employer. It is based on a statutory provision of Worker's Compensation Laws and the Labor Code. It is filed with the Worker's Compensation Appeals Board and personally served on the employer. Thereafter, the procedure is the same.

15.2 APPLICATION FOR SUBSEQUENT INJURIES FUND BENEFIT

BEFORE THE WORKMEN'S COMPENSATION APPEALS BOARD
OF THE STATE OF _____

_____,   )   NO.
       Applicant,   )
)   APPLICATION FOR
)   SUBSEQUENT INJURIES
)   FUND BENEFIT
)
vs.   )
)
_____,   )
       Defendants.   )
_____   )

COMES NOW applicant and alleges for benefits against the Subsequent Injuries Fund of the State of _____ as follows:

I

On November 15, 19___, applicant was permanently disabled by reason of an injury to his back and left lower extremity which arose out of and occurred in the course and scope of his employment as a maintenance man for _____, doing business as _____ at _____, _____, which caused pain and stiffness in his leg and knee; he suffered constant pain; the knee gives way frequently; he cannot kneel or squat and he has a great deal of difficulty walking up and down steps.

II

At the time of, and prior to his injury, applicant suffered disability of his left lower extremity, chest and back.

III

The combined effect of the pre-existing disability or impairment affected the right lower extremity and the permanent disability resulting from the subsequent injury affects the opposite and corresponding member, and such latter permanent disability, when considered alone and without regard to, or adjustment for, the occupation or age of the applicant, is equal to five (5%) percent or more of the total disability.

IV

The permanent disability resulting from the subsequent injury when considered alone and without regard to, or adjustment for, the occupation and age of the applicant, is equal to thirty-five (35%) percent or more of the total disability.

WHEREFORE, applicant requests that he be awarded the additional benefits provided by Labor Code Sections _____.

Dated: August 18, 19____.

_____

Attorney for Applicant

COMMENTS

Form 15.2   Application for Subsequent Injuries Fund Benefit

This application seeks to compensate an employee for his on-the-job injury, as well as any other pre-existing disability, whether the prior injury is job-related or not.

It should be filed with the Appeals Board with a copy to the Attorney General's Office (or other appropriate agency); together with a copy or copies of any and all medical reports applicable to the applicant's injury or injuries, past and present.

The Board will thereafter set a date for a hearing on the application, where the applicant, his attorney and the Attorney General's representative will be present to argue the matter.

15.3   PETITION TO REOPEN FOR NEW AND FURTHER DISABILITY BASED ON CHANGE IN CONDITION

BEFORE THE WORKMEN'S COMPENSATION APPEALS BOARD
STATE OF _____

)	NO.
)	
_____,)	PETITION TO REOPEN FOR
)	NEW AND FURTHER
Applicant,)	DISABILITY BASED ON
)	CHANGE IN CONDITION
vs.)	
)	
_____,)	
Defendants.)	
)	

COMES NOW your petitioner _____, and respectfully alleges as follows:

I

Your petitioner sustained an industrial injury to his back, hip and legs on April 27, 19___. As a result of proceedings before the Wormen's Compensation Appeals Board, a Findings and Award was issued in the above matter, awarding your petitioner temporary disability, and permanent disability benefits and medical-legal expenses.

II

Since the date of last evidence in the above-entitled case, there has been a change in the petitioner's condition, causing a further period of disability, a need for specific type of medical care and an increase in his permanent disability.

III

In support of the above allegation, we have attached the medical report of Dr. _____, dated August 14, 19___, and by this reference, said medical report is made a part of this Petition as though set forth in full herein.

WHEREFORE, your petitioner respectfully prays that this case be set for further proceedings and that thereafter he be awarded further temporary disability benefits, further necessary medical treatment, an increase in permanent disability and the reasonable value of the medical expense necessarily incurred on account of said recurrence of disability.

Dated: September 2, 19___.

_____
Attorneys for Petitioner

COMMENTS

Form 15.3   Petition to Reopen for New and Further
Disability Based on Change in Condition

This document is filed after it has been established, through documentation, i.e., a current medical report, that there is a recurring or increased disability (new and further, based on change in condition of original injury); or that the disability has diminished or terminated (which petition for the latter would be brought by the insurance company).

Note, however, that this petition must be filed within five years from the date of the original injury and that the defendant insurance company has the right to seek relief by filing a counter-petition objecting to the Petition to Reopen filed by the applicant.

15.4   PETITION FOR RECONSIDERATION

Attorney Information

WORKER'S COMPENSATION APPEALS BOARD
STATE OF _____

Parties	) Case No. _____)) PETITION FOR) RECONSIDERATION))

Applicant, _____, being aggrieved by Order of Dismissal heretofore made, and served by mail July 8, 19___, Petitions for Reconsideration on each of the following grounds:

(a) That by such order, decision, or award made and filed by the Appeals Board, the Appeals Board acted without or in excess of its powers.

(b) That the order, decision or award was procured by fraud.

(c) That the evidence does not justify the findings of fact.

(d) That the findings of fact do not support the order, decision or award.

(e) The order, decision or award was unreasonable.

Labor Code Section _____.

Specifically, your petitioner is aggrieved by:

1. Said Order for Dismissal deprives him of his Constitutional Rights to the Equal Protection of the Law and Due Process of Law under the *Fifth and Fourteenth Amendments to the United States Constitution.*

2. Said Order of Dismissal deprives him of his Constitutional Rights under *Article XX, Section 21, of the (State)* _____ *Constitution.*

The Order of Dismissal deprives applicant of his rights to a liberal construction of the Workmen's Compensation Law with its purpose of extending its benefits for the protection of persons injured in the course of their employment.

Labor Code Section 3202* provides that the Workmen's Compensation Insurance Law "shall be liberally construed by the courts with the purpose of extending their benefits for the protection of persons injured in the course of their employment." A dismissal in the present circumstances is far from extending benefits of the law to the injured workman, but is in fact a liberal construction in favor of the self-insured defendant.

3. Said Order being in excess of the powers granted the Worker's Compensation Appeals Board by the legislature and by the Labor Code, as the only grant of power to dismiss in the Labor Code is the grant of power to dismiss contained in *Labor Code Section 5507**, that is, when the application fails to state a cause of action on its face. *C.C.P. Section 583** would seem to apply to specific Courts and not to the Appeals Board. *Section 10582 of the Board's Rules** is an illegal and unlawful grasp for power on the part of the Appeals Board. In Applicant's case, no dismissal is possible under Section 5507.* The legal principle "expressio unius est exclusio alterius," stands for the proposition that when the legislature enumerates one or more of a class, that all the others within that class not so enumerated are excluded. It is, therefore, our contention that since the legislature has seen fit to state only one set of circumstances upon which an Application may be dismissed, no dismissal may be had upon other non-enumerated grounds.

In formulating Rule 10582* as a rule of technical procedure, the Board has taken in upon itself to defeat the clear and unequivocal leglislative purpose in establishing a plenary system of Workmen's Compensation. What we, therefore, have is a situation in which a case has been dismissed despite the fact that the Application clearly shows upon its face that the applicant is entitled to benefits, and despite the knowledge that medical evaluation herein establishes industrial injury and disability. *Colonial Insurance Company v. Industrial Accident Commission*, (1945) 164 P.2d 490 at 492 held that the provisions of the Workmen's Compensation Law dealing with limitation of time within which proceedings for compensation may be commenced are to be liberally construed, to the end that the beneficial features thereof *will not be lost to the employees.*

4. Said Order of Dismissal is in violation of the rights to Equal Protection of the Law in comparison to that of a defendant who fails to appear or answer, as Labor Code Section 5506* provides, that no default shall be taken against such defendant.

5. That neither defendant's letter of February 25, 19___, nor of March 6, 19___, or March 12, 19___, makes any showing of "Prejudice," and failing such, good cause to dismiss should not be presumed, and dismissal is in excess of the power of the Board.

---

* Refers to California Law

6. Dismissal herein one year, nine months, and twelve days following the filing of Application is much earlier than the three years provided for, for Civil Courts in *C.C.P. 581(a)*. (California Law)

7. This case has been on the calendar of the Worker's Compensation Appeals Board only once, that is July 6, 19___, and that only by action of the Presiding Judge without any filing of a "Declaration of Readiness to Proceed" being filed by any of the parties. Such setting resulted from defendant's letter of March 12, 19___, (a copy of which is attached hereto) requesting dismissal, applicant's attorney's letter of March 17, 19___, (a copy of which is attached hereto) asking for issuance of award rather than dismissal and therein *offering in evidence defendant's medical reports*, defendant's letter of March 25, 19___, (a copy of which is attached hereto) opposing award and Judge _____ letter of March 30, 19___, (a copy of which is attached hereto) stating the case would be calendared and *decision would issue* based on the file existing as of May 31, 19___. _____ filed appearance as defendant's counsel on June 22, 19___, and on the date of trial, July 6, 19___, served an Answer (a copy of which is attached hereto) which *admits*, among other matters, *employment*, industrial *injury* and some *periods* of temporary disability.

On July 6, 19___, the undersigned repeatedly requested to go on the record, and repeatedly offered defendant's medical reports in evidence, but such requests were continuously refused. The purported "Minutes of Hearing and Order of Dismissal" (a copy of which is attached hereto) are fictitious, as no reporter was present, and is also in error in stating applicant was present and that there were "no exhibits," in spite of the repeated offer of defendant's medical reports (copies of the twelve sheets attached hereto). There has been no abuse of the Worker's Compensation Appeals Board Calendar and personnel, and no cost to the taxpayers, hence, no grounds for Dismissal.

8. That in fact no notice has been served on defendant, as communication has been lost with him and his present residence address in unknown.

9. The Order is ambiguous as stated since it does not state whether it is dismissed "with prejudice" or "without prejudice."

WHEREFORE, petitioner/applicant prays that reconsideration be granted, and that decision issue, based on defendant's medical reports and the admissions in defendant's Answer that applicant did sustain industrial injury to his right major hand on July 11, 19___, that he was paid temporary disability of $806.19, and was temporarily disabled from June 12, 19___, through August 7, 19___, and again August 20, 19___, through September 24, 19___, for which he has been adequately compensated and at the Board's discretion, under the provisions of Labor Code Section 5802*, a nominal award be granted, and for such other relief as the Appeals Board sees fit.

DATED: July 29, 19___

Respectfully submitted,

_____
Counsel for Applicant

_____
* California Law

COMMENTS

Form 15.4   Petition for Reconsideration

This Petition is an appeal vehicle which must be filed within 20-days from the date of the judge's (referee's) decision on the original hearing of the claim. You are cautioned to check your local rules to verify this time limitation.

Note that your Petition will be denied if you merely set forth statutory grounds. For this reason you should make specific reference to the record and supply supporting law and case authority as to the allegations when utilizing the following grounds:

1. That the decision was obtain by fraud;
2. That the evidence did not justify the findings of fact;
3. That the findings of fact did not support the order;
4. That new evidence has been discovered which was undiscoverable at the time of the original hearing; and/or
5. That the order so rendered exceeded the power of the Appeals Board.

15.5   ANSWER TO PETITION FOR RECONSIDERATION

Attorney for Applicant

BEFORE THE WORKMEN'S COMPENSATION APPEALS BOARD
STATE OF _____

Applicant,	CASE NO. _____
	ANSWER TO PETITION
	FOR RECONSIDERATION
vs.	
Defendant.	

COMES NOW, the Defendant _____, and in answer to the Petition for Reconsideration filed herein, denies that:

1. By the order, decision or award of the Appeals Board it acted without or in excess of its powers.
2. The evidence does not justify the Findings of Fact.
3. The Findings of Fact do not support the order, decision or award.

SUMMARY OF EVIDENCE

A Findings and Award issued in the above-captioned case wherein the Applicant was awarded permanent disability of 47-1/2% of $_____ per week for a period of 190 weeks in the total sum of $_____ payable beginning January 10, 19___, less credit for advances previously made on permanent disability.

The defendant petitioned for reconsideration on the basis that the Applicant should be subjected to an operation before a condition could be considered permanent and stationary. This petition was denied. The Applicant secured an opportunity to purchase an interest in a gas station for the sum of $3,500.00, whereby he would be able to earn an income to support his family and would be required to do but the lightest type of work. He also needed money to purchase a transportation car and to move to the area closest to his business.

The Applicant filed a Petition for Commutation which was objected to by the defendants and on August 21, 19___, the matter came up for hearing on the issue of whether the Petition for Commutation should be granted. An overwhelming weight of the evidence supported the Referee's decision that the Petition for Commutation for the payments should be granted.

I

AN OVERWHELMING WEIGHT OF THE EVIDENCE SUPPORTS THE REFEREE'S DECISION TO GRANT COMMUTATION.

The whole purpose of permanent disability payments is to assist a disabled worker to rehabilitate himself and to assist him in again becoming a self-sufficient member of the community.

The Applicant in this case had a wonderful opportunity to become a partner in a service station, which would utilize his abilities, and to work within his physical limitations. He would be a partner of someone he had known for a number of years and with whom he had a good rapport. He had no experience in the service station business, but his partner, who is the present owner of the service station in this case, had a great deal of experience in the service station business and related businesses.

The other money sought was absolutely necessary for him to secure transportation and move his large family to a better location nearer the site of his business.

II

DEFENDANTS HAVE ULTERIOR MOTIVES IN RESISTING THIS PETITION FOR COMMUTATION.

The defendants' objection to this Petition for Commutation is that they are unhappy with the original decision of your Board and the Board's refusal to overrule it; even though at the time of the writing of the Petition for Reconsideration and at the time of the hearing of the Petition for Commutation, they had no evidence that the Applicant's condition had become less than disabling. It is their intention to secure additional evidence from the same doctor who had previously examined the Applicant that his condition was better. They are objecting strenuously that the Applicant did not keep appointments with their doctor to help them cut the rating. The defendants, of course, have no basis for this objection for two reasons: 1) they did not provide the Applicant with transportation money to reach the doctor; 2) the Applicant has made efforts to make appointments with their doctor and in fact, has presently an appointment with their doctor.

In conclusion, the entire theory of permanent disability is to encourage and prepare a person to work within his industrial disability. It is not proper to deny a Petition for Commutation on the grounds that possibly the Applicant's condition will probably become better. If that were the case, all petitions for commutation should be denied, not only on the basis that the Applicant's condition may become better, but perhaps the Applicant will die tomorrow and the insurance company will not be required to make payment. Petitions for commutation were created to benefit the applicant. There should be absolutely no consideration as to whether the insurance company may eventually be hurt if the Petition for Commutation is granted. The only real problem in this case is what should the liability be against the insurance company if by reason of its strenuous and dilatory tactics, the applicant loses this opportunity to purchase his interest in the service station and it does become successful!

WHEREFORE, the Applicant respectfully requests that the defendants' Petition for Reconsideration be denied.

Respectfully submitted this ____ day of October, 19___.

_____

Attorney for Applicant

COMMENTS

Form 15.5   Answer to Petition for Reconsideration

This document would be prepared the same as any other answer, with the same time limitation according to Worker's Compensation and Labor Code rules and regulation; and the same explanatory procedure as set forth in the Comments to Form 15.4

15.6   COMPLAINT IN INTERVENTION

Attorney for Intervenor.

)	NO.
)	
)	COMPLAINT IN
)	
)	INTERVENTION (PURSUANT
)	TO LABOR CODE
)	SECTION _____)
)	
_____)	
a corporation,)	
Intervenor.)	
_____)	

INTERVENOR alleges:

I

At all times herein mentioned, the intervenor, _____, was and now is, a corporation doing business under the laws of the State of _____ and is authorized to transact general workmen's compensation insurance business.

II

The true names or capacities, whether individual, corporate, associate or otherwise, of defendants names herein as DOE _____ are unknown to intervenor, who therefore sues said defendants by such fictitious names and plaintiff will amend this complaint to show such names and capacities when same have been ascertained.

III

That intervenor is informed and believes, and on that information and belief, alleges that each defendant designated herein as a Doe is negligently responsible in some manner for the events and happenings herein referred to, and negligently caused injury and damages proximately thereby to the plaintiff.

IV

At all times herein mentioned, plaintiff was employed by _____ and both plaintiff and his employer were subject to the workmen's compensation provisions of the Labor Code of the State of _____.

V

On or about _____, while plaintiff was engaged in the course and scope of his employment for said employer, the defendants, and each of them, through their agents, servants and employees, carelessly and negligently injured the plaintiff and such conduct on the part of the defendants proximately caused plaintiff severe and permanent injuries to his person, all as more fully set out in plaintiff's complaint on file herein.

VI

As a direct and proximate result of the injuries sustained by said plaintiff, intervenor has heretofore paid to plaintiff, pursuant to the provisions of the Labor Code of the State of _____, the following sums:

Medical expenses _____

Temporary disability benefits _____

Permanent disability benefits _____

Total _____

VII

Intervenor is informed and believes, and upon such information and belief alleges, that it will be required to pay further sums by way of medical expenses for the treatment of plaintiff, and disability indemnity benefits and other benefits as provided by the workmen's compensation law of the State of _____; that intervenor will ask leave of court to amend its Complaint in Intervention to show the true amounts of such expenditures when the amounts are ascertained.

WHEREFORE, intervenor prays for judgment against the defendants, and each of them, in any amount intervenor may be required to pay or may become due the injured plaintiff on account of compensation and medical expenses according to proof at time of trial; for costs of suit; and for all the relief that the Court considers just and proper.

BY _____
Attorney for Intervenor

PROOF OF SERVICE BY MAIL
(_____ and _____.)*

I am a citizen of the United States and a resident of the County of _____; I am over the age of eighteen and not a party to the within action; my business address is _____, _____, _____ _____,

On _____, I served the within COMPLAINT IN INTERVENTION PURSUANT TO LABOR CODE SECTION _____ on the parties in said action, by placing a true copy thereof, enclosed in a sealed envelope with postage thereon fully prepaid, in the United States mail at _____, _____, addressed as follows:

I declare under penalty of perjury that the foregoing is true and correct.

Executed on _____, at _____, _____.

_____

DECLARANT

COMMENTS

Form 15.6   Complaint in Intervention

This complaint is basically the same as any other complaint with the exception that the intervenor is seeking to become a part of the action to minimize or possibly negate its (their) liability in action; and/or to protect its (their) rights therein.

15.7   DECLARATION FOR ORDER GRANTING LEAVE TO INTERVENE AND ORDER...

Attorney for Intervenor

	) NO.
	)
	) DECLARATION FOR ORDER
	) GRANTING LEAVE TO
_____	) INTERVENE AND ORDER;
	) POINTS AND AUTHORITIES
	)
, a corporation,	)
Intervenor.	)
_____	)

_____

* Your Local Applicable Code Sections

_____ states;

I am one of the attorneys for the intervenor, _____, a corporation, the Workmen's Compensation insurer of the employer of the plaintiff in the above-entitled action. Said insurer has an interest in the matter in litigation in that it has paid Workmen's Compensation benefits to the plaintiff pursuant to the provisions of a policy of Workmen's Compensation Insurance existing between itself and plaintiff's employer for the benefit of plaintiff at the time of the accident complained of in plaintiff's complaint, and now desires leave, pursuant to the provisions of Section _____, Labor Code, to file in this action a Complaint in Intervention. The proposed Complaint in Intervention is submitted for filing herewith.

I declare under penalty of perjury that the foregoing is true and correct.

Executed on _____, at _____,

_____
Declarant

ORDER

Upon reading the declaration of _____ filed herewith and good cause appearing therefore, _____, a corporation, is hereby granted leave to file its Complaint in Intervention.

DATED: _____

_____
JUDGE

POINTS AND AUTHORITIES

I

Any person who is a real party in interest may intervene in any type of action or proceedings.

Cohen vs. *County Board of Supervisors, etc.,* 135 Cal. App. 2d. 180, 184 (3).

Robinson vs. *Crescent City Mill and Transportation Co.,* 93 Cal. 316, 318-319.

II

The purposes of intervention are to protect the interests of those who may be affected by the judgment and to obviate delays and multiplicity of actions.

Baroldi vs. *Denni* (1961),
197 Cal. App. 2d. 472-480(6).

Code of Civil Procedure, Section 387.
Labor Code, Section 3852.

Note: The above would have to be Shepardized.

COMMENTS

Form 15.7   Declaration for Order Granting Leave to Intervene and Order; Points and Authorities

This document is self-explanatory.

Just be sure that your Points and Authorities have been Shepardized and that the cases submitted are on point.

Contents—Chapter 16
Checklists

16

CHECKLISTS

16.1 THE ELEVEN CIRCUITS OF THE UNITED STATES COURTS OF APPEAL

FIRST
CIRCUIT

Maine
Massachusetts
New Hampshire
Puerto Rico
Rhode Island

SECOND CIRCUIT

Connecticut
New York
Vermont

THIRD CIRCUIT

Delaware
New Jersey
Pennsylvania
Virgin Islands

FOURTH CIRCUIT

Maryland
North Carolina
South Carolina
Virginia
West Virginia

FIFTH CIRCUIT

Alabama
Canal Zone
Florida
Georgia
Louisiana
Mississippi
Texas

SIXTH CIRCUIT

Kentucky
Michigan

SIXTH CIRCUIT
Ohio
Tennessee

SEVENTH CIRCUIT
Illinois
Indiana
Wisconsin

EIGHTH CIRCUIT
Arkansas
Iowa
Minnesota
Missouri
Nebraska
North Dakota
South Dakota

NINTH CIRCUIT
Alaska
Arizona

NINTH CIRCUIT
California
Hawaii
Idaho
Montana
Nevada
Oregon
Washington
Territory of Guam

TENTH CIRCUIT
Colorado
Kansas
New Mexico
Oklahoma
Utah
Wyoming

DISTRICT OF COLUMBIA CIRCUIT
Washington, D.C.

16.2   CHECKLIST FOR BASIC PLEADINGS
FILED BY PLAINTIFF

1. Complaint
2. Demurrer to Answer
3. Answer to First Amended Answer
4. Demurrer to First Amended Answer
5. Answer to Cross-Complaint
6. Demurrer to Cross-Complaint
7. Answer to First Amended Cross-Complaint

16.3   CHECKLIST FOR BASIC PLEADINGS
FILED BY DEFENDANT

1. Answer to Complaint
2. Demurrer to Complaint
3. Answer to First Amended Complaint
4. First Amended Answer
5. Cross-Complaint

16.4   CHECKLIST FOR LEGAL RESEARCH

Introduction

There are basically four methods of legal research, and they are as follows:
1. Topical approach;
2. Descriptive work approach
3. Table of cases or statutes;
4. Words and phrases;

The following are two examples of the tools which can be utilized by a legal assistant in researching the law:
1. Shepardizing
2. American Law Reports

16.4(a) When Shepardizing a case, you should know the following:

A...Affirmed
CC...connected case ...
D...Dismissed
M...Modified
r...reversed
s...same case
S...superseded
v...vacated
US cert den
US cert dis
US reah den
US reah dis
This is the history of the case as set forth in your Shepardizing.

The treatment of the case is as follows:
c...criticized
d...distinguished
e...explained
f...followed
h...harmonized
i...dissenting opinion
L...Limited
O...Overruled
p...parelleled
q...question
v...vacated

16.5   19-POINT CHECKLIST
OF SUGGESTED DUTIES OF A GENERAL
LEGAL ASSISTANT IN A LAW OFFICE

No.	GENERAL LEGAL ASSISTANT
1	Provide example and ideas for other employees
2	Inquire into proof of facts and reasons for events
3	Organize descriptive information into workable pattern
4	Initiate needed action based on knowledge
5	Manage and control release of information
6	Finish assigned work according to standards.
7	Establish practical interpersonal status
8	Maintain practical interpersonal status
9	Keep apparel and grooming non-distracting
10	Use criticism to evaluate work methods
11	Structure critique so as to be usable.
12	Provide direction to others in a tolerable manner.
13	Control expression of own feelings.
14	Maintain adult and ethical behavior under pressure.
15	Listen to moods of others and manage self to fit.
16	Exchange messages with others to verify intentions.
17	Interview others to get valid, complete information.
18	Listen to oral reports to grasp facts and anticipate implications.
19	Read forms to formulate research questions and topics.

16.6 12-POINT CHECKLIST OF SUGGESTED DUTIES OF A LEGAL ASSISTANT AS A LAW OFFICE MANAGER

1	Office management
2	Plan and direct maintenance repair and decor
3	Plan and direct accounting and bookkeeping
4	Plan and direct financial and statistical reporting.
5	Design and direct office records system.
6	Compile and monitor purchase of office services.
7	Direct operation of law library
8	Plan and direct selection and training of employees
9	Supervise employees
10	Plan and direct machine word processing
11	Direct recording of employee working hours
12	Professional and Interpersonal work

APPENDIX

A.—CORRELATION TABLE
Civil Case Procedure (Federal)

NAME OF DOCUMENT	SECTION
Commencement of Action	Rule 3
Procedure:	
a. Summons	
b. Form	Rule 4
c. Service	Rule 5
Computation of Time	Rule 6 (a)-(e)
Pleadings and Motions	Rule 7
General Rules re Pleadings	Rule 8
Special Pleadings	Rule 9
Form of Pleadings	Rule 10
Signing of Pleadings	Rule 11
Defenses and Objections	Rule 12
Counterclaim and Cross-Claim	Rule 13
Third-Party Practice	Rule 14
Amended and Supplemental Pleadings	Rule 15
Pretrial Procedures	Rule 16
Parties	Rule 17-22
Class Actions	Rule 23
Derivative Actions by Shareholders	Rule 23.1

Intervention	Rule 24
Substitution of Parties	Rule 25
Depositions and Discovery Procedure	Rules 26-37
Trial Procedures	
(by jury)	
(by the court)	Rules 38-53

B.—CORRELATION TABLE
(CRIMINAL PROCEDURE)

RULES OF EVIDENCE OF U.S. COURTS AND MAGISTRATES		FEDERAL RULES REVISED TITLE 18 U.S. CODE
Rule	Name of Document	Rule
1101	Complaint	3
1101	Summons	4(a-c)
1101	Preliminary Examination	5
606	Indictment and information	6
	Pleadings allowed; Form of Motions	7
	Arraignment and Preparation for Trial	10
1007; 106; 612	Pleadings and Motions Defenses and Objections	12
106; 706; 1007	Amended and Supplemental Pleadings	15 (a-f)
104; 1101	Pretrial Procedures	16 (a-q)
613	Parties	17 (a-g)
	Joinder of Claims	18, 20, 22
201; 615	Joinder of Parties	19
	Class Action	23
	Intervention	24
614; 1101	Discovery Process	26-33
803; 103	Judgment	36
609; 612; 803; 901; 1101	Jury Trial	38
1101	Searches and Seizure	41-41(H)
	Motions	47
	Service and Filing of Pleadings	49

LIST OF RELEVANT POSTAL ZIP CODES

AKRON, OH	44300	HARRISBURG, PA	17101
ALBANY, NY	12200	HARTFORD, CT	06100
ALBURQUERQUE, NM	87100	HELENA, MT.	59601
ALLENTOWN, PA	18100	HONOLULU, HI	96800
ANNAPOLIS, MD	21400	HOUSTON, TX	77000
ANN ARBOR, MICH	48103	INDIANAPOLIS, IN	46200
ATLANTA, GA	30300	JACKSON, MS	39200
AUGUSTA, ME	04301	JACKSONVILLE, FL	32200
AUSTIN, TX	78700	JEFFERSON CITY, MO	65101
BALTIMORE, MD	21200	JUNEAU, AK	99801
BARTLESVILLE, OK	74003	KANSAS CITY, MO	64100
BATON ROUGE, LA	70800	LANSING, MI	48900
BIRMINGHAM, AL	35200	LAS VEGAS, NV	89100
BISMARCK, ND	58501	LINCOLN, NB	68500
BOISE, ID	83700	LITTLE ROCK, AR	72200
BOSTON, MA	02100	LOUISVILLE, KY	40200
BRIDGEPORT, CT	06600	MADISON, WI	53700
BROOKLYN, NY	11200	MEMPHIS, TN	38100
BUFFALO, NY	14200	MIAMI, FL	33100
CARSON CITY, NV	89701	MILWAUKEE, WI	53200
CHARLESTON, WV.	25300	MINNEAPOLIS, MN	55400
CHATTANOOGA, TN.	37400	MOBILE, AL	36600
CHEYENNE, WY	82001	MONTGOMERY, AL	36100
CHICAGO, IL	60600	MONTPELIER, VT	05601
CINCINNATI, OH	45200	NASHVILLE, TN	37200
CLEVELAND, OH	44100	NEWARK, NJ	07100
COLUMBIA, SC	29200	NEW HAVEN, CT	06500
COLUMBUS, OH	43200	NEW ORLEANS, LA	70100
CONCORD, NH	03300	NEW YORK, NY	10000
DALLAS, TX	75200	OGDEN, UT	84400
DAVENPORT, IA	52800	OKLAHOMA CITY, OK	73100
DAYTON, OH	45400	OMAHA, NB	68100
DENVER, CO	80200	OLYMPIA, WA	98501
DES MOINES, IA	50300	PEORIA, IL	61600
DETROIT, MI	48200	PHILADELPHIA, PA	19100
DOVER, DE	19901	PHOENIX, AZ	85000
DULUTH, MN	55800	PIERRE, SD	57501
EL PASO, TX	79900	PITTSBURGH, PA	15200
ERIE, PA	16500	PORTLAND, OR	97200
EVANSVILLE, IN	47700	POUGHKEEPSIE, NY	12600
FT. WAYNE, IN	46800	PROVIDENCE, RI	02900
FORT WORTH, TX	76100	RALEIGH, NC	27600
FRANKFORT, KY	40601	RENO, NV	89500

RICHMOND, VA	23200	SYRACUSE, NY	13200
ROCHESTER, NY	14600	TACOMA, WA	98400
ST. LOUIS, MO	63100	TALLAHASSEE, FL	32301
ST. PAUL, MN	55100	TOLEDO, OH	43600
SALEM, OR	97301	TOPEKA, KS	66600
SALT LAKE CITY, UT	84100	TRENTON, NJ	08600
SAN ANTONIO, TX	78200	TUCSON, AZ	85700
SANTA FE, NM	87501	TULSA, OK	74100
SEATTLE, WA	98100	WASHINGTON, DC	20000
SKOKIE, IL	60076	WICHITA, KS	67200
SPOKANE, WA	99200	WILMINGTON, DE	19800
SPRINGFIELD, IL	62700	YOUNGSTOWN, OH	44500

INDEX